INTERNATIONAL CAPITAL MARKETS IN A WORLD OF ACCOUNTING DIFFERENCES

INTERNATIONAL CAPITAL MARKETS IN A WORLD OF ACCOUNTING DIFFERENCES

Edited by

Frederick D. S. Choi
and
Richard M. Levich

NEW YORK UNIVERSITY SALOMON CENTER
Leonard N. Stern School of Business

IRWIN
Professional Publishing
Burr Ridge, Illinois
New York, New York

Senior sponsoring editor: Amy Hollands Gaber
Project editor: Susan Trentacosti
Production manager: Laurie Kersch
Cover designer: Tim Kaage
Printer: Book Press

Library of Congress Cataloging-in-Publication Data

International capital markets in a world of accounting differences /
   edited by Frederick D. S. Choi and Richard M. Levich.
      p.   cm.
   "Proceedings of a conference sponsored by the New York University
Salomon Center at the Leonard N. Stern School of Business of New York
University, and held at NYU on October 16, 1992"—Pref.
   Includes bibliographical references and index.
   ISBN 1–55623–601–8 (alk, paper)
      1. Financial instruments—Accounting—Congresses.   2. Securities—
Accounting—Congresses.   3. Disclosure in accounting—Congresses.
4. Comparative accounting—Congresses.   I. Choi, Frederick D. S.
II. Levich, Richard M.
HF5681.F54I58   1994
657—dc20   93–7313

PREFACE

This book contains the proceedings of a conference sponsored by the New York University Salomon Center at the Leonard N. Stern School of Business of New York University, and held at NYU on October 16, 1992. We wish to express our appreciation to the NYU Salomon Center for underwriting the expenses associated with this research conference. We thank Ingo Walter, the director of the Salomon Center, for encouraging us to organize this event. We also thank Mary Jaffier for assisting with the administrative arrangements for the conference. Finally, thanks are due to the conference participants for contributing their ideas and research findings to this permanent record of the conference.

CONTRIBUTORS

Ravi Bhushan, Massachusetts Institute of Technology

Gary C. Biddle, University of Washington

Frederick D. S. Choi, New York University

James L. Cochrane, New York Stock Exchange

Robert P. Fisher, Jr., Goldman Sachs & Co.

Paul Guy, International Organization of Securities Commissions

Charles Hall, Columbia University

Yasushi Hamao, Columbia University

Sara Hanks, Rogers & Wells

Trevor S. Harris, Columbia University

Changwoo Lee, Seoul National University

Donald R. Lessard, Massachusetts Institute of Technology

Richard M. Levich, New York University

Eric B. Lindenberg, Salomon Brothers, Inc.

Bevis Longstreth, Debevoise & Plimpton

Terrence O'Rourke, Price Waterhouse

Peter F. Pope, University of Lancaster

William P. Rees, University of Strathclyde

Shahrokh M. Saudagaran, Santa Clara University

Clyde P. Stickney, Dartmouth College

Kishore Tandon, Baruch College

Raman Uppal, University of British Columbia

CONTENTS

CHAPTER 1

INTERNATIONAL CAPITAL MARKETS IN A WORLD OF ACCOUNTING DIVERSITY

Frederick D. S. Choi
Richard M. Levich

INTRODUCTION

In the spring of 1988, we began a research project designed to examine whether or not international accounting differences; i.e., differences in accounting measurement rules, financial disclosure requirements, and/or differences in auditing standards, had an impact on behavior in capital markets. This research, built around interviews with various capital market participants, resulted in a report, *The Capital Market Effects of International Accounting Diversity* (Choi and Levich, 1990). The papers appearing in this volume are an outgrowth of our earlier inquiry and our ongoing interest in the relationship between international accounting diversity and capital markets.

In the past, much of the research pertaining to international accounting focused on documenting differences that characterize accounting principles and reporting practices in various national settings (e.g., see Nobes and Parker, 1991; UBS-Philips & Drew, 1987; Simmonds and Azieres, 1989; and Peller and Schwitter, 1991). As a logical extension of that effort, academics have begun to examine the effects of such differences on reported accounting numbers (see Davidson and Kohlmeier, 1966; Abel, 1969; Gray, 1980; and Weetman and Gray, 1990). Motivating this work is the presumption that accounting differences lead to problems of understanding and interpretation when accounting numbers are prepared according to one set of accounting and reporting norms and used by those familiar with another. These concerns have, in turn, sparked a renewed interest in institutional efforts to harmonize accounting and reporting standards the world over (Wyatt and Yospe, 1993).

While significant resources are currently being expended on efforts to formulate a set of accounting standards that will be internationally accepted, little empirical evidence has been garnered as to whether or not such differences are actually a problem in the sense that they impact user decisions. Accordingly a question raised nearly 30 years ago by Davidson and Kohlmeier (1966) has largely gone unanswered. To wit:

> ... there remains the question of how differences in financial reporting affect individual investment decisions and the aggregate international flow of capital.

The above question is fundamental, especially now that technological and regulatory changes allow more international investors in securities and corporate issuers of securities to consider tapping capital markets in distant corners of the world. Given these technological advances, it is especially worth asking whether international accounting diversity represents a serious barrier to the globalization of financial markets.

Naturally, international accounting differences are important in the trivial sense that the reader must know whether he or she is about to read financial statements prepared according to U.S., French, or Japanese accounting principles—exactly as anyone must know whether a distance is expressed in miles or kilometers before making travel decisions. In the traveling example, we would expect that the choice of units of measurement had no impact on travel decisions. Can it also be said that the choice of accounting principles has no impact on capital market decisions?

Elsewhere (Choi and Levich, 1991), we have developed the argument that accounting differences could be characterized as either real or nominal. Real accounting differences are those that would affect a corporation's after-tax cash flows or the quality of the information transmitted to investors. When accounting difference are real, two firms undertaking identical business projects would achieve different market valuations because real cash flows or the quality of information about cash flows differed. Nominal differences are those that affect externally reported accounting values, but not cash flows or the quality of available information. When financial analysts can "see through" available accounting statements—perhaps relying on restatement algorithms or additional corporate explanations—then two firms undertaking identical business projects would achieve identical market valuations in spite of their accounting differences.

Since financial analysts have obvious financial incentives to unlock the apparent mysteries in accounting statements prepared according to diverse principles, it is reasonable to hypothesize that coping mechanisms have developed to blunt the impact of accounting differences. If so, accounting differences might be largely nominal. But since some accounting differences have immediate cash-flow implications and could affect the quality of data presented to the market, accounting differences could have a real impact. The overall impact of accounting diversity on capital market decisions remains an empirical question.

CAPITAL MARKETS INVESTIGATION

When we began our investigation into the capital market effects of international accounting diversity, we did not know which accounting measurement principles or items of financial disclosure, were problematic. Nor were we in a position to quantify the effects of these accounting differences on market decisions. Hence we decided on a two-phased inquiry. The first phase was intended to be exploratory in nature. It encompassed interviews with institutional investors, corporate issuers, investment underwriters and market regulators in major financial centers in Germany, Japan, Switzerland, the United Kingdom, and the United States. The object of our interviews was to ascertain the perceived effects of accounting differences on the behavior of international market participants, all of whom had direct decision responsibility for their organizations' investing, funding, underwriting and regulatory decisions.

Approximately one-half of those interviewed reported being bothered by national accounting differences. These differences, moreover, were associated with market effects ranging from the location of market activity to the pricing of international securities. It thus appears that for some, problems caused by international accounting differences are non-trivial.

The following chapters in this volume constitute the second phase of our capital markets inquiry. In this stage, we marshal empirical evidence in an attempt to quantify the market effects of international accounting diversity. The chapters are based on papers commissioned for and presented at a New York University Salomon Center conference on October 16, 1992, entitled, "International Capital Markets in a World of Accounting Differences."

FINANCIAL MARKET EFFECTS OF MARKET SEGMENTATION

The first part of the book explores to what extent accounting differences either contribute to or help to explain market segmentation. The chapter by Raman Uppal examines why investors bias their investments toward domestic equities despite evidence suggesting that significant gains are to be had by diversifying internationally. He focuses on three potential explanations.

Uppal first examines if the high proportion of domestic assets in investor portfolios can be explained by their desire to hedge domestic inflation. The analytical model he develops shows this not to be the case. He then examines whether institutional barriers, such as direct controls on foreign investments, might limit the extent of foreign investment. While there were substantial controls on capital flows before the 1980s, he contends that this is no longer the case for most developed countries. The author finally examines whether discriminatory and other transactions costs incurred in investing abroad might be possible explanations. He concludes that these costs are sufficiently low so as not to unduly inhibit international investments.

On the basis of his findings, Uppal ponders other possible explanations for the bias toward home country securities in investment portfolios. While inefficiencies of smaller stock exchanges and delays in transactions settlement are potential explanatory variables, Uppal raises the specter of international accounting differences as a plausible hypothesis. As unfamiliarity with foreign accounting rules increases the information cost of cross-country comparisons, concentrating more investments at home would be a logical outcome.

While the Uppal hypothesis seems intuitively plausible, Charles Hall, Yasushi Hamao, and Trevor Harris (HHH), issue a note of caution in Chapter 3. Their basic message: before concluding that accounting may be a variable explaining market segmentation, we need to first determine if the market actually uses accounting numbers. To shed some light on this issue, HHH focus on price-to-earnings (P/E) comparisons between Japan and the United States.

Prior studies have asserted that one reason for Japan-U.S. P/E differentials lies in alternative accounting measures of "E" in the P/E multiple (Aaron 1991). The authors raise a fundamental question: "Is P related to E?" Specifically, HHH examine the association between stock returns and accounting earnings during the 1970s and 1980s for Japanese and U.S. firms. They find much lower correlations between returns and earnings for Japanese sample firms than for U.S. firms. Contrary to what one might expect, given the evidence accumulated by earlier information content studies (Hawawini 1984), the Japanese do not appear to rely heavily on accounting information. This seems to have been especially true during the boom period of the mid-1980s. Thus, HHH conclude that accounting differences may not be the cause of valuation differences across countries, at least not for Japan.

INTERNATIONAL GAAP DIFFERENCES AND THEIR EFFECTS ON FIRMS

Part 2 of this volume examines the capital market effects of international GAAP differences at the level of the firm. While the association between reported earnings and share prices may not be strong in Japan, is this necessarily the case in other markets? Chapter 4, by Peter F. Pope and William P. Reese, not only examines this association for the United Kingdom, but goes a step further and examines the incremental information content of U.K. earnings that have been restated to U.S. GAAP.

The authors' treatment sample consists of British firms that have cross-listed their shares in the United States in the form of American Depositary Receipts. Pope and Reese then proceed to examine whether U.S. GAAP earnings have incremental explanatory power relative to U.K. GAAP earnings. The authors find that U.K. GAAP earnings changes are indeed impounded by market prices. What is more, U.K. GAAP earnings changes appear to have greater information content than U.S. GAAP earnings changes. While earnings levels measured under U.S. GAAP appear to have some information content relative to U.K. GAAP earnings, that relationship appears to be weak.

In chapter 5, Frederick D. S. Choi and Changwoo Lee examine whether GAAP differences manifest themselves in other ways. Specifically, they examine whether there is any empirical validity to the popular notion that differences in national accounting treatments for purchased goodwill give foreign companies a competitive edge when bidding for U.S. target companies. To quantify this market effect, the authors: (1) assess whether U.K., Japanese, and German acquirers consistently pay higher premiums on average for U.S. targets than U.S. acquirers, (2) whether these premiums are associated with accounting measures of goodwill, and (3) whether observed premium differentials are attributable to differences in goodwill accounting treatments.

The authors find that foreign acquirers do on average pay higher premiums for U.S. acquisition targets, and that premium differentials do appear to be associated with differences in accounting for goodwill. While their findings should be viewed as preliminary pending additional controls, the results provide systematic evidence in support of the notion that national GAAP differences do indeed affect market decisions.

ACCOUNTING DIFFERENCES AND SECURITIES MARKETS REGULATION

While chapters 4 and 5 deal with the market effects of national GAAP differences, chapters 6 and 7 focus on corporate financial disclosure. In chapter 6, Ravi Bhushan and Donald Lessard examine the benefits and costs of greater disclosure uniformity as perceived by international investment managers. They survey investment managers in the United Kingdom and United States as to the desirability of reduced disclosure diversity by means of either (1) more uniform disclosure standards, (2) reconciliation of foreign accounting numbers to conform with domestic GAAP, or (3) harmonization of diverse national accounting standards. While all of these reporting accommodations were regarded as desirable, none were viewed as necessary for the effective management of international portfolio investments as managers were able to achieve their objectives using local financial statements and valuation norms.

This finding suggests that policy efforts aimed at reducing international accounting diversity must address the costs as well as the benefits of greater accounting uniformity. Moreover, although fund managers sampled feel that they can manage quite well with existing data constraints, this begs the question of whether their decisions would be even better if they had access to more uniform information.

Chapter 7, authored by Gary Biddle and Shahrokh Saudagaran, asks whether differences in the level of national disclosure requirements impose costs on foreign companies sufficient to affect the location of their foreign listing decisions. To answer this question, the authors test two major hypotheses: (1) the probability that firms will list their shares on a given foreign stock exchange is inversely related to that exchange's required disclosure level, and (2) the probability that a firm will list its shares on a given foreign stock exchange will vary inversely to the exchange's disclosure level when the exchange's disclosure level is higher than the firm's current level. Although their test results only support the first hypothesis, this chapter presents strong evidence that accounting diversity does have a significant effect on the location of capital market activity.

POLICY ALTERNATIVES AND STRATEGIC OPTIONS FOR A WORLD WITH ACCOUNTING DIFFERENCES

The concluding part to this anthology contains four articles—each intended to present a perspective on current policy alternatives in a world characterized by accounting differences. The authors are all practicing participants in various roles in the field of international investments. In the first paper, Robert P. Fisher, Jr., of Goldman Sachs & Co., provides an investment underwriter's assessment of the recent accord reached between the United States and Canada. The essential principle underlying this bilateral agreement, known as the Multijurisdictional Disclosure System (MJDS), is that large companies in both countries may satisfy the other country's disclosure requirements simply by providing whatever they currently disclose in their home country. The MJDS is intended to permit easier access by U.S. firms to the Canadian market and vice versa. But to date, the agreement has primarily been used to allow Canadian firms easier access to the U.S. market. As the MJDS agreement is a recent development, Fisher comments on its performance to date and its future prospects.

In the next piece, Bevis Longstreth of Debevoise and Plimpton and former SEC Commissioner, argues, in effect, for the extension of the MJDS system to all foreign issuers that meet certain size requirements. At the present time, non-U.S. companies that list their shares on a recognized United States exchange are permitted to prepare financial accounts filed with the Commission based on their home country accounting standards. They must, however, provide in a separate schedule, a reconciliation of major differences between those principles and generally-accepted accounting principles in the United States. Longstreth questions the "value added" of such information given that accounting standards are shaped by unique social, economic and political considerations that are country-specific. In doing so, he offers a vivid example of the complexities that are involved in this contemporary reporting issue.

James Cochrane of the New York Stock Exchange addresses the competitive effects of disparate accounting requirements in his article, "Helping to Keep U.S. Capital Markets Competitive: Listing World Class Non-U.S. Firms on U.S. Exchanges." In discussing these effects, he identifies practical considerations that need to be factored into any cost/benefit calculus of the SEC's stance with respect to foreign issuers. Cochrane argues that special disclosure standards for "world-class" companies could be adopted to permit listing and trading on U.S. exchanges, yet still be consistent with the broad notion of investor protection.

In the final article of this section, Paul Guy, Secretary General of the International Organization of Securities Commissions, identifies another policy option that would facilitate multinational equity offerings in a world of accounting differences. This option embraces a set of uniform accounting principles and auditing standards that would be adopted as minimum requirements by securities regulators around the world. With the support of this international organization, the international standards movement, which floundered in the 1980s, appears to be cutting new teeth.

Overall, the papers in this volume demonstrate that accounting diversity and regulatory diversity as they pertain to the accounting and disclosure requirements placed upon corporate share issuers may have an impact on financial market decisions. Accounting diversity can impact the real cash flows of firms. Accounting diversity and regulatory diversity can impact the listing cost and listing decisions of firms. Investment analysts use costly resources to deal with accounting diversity. So even if analysts eventually see through accounting differences, they would prefer less diversity as long as the quality of information released is kept constant. Market organizers and regulators have begun to harmonize their requirements more than in the past. Even in the United States where the requirements for the standardization of accounting principles and disclosure have been the most stringent, there are signs of cooperation with Canadian regulatory agencies.

We hope that the reader will find the papers in this volume to be stimulating. If the case for a financial market impact of accounting diversity has been established, perhaps the next stage will be to quantify and detail the effects more thoroughly in future research.

REFERENCES

Abel, Rein. (1969). "A Comparative Simulation of German and U.S. Accounting Principles." *Journal of Accounting Research.* Spring, pp. 1–11.

Aron, Paul. (1991). "Japanese P/E Ratios n an Environment of Increasing Uncertainty," in F.D.S. Choi (ed.), *Handbook of International Accounting.* New York: John Wiley & Sons.

Choi, Frederick D.S., and Richard M. Levich. (1990). *The Capital Market Effects of International Accounting Diversity.* Homewood, IL: Dow Jones-Irwin.

Choi, Frederick D.S., and Richard M. Levich. (1991). "International Accounting Diversity and Capital Market Decisions," in F.D.S. Choi (ed.), *Handbook of International Accounting.* New York: John Wiley & Sons.

Davidson, S., and J. M. Kohlmeier. (1966). "A Measure of the Impact of Some Foreign Accounting Principles." *Journal of Accounting Research.* Autumn, pp. 183–212.

Gray, S. J. (1980). "The Impact of International Accounting Differences From a Security Analysis Perspective: Some European Evidence." *Journal of Accounting Research.* Spring, pp. 64–76.

Hawawini, Gabriel. (1984). *European Equity Markets: Price Behavior and Efficiency.* New York University Monograph Series in Finance and Economics, No. 1984–4/5.

Nobes, Christopher, and Robert Parker. (1991). *Comparative International Accounting.* Third edition. Englewood Cliffs, NJ: Prentice–Hall, Inc.

Peller, Philip R., and Frank J. Schwitter. (1991). "A Summary of Accounting Principle Differences Around the World," in F.D.S. Choi (ed.), *Handbook of International Accounting.* New York: John Wiley & Sons, Inc.

UBS-Phillips & Drew. (1987). *Understanding European Financial Statements.* Geneva: UBS-Phillips & Drew Global Research Group.

Simmonds, Andy, and Olivier Azieres. (1989). *Accounting for Europe-Success by 2000 AD?* London: Touche Ross.

Weetman, P., and S. J. Gray. (1990). "International Financial Analysis and Comparative Corporate Performance: the Impact of U.K. versus U.S. Accounting Principles on Earnings." *Journal of International Financial Management and Accounting.* Summer and Autumn, pp. 111–30.

Wyatt, Arthur R., and Joseph F. Yospe. (1993). "Wake-Up Call to American Business: International Accounting Standards Are on the Way." *Journal of Accountancy.* July, pp. 80–85.

PART ONE

FINANCIAL MARKET EFFECTS OF CAPITAL MARKET SEGMENTATION AND ACCOUNTING DIFFERENCES

CHAPTER 2

THE ECONOMIC DETERMINANTS OF THE HOME COUNTRY BIAS IN INVESTORS' PORTFOLIOS: A SURVEY

Raman Uppal

In this chapter, we survey the literature to investigate why investors bias their portfolios towards domestic assets, even though there are significant gains to diversifying internationally. We examine three factors that have been proposed to explain the bias in investors' portfolios towards home equity. First, we analyze if the bias in investors' portfolios, towards home equity, can be explained by the desire to hedge domestic inflation. The models of Krugman (1981), Sercu (1980), Adler and Dumas (193), Stulz (1981a, 1983) predict that this is the case. However, in the general equilibrium model of Uppal (1993), with costs for the international transfer of goods, investors bias their assets towards domestic equity only if their relative risk aversion is less than one. Second, we present evidence (Halliday, 1989) to show that the prevailing institutional barriers to foreign investment cannot explain the magnitude of the bias in portfolios towards home assets. Third, we consider the discriminatory tax treatment of income from domestic and foreign assets. Cooper and Kaplanis (1986, 1991) and French and Porterba (1991) estimate that the taxes required to explain the observed bias

The author thanks the discussants Eric Lindenberg and Clyde Stickney for their suggestions.

are much larger than those investors actually face. Thus, it is unlikely that these three factors can explain the observed home equity bias.

The benefits of international diversification have been well documented. Grubel (1968) shows that, given that different national stock markets are not perfectly correlated,[1] international diversification allows investors to attain lower return variances than those achievable by diversifying just domestically. The results of Levy and Sarnat (1970) support these conclusions. Lessard (1973) demonstrates that the gain from international diversification, given diversification across industries, is greater than the gain from diversifying across industries, given international diversification. Solnik (1974a), while confirming the above results, shows that hedging the exchange risk further improves the performance of the internationally diversified portfolios.[2] Errunza (1983) shows that the advantages from diversifying internationally, by investing in emerging countries, is even greater. These benefits arise from the fact that the correlations of the stock markets of developing countries with those of developed nations are lower than the correlations between the stock markets of developed nations. Eun and Resnick (1988) show that international portfolio strategies that take into account exchange risk significantly outperform a U.S. domestically diversified portfolio even in out-of-sample periods.[3]

The portfolios that investors actually hold, however, are markedly different from those predicted by the above studies. Cooper and Kaplanis (1991) and French and Porterba (1991) find that the portfolios of investors have a disproportionately high share invested in domestic equities, relative to the market portfolio. In Table 2–1, we report the results of Cooper and Kaplanis. From this table, we see that U.S. investors have 98 percent of their portfolio in domestic equity while the world market capitalization of the U.S. stock market is only 36.4 percent. This bias is even greater when considering the portfolios of other countries. For example, in Italy, 91 percent of the portfolio is in domestic equities while the market capitalization of the Italian stock market is only 1.9 percent. Glassman and Riddick (1990) also find that there is a large divergence between the actual portfolio that international investors hold and that predicted by a mean-variance model.

We examine three arguments that have been put forth to explain this bias in investors' portfolios. These three factors are (a) the need to hedge domestic inflation, (b) institutional barriers that limit the extent of foreign investment, and (c) discriminatory taxes on foreign income and other costs of net foreign investment. We discuss these in greater detail below.

The major part of this chapter will be devoted to analyzing if the

TABLE 2–1
Proportion of Portfolio in Domestic Equity, from Cooper and Kaplanis (1991)

Country	Market Capitalization	Proportion in Domestic Equities (percent)	Return Index
France	2.6	64.4	Inol Tendance
Italy	1.9	91.0	Bancu Com Itul
Japan	43.7	86.7	Tokyo SE
Spain	1.1	94.2	Madrid SE
Sweden	0.8	100.0	Jacobson
United Kingdom	10.3	78.5	FTA
United States	36.4	98.0	SP Composite
West Germany	3.2	75.4	Commerzbank
Total	100.0		

Sources: Market capitalization are Morgan Stanley Capital International Indices (1987), index returns are from the London Share Price Database, London Business School (LSPD). Price indices are consumer price indices from *IMF International Financial Statistics* (various issues). The domestic proportion for Japan is for bonds and shares combined. The source of portfolio holdings for the United States is survey of current business for the *U.K. CSO Financial Statistics* (February 1990), for the remaining countries *Financial Accounts Statistics* (OECD) (1988–1989). The source for equity indices and exchange rates is the LSPD.

relatively larger demand for domestic assets stems from the need to hedge against domestic inflation. Solnik (1974b), Sercu (1980), Krugman (1981), Stulz (1981b, 1983), Adler and Dumas (1983), and Branson and Henderson (1985) develop models to examine this hypothesis and find that as the fraction of domestic goods in total consumption increases, or as risk aversion increases, the demand for home equity also increases. In these articles, with the exception of Stulz (1983), the processes for prices, the exchange rate and the risk-free interest rate are specified exogenously.

Uppal (1993) endogenizes the process for the interest and exchange rates. In this model a cost is introduced for transferring capital from one location to another. As a consequence of this "shipping" cost, deviations from the law of one price (LOP) arise endogenously. The major result of this model is that the deviations from LOP lead to a preference for home equity only if the investor has relative risk aversion *less* than one. Relatively more risk averse investors prefer the foreign stock for two reasons: (a) the exchange rate change is negatively correlated with the return on the foreign stock, and (b) the share of the foreign good in total domestic consumption increases with risk aversion. Thus, as risk aversion increases, the foreign asset is preferred because its translated return is less risky, in real terms, than the return on the domestic stock.

Given that most asset pricing studies find that relative risk aversion is greater than one,[4] the results of Uppal (1993) suggest that it is unlikely that the portfolios that one observes empirically can be explained by the bias in consumption toward domestic goods. Even if one were willing to accept that relative risk aversion is less than one, the extent of the portfolio bias explained by the constraint on consumption is quite small. Thus, this model suggests, it is unlikely that the home equity bias is a consequence of the demand for hedging domestic inflation. The empirical test of Cooper and Kaplanis (1991) also rejects the hedging motive as an explanation for the home equity bias. They find that domestic equities do not provide a good hedge against deviations from purchasing power parity.

The second explanation for the bias towards domestic equity is based on the institutional constraints on foreign investment, such as restrictions on the maximum fraction of a firm that can be held by foreigners. Cohn and Pringle (1973) suggest that it is markets with low correlations with the developed stock markets that usually have such restrictions on capital flows. Thus, the markets that are most attractive to investors [see Errunza (1983)] are also those in which it is difficult to invest. We will look at some of the evidence on the prevailing institutional constraints and investigate if these are sufficiently strong to generate the proportion of the observed bias in portfolios.

Third, Black (1974) and Stulz (1981b) analyze models of international capital market equilibrium where there are taxes on foreign investment. In these models, taxes capture the effect of the existence of the various costs of investing abroad. Cooper and Kaplanis (1986, 1991) and French and Porterba (1991) estimate that the level of taxes and other costs for investing abroad required to explain the observed bias is much larger than that investors actually face.

We conclude that it is unlikely that the three factors discussed above are significant enough to explain the degree of the bias in portfolios that is observed empirically.

The aim of this chapter is not to provide an exhaustive survey of the literature on international portfolio choice models. Our objective is a limited one: to evaluate if the three factors under consideration can explain the home equity bias. For a comprehensive survey of the literature on international portfolio choice and asset pricing, see Adler and Dumas (1983), Dumas (1993), and Stulz (1992).

The rest of the chapter is organized as follows. In the first section below, using the models of Krugman (1981), Sercu (1980), Adler and

Dumas (1983), and Stulz (1981a, 1983), we explain why the demand for hedging domestic inflation leads to home equity bias. In the second section below, we analyze the effect of this demand for hedging inflation, on investors' portfolios, in the context of the general equilibrium model developed in Uppal (1993). In the third section, we examine whether the prevailing institutional controls on foreign investment can explain the magnitude of the home equity bias that is observed. In the fourth section below, we examine the costs of investing abroad, and how large these costs need to be to explain the observed home equity bias. We present our conclusions in the final section.

THE EFFECT ON PORTFOLIO CHOICE OF THE DESIRE TO HEDGE INFLATION

In this section we examine how the need to hedge against domestic inflation affects an investor's portfolio choice. We analyze the effect of this demand for hedging in the context of the models of Krugman (1981), Sercu (1980), Adler and Dumas (1983) and Stulz (1981a, 1983). The main result of these models is that as an investor become more risk averse, the proportion of domestic assets in the portfolio increases. In the next section, we consider the same issue in a model where it is costly to transfer goods from one country to another.

   We start by recalling the example in Krugman (1981). In this example, an investor has to choose between the domestic and foreign bond, both of which have the same riskless return. However, the foreign bond is exposed to exchange risk. Given the effect of Jensen's inequality, the foreign bond has a positive expected return in terms of the home currency. Thus, investors who are risk neutral choose to invest entirely in the foreign bond. Infinitely risk averse investors hold only the domestic bond, in order to avoid taking on any exchange risk. As is well known, investors with relative risk aversion equal to one hold the market portfolio. Thus, only investors who have risk aversion greater than one will exhibit a bias towards the domestic asset. This is because, for them, the excess return earned by holding the foreign bond is insufficient to compensate for the exchange risk that this entails. Krugman generalizes this example to show that an increase in the demand for domestic goods will lead to greater demand for the domestic asset only if relative risk aversion is greater than one.

   Note, however, that there are several assumptions underlying the model analyzed in Krugman (1981). The most important assumption is that the variance of the exchange rate and asset returns is independent of investors' risk aversion and their preferences for the domestic good.

Sercu (1980) extends this argument to an equilibrium setting. He generalizes the capital asset pricing model (CAPM) to an international setting, where he allows for exchange risk, but assumes that there is no inflation. As is well known, in the standard CAPM economy, an investor's optimal portfolio can be decomposed into demand for two funds: the market portfolio and the riskless asset. With exchange risk, however, the efficiency frontier that investors from different nations face is no longer the same. Thus, to obtain the separation results, we need to find a fund that is common to investors across nations. Sercu's result is based on the clever insight that one can recover the separation property by using the log investor's portfolio instead of the portfolio of all risky assets. The log portfolio is independent of the measurement currency that is being used,[5] and therefore, is the same for investors of all nationalities.

More formally, Sercu considers the problem of an investor who has a constant relative risk averse utility function, with relative risk aversion given by RRA, and wishes to choose a portfolio to maximize the expected utility of consumption over her lifetime. This problem is equivalent to maximizing the difference between the expected return of a portfolio and its variance. Define $\mathbf{X}_i$ to be the $N \times 1$ vector weights on the risky asset in the portfolio of investor residing in country i. Let $\mathbf{X}_i^f = [\mathbf{X}_i, x^f]$ be the $(N+1) \times 1$ vector of weights where the $N + 1^{st}$ component is the investment in the risk-free asset, x^f. The components of $\mathbf{X}_i^f$ sum to one. Also, let $\mathbf{R}$ be the $N \times 1$ vector of excess returns on the risky assets and $\mathbf{V}$ the $N \times N$ variance-covariance matrix. Then, the investor's problem is:

$$\max_{\mathbf{X}i} \ \mathbf{X}_i' \mathbf{R} - (\text{RRA}_i/2) \, \mathbf{X}_i' \mathbf{V} \mathbf{X}_i.$$

The first order condition for this problem is:

$$\mathbf{X}_i = T_i \mathbf{V}^{-1} \mathbf{R}_i,$$

where T_i is the risk tolerance of the investor in country i, and is equal to $1/\text{RRA}_i$. As in the standard CAPM, investor i's optimal portfolio can be decomposed into:

$$[\mathbf{X}_i^f] = T_i(\mathbf{1}' \, \mathbf{V}^{-1} \, \mathbf{R})\begin{bmatrix} \mathbf{Y} \\ 0 \end{bmatrix} + (1 - T_i \mathbf{1}' \, \mathbf{V}^{-1} \, \mathbf{R})\begin{bmatrix} \mathbf{0} \\ 1 \end{bmatrix} \qquad (2.1)$$

where $\mathbf{Y}$ is the portfolio containing just the risky assets, $\mathbf{Y} = \mathbf{V}^{-1}\mathbf{R}/\mathbf{1}'\mathbf{V}^{-1}\mathbf{R}$. The second portfolio is, of course, the risk-free asset.[6] Sercu then shows that the above portfolio can be decomposed differently, in terms of the following two funds:[7]

$$[\mathbf{X}_i^f] = T_i \begin{bmatrix} \mathbf{V}^{-1}\mathbf{R} \\ 1 - (\mathbf{1}'\mathbf{V}^{-1}\mathbf{R}) \end{bmatrix} + (1 - T_i) \begin{bmatrix} \mathbf{0} \\ 1 \end{bmatrix} \qquad (2.2)$$

An investor with relative risk aversion equal to one (the 'log' investor) invests only in the first fund. This fund may contain both risky and riskless assets. The investor who is infinitely risk averse, invests only in the second fund, which is the domestic riskless asset. The implication of the above result, for home asset bias, is that as an investor's risk aversion increases she invests an increasing proportion of her wealth in the domestic riskless asset. Thus, the bias towards domestic assets increases with risk aversion.[8]

The above result depends on the assumptions that (a) there is no home inflation, and therefore, the domestic bond is riskless in real terms, and (b) that the exchange rates and interest rates are determined exogenously. Adler and Dumas (1983) and Stulz (1981a) extend the work of Sercu (1980) by explicitly allowing for inflation. Adler and Dumas assume that the stochastic process for price levels is different across countries. Stulz, on the other hand, specifies that while the law of one price holds for traded goods, deviations in purchasing power arise as a consequence of the differences in consumption opportunity sets across countries. As a result of these assumptions, in these models the domestic bond is no longer riskless. Thus, the domestic bond is not the asset that an infinitely risk averse agent would like to hold. The two funds separation in this case, as derived in Adler and Dumas, is given by:

$$[\mathbf{X}_i^f] = T_i \begin{bmatrix} \mathbf{V}^{-1}\mathbf{R} \\ 1 - (\mathbf{1}'\mathbf{V}^{-1}\mathbf{R}) \end{bmatrix} + (1 - T_i) \begin{bmatrix} \mathbf{V}^{-1}\Sigma_{\mathbf{R}i} \\ 1 - (\mathbf{1}'\mathbf{V}^{-1}\Sigma_{\mathbf{R}i}) \end{bmatrix} \qquad (2.3)$$

where $\Sigma_{\mathbf{R}i}$ is the vector of covariances of the risky asset returns with the rate of inflation in country i. Thus, in the Adler and Dumas model, the optimal portfolio for an investor in country i is a combination of (a) the log portfolio, and (b) investor i's global minimum variance portfolio in real terms. A similar result holds in Stulz (1981a). Adler and Dumas also show that the second fund is one whose nominal return is most highly correlated with the rate of inflation in country i. That is, it is the portfolio that provides investor i with the best hedge against domestic inflation.

To deduce the implications of the above result for the bias in an investor's portfolio, note that as risk tolerance decreases, the weight on the minimum variance portfolio increases. Adler and Dumas find that the minimum variance portfolio consists mainly of domestic T-bills. Thus, as in the model of Sercu (1980), when an investor's risk aversion increases, she increases her holding of domestic bonds. Cooper and Kaplanis (1991) test the model of Adler and Dumas and strongly reject the hypothesis that the home equity bias is a consequence of investors' attempt to hedge against deviations from purchasing power parity.

Stulz (1983) extends the Krugman (1981) model by considering utility functions that do not restrict expenditure shares to be fixed. Also, in his model the exchange rate is determined endogenously. Stulz shows that, with an increase in risk aversion, an investor is less willing to take on price gambles. The agent does this by investing a larger proportion in the domestic bond.

The main conclusion of the models discussed in this section is that an increase in an investor's risk aversion leads to a greater investment in home assets, typically the domestic riskless bond. In the next section, we consider the model in Uppal (1993). This model extends the work that has been discussed in this section, by constructing a model where there are costs for transferring capital from one country to another and consequently, deviations from LOP arise endogenously. We then examine how this shipping cost affects an investor's optimal portfolio choice.

PORTFOLIO CHOICE IN AN ECONOMY WITH SHIPPING COSTS

In this section, we examine the optimal portfolio that an investor would choose in an economy where the financial markets are integrated but markets for real capital are not. Uppal (1993) develops a two-country, general equilibrium model with costs for transferring physical capital between these two countries. The main finding is that the optimal portfolio of an investor is biased towards domestic equity only if the investor's relative risk aversion parameter is less than one. Investors with risk aversion greater than one, prefer to hold more of the foreign equity, relative to the market portfolio. This result is in contrast to the that of the models considered in the previous section. However, as we explain below, the result is consistent with that of the models discussed in the section above.

By explicitly introducing a cost for transferring goods from one location to another, the decision as to whether a good is traded or not is endogenized in Uppal (1993). This is in contrast to models where investors find it optimal to bias their portfolio towards domestic stocks because of the presence of non-traded goods. For example, Stockman and Dellas (1989) assume the existence of a non-traded good and that the utility from consuming this good is separable from that from the traded goods.[9] Thus, the domestic investor holds all the shares in the firm producing the non-traded good, which biases the portfolio towards domestic assets. However, this model begs the question why certain goods are not traded.

We now briefly describe the model in Uppal (1993).[10] There are two countries and two goods. Each country has a single representative investor. The representative investors in the two countries are identical in all respects—they have the same preferences, represented by a constant relative risk averse utility function, with the same degree of risk aversion and time preference. These assumptions are motivated by the desire to ensure that, other than the cost for transferring goods described below, there is no other factor that biases the portfolio of the investors in any direction. The objective of the home (foreign) investor is to maximize the expected utility of consumption over her lifetime.

There is one risky production technology in each country. The production processes in both countries are assumed to identical: they have the same expected return and instantaneous variance, and are uncorrelated. It is also assumed that there is a proportional cost for transferring goods from one country to another.

Each investor can potentially invest in four assets: the foreign and domestic equities and riskless bonds. The home investor's problem is to maximize her lifetime expected utility by choosing the optimal consumption policy, portfolio strategy, and a rule that determines when goods are to be transferred from the domestic location to the foreign location. Given that the investors in the two locations are symmetric and that the output shocks are uncorrelated, in the absence of a shipping cost, the solution to the investor's problem would be to hold the market portfolio. Thus, in this case there would not be any home equity bias. But, in the presence of the shipping costs, holding the market portfolio is no longer optimal.

In the presence of proportional transfer costs, it is certainly not optimal to correct the imbalance by shipping at each instant. Given the continuous time construct of this model, if one corrected the imbalance every instant, the cumulative cost of doing this would be ruinous. Instead, within a certain range, it may be desirable to rebalance through different consumption rates—consumers in the land of abundance consuming more than those in the land of scarcity. This is because the diversification benefits obtained from shipping may be less than the cost of shipping.

Also, within this range of no shipping, the price of the consumption good abroad, relative to that of the good at home, is not equal to one. This gives rise to deviations from the Law of One Price. Since, within the zone of no shipping, the home and domestic investors consume at different rates and face different prices for consumption, it will no longer be optimal for them to hold the same portfolio, the market portfolio.

The optimal portfolio of the home investor, for different levels of risk aversion, is given in Table 2–2 (Panels A and B). The results in this table raise two questions. One, given that the home investor only consumes from the domestic capital stock, why does she invest in the foreign stock at all. Two, what explains the direction of the bias in the home investor's portfolio.

To answer the first question, recall that the home and the foreign investor are similar in all respects except that, given the transfer cost, each investor is constrained to consume only out of the capital stock located in her country. Given that each investor consumes only out of the capital stock located in her country of residence, one may expect investors to invest only in local assets. But this is true only for a risk neutral investor. Risk averse investors will always invest a positive amount in the other country's equity to hedge against the likelihood of shipping, that is, the possibility of having to consume from the foreign stock of goods, following a transfer from abroad. Thus, the possibility of shipping in the future affects today's portfolio choice.

Note that the difference in the individual and market portfolios will be largest when the likelihood of shipping is the smallest. This is the point where the capital stocks are perfectly balanced in the two countries (Table 2–2, column 4). As the imbalance increases (columns 2 and 6), and the likelihood of shipping increases, the difference in the two portfolios declines.

To answer the second question, note that the consumption of the home investor is not equal to half of the aggregate consumption. Given the presence of the shipping cost, it will be optimal in some periods to correct the imbalance in the physical capital stocks by consuming unequal amounts in the home and foreign countries. Thus, since the consumption stream that must be financed is not half of the aggregate consumption, the portfolio held to finance this will not be the market portfolio. If the relative risk aversion of the home investor is less than 1, the home investor exhibits a bias for the home equity. For the case where the home investor is relatively more risk

TABLE 2–2
Fraction of Total Investment in Home Equity[a]

Model Parameters	Fraction of Total Investment in Domestic Equity				

Panel A: RRA = 0.5, 1 − *s* = .18

Model Parameters					
Market portfolio weight in domestic equity	0.2258	0.3684	0.5000	0.6316	0.7742
Home investor's portfolio weight in domestic equity	0.2258	0.4146	0.5698	0.6777	0.7742
Home equity bias	0.0000	0.0461	0.0698	0.0461	0.0000

Panel B: RRA = 1.5, 1− *s* = .18

Market portfolio weight in domestic equity	0.2974	0.4041	0.5000	0.5959	0.7026
Home investor's portfolio weight in domestic equity	0.2974	0.3967	0.4882	0.5885	0.7026
Home equity bias	0.0000	-0.0074	-0.0118	-0.0074	0.0000

Panel C: RRA = 0.5, 1− *s* = .01

Market portfolio weight in domestic equity	0.3802	0.4376	0.5000	0.5624	0.6198
Home investor's portfolio weight in domestic equity	0.3802	0.4391	0.5022	0.5639	0.6198
Home equity bias	0.0000	0.0015	0.0022	0.0015	0.0000

Panel D: RRA = 0.5, 1 − *s* = .50

Market portfolio weight in domestic equity	0.2198	0.4073	0.5000	0.5820	0.7802
Home investor's portfolio weight in domestic equity	0.2198	0.5119	0.6156	0.6866	0.7802
Home equity bias	0.0000	0.1046	0.1156	0.1046	0.0000

[a] Simulation results from Uppal (1993).
This table describes the extent of the home equity bias for different parameters of the model. The parameters considered are different levels of relative risk aversion, RRA, and different levels of shipping cost, 1−*s*. The home equity bias is measured by the difference between the proportion of the home investor's portfolio in domestic equity *less* the market portfolio weight in the domestic equity. Comparing Panel A and B, we find that as RRA increases the home equity bias decreases. Comparing Panels A, C, and D, we find that as the shipping cost increases, the increase in the home equity bias is quite small. For the above simulations, the volatility of the production processes is assumed to be 20 percent per annum.

averse, the direction of the bias is reversed.

The direction of the bias in the individual investors' portfolios will depend on two factors: (a) the frequency of shipping and (b) the variance of the return on the foreign equity, translated into domestic terms. Given the general equilibrium nature of the model, these factors are not independent of the degree of risk aversion. The frequency of shipping is directly related to the investors risk aversion. As risk aversion increases, the diversification benefits from balancing capital stocks increase, and therefore, the cone narrows and the frequency of shipping increases.

Also, in this model, the exchange rate is negatively correlated with the return on the foreign equity.[11] As the foreign good becomes relatively more abundant, its price, the exchange rate declines. Thus, the variance of the translated foreign return is always less than that before translation. This implies that, from the domestic investor's point of view, the foreign security is *less* risky than the domestic asset.

Thus, as risk aversion increases: (a) the frequency of shipping, and thus, the likelihood of consuming from the foreign capital stock increases, and (b) the riskiness of the return from the foreign asset, translated into domestic terms declines. Therefore, the more risk averse investor chooses to bias her portfolio towards the asset that is less risky in real terms—the foreign asset.

Most empirical asset pricing studies [see, for example, Singleton (1990)], estimate the relative risk aversion parameter of the aggregate investor is significantly greater than one. This implies that it is unlikely that the Uppal (1993) model can explain the home equity bias. Even if one were willing to assume that the degree of relative risk aversion is less than one, it is unlikely that the level of the bias observed in the data can be explained by this model (see Table 2–2, Panel D where the shipping cost is 50 percent). Thus, this model only serves to deepen the home equity puzzle.

Note that the investor in the Uppal (1993) model behaves the same as the investor in the Krugman (1981), Sercu (1980) or Stulz (1983) models: as risk aversion increases, she holds a portfolio that is weighted towards the less risky asset. The only difference is that in the Uppal model, given the negative correlation between the exchange rate and the foreign equity, the less risky asset is the foreign stock. In the other models, as risk aversion increases, the investor holds an increasing proportion of the domestic bond.

THE EFFECT OF INSTITUTIONAL BARRIERS ON FOREIGN INVESTMENT

In this section, we examine the effect of direct controls on foreign investment. The controls may either limit foreign investment into a country or restrict domestic residents from investing abroad. Restrictions on foreign investment into a country may be imposed in different ways—in the form of a limit on the fraction of equity that can be held by foreigners or a restriction on the types of industries in which foreigners can invest. Details on the type and magnitude of these restrictions can be found in Eun and Janakiramanan (1986, Table 1). There may also be domestic controls on how much a resident can invest abroad. For example, Japanese insurance companies may not invest more than 30 percent of their portfolio in foreign assets, and only 30 percent of the assets of Spanish pension funds may be invested abroad.

We ask two questions in this section. One, if these restrictions exist, do they then have a significant impact on the choice of the optimal portfolio. Two, how significant are these constraints today.

Bonser-Neal, Brauer, Neal, and Wheatley (1990) examine if the restrictions on investing abroad are binding. They examine closed-end country funds and find that these trade at premiums relative to their net asset values, indicating that the French, Japanese, Korean, and Mexican markets are at least partially segmented from the U.S. capital market. Hietala (1989) studies the effects of the Finnish law that prevented investors from investing in foreign securities and finds that there is a significant difference between the returns on domestic assets required by residents compared to foreigners. Gultekin, Gultekin, and Penati (1989) also find strong evidence that the U.S. and Japanese markets were segmented prior to 1980.[12]

However, while there were substantial controls on capital flows before the 1980s, this is no longer true. Halliday (1989) reports that there are few constraints on investing in foreign stock markets. This is especially true for investing in the markets of developed countries. For example, there are no controls on investment by foreigners into Austria, Belgium, Denmark, Ireland, Italy, Japan, Netherlands, United Kingdom, United States, and West Germany. Not surprisingly, Gultekin, Gultekin, and Penati (1989) find that there is no significant evidence of segmentation between the U.S. and the Japanese stock markets after the enactment of the Foreign Exchange and Foreign Trade Control law in 1980.[13] Also, looking at restrictions that limit domestic residents from investing abroad, one sees that these constraints are often not binding. For example, Fairlamb (1989) reports that in 1988 only 8 percent of Spanish funds were actually invested in foreign assets, while the limit was 30 percent.

Thus, we conclude that while the direct controls on foreign investment may have been important in the past, they are probably not the reason for the lack of international diversification that we observe today.

THE EFFECT OF DISCRIMINATORY TAXES AND
OTHER COSTS OF INVESTING ABROAD

In this section, we first examine models that study how discriminatory taxes on foreign investment affect an investor's optimal portfolio. In these models the tax captures the effect of withholding taxes, stamp duties, turnover taxes and also the effects of political risk, or information costs that arise because of unfamiliarity with foreign markets. We then look at the data to see if the costs of investing abroad are sufficiently large to explain the observed bias in investors' portfolios.

Black (1974) develops a model of international capital market equilibrium with a proportional tax on foreign investment. Black makes the strong assumptions that unlimited short sales are permitted, and that a subsidy (negative tax) is received on the short position in foreign assets. The net effect of the tax on foreign investment is to bias the optimal portfolio towards domestic assets. Of course, given that one earns a subsidy on short positions in foreign assets, if these taxes were very high, the model predicts that investors would hold large short positions in these assets.

Stulz (1981b) considers a model similar to that of Black (1974), but where the cost of holding foreign assets is applied to the absolute asset position. That is, there is a positive tax on both long and short positions in foreign assets. This captures the effect that there are barriers to investing abroad—irrespective of whether one takes a long or short position. With such a tax, some foreign assets will not be held at all by investors in the other country. An important implication of this model is that investing abroad by buying the market portfolio of the foreign country may not be efficient.

Cooper and Kaplanis (1986), using a model similar to that of Black (1974), estimate the implied deadweight costs given the portfolios that investors hold. Their estimate of the costs of investing abroad is of the order of 3–4 percent of the value of the foreign investment. Cooper and Kaplanis (1991) extend this model to allow for deviations from purchasing power parity. Using this model, their estimate of the costs of investing abroad is between 2 percent and 14 percent p.a. French and Porterba (1991) find that, to explain the observed portfolios, the difference in expected returns needs to be substantial. For example, they find that U.S. investors expect the return on U.S. stocks to be 2.5 percent p.a. more than that on Japanese stocks. Japanese investors, on the other hand, expect the return from their home assets to exceed the U.S. return by 3.5 percent p.a.

How large are the costs of investing abroad? Typically, the withholding tax is 15 percent on dividends from foreign assets (*Capital International Perspectives II*, 1986, and the *Montreal Exchange Guide to World Equity Markets*, 1988). However, one can usually receive a tax credit for this in the home country, and thus, this tax should not have any impact on an investor's portfolio. The only exception to this is the case where investors are tax-exempt, as are pension funds.

Transactions costs for trading in international markets also seem to be quite low. Kemp (1987) estimates these costs to range from 0.5 percent to 7 percent. More importantly, often these costs are the same for domestic and foreign residents, so their affect should be to bias an investor's portfolio towards markets with low trading costs rather than towards domestic assets. Similarly, in some countries stock markets are quite thin and there may be problems with lack of liquidity. This is especially true of the secondary markets in Holland, Italy and France (Kirzner and Dickinson, 1987). But even when one includes the effect of market impact in the implicit transactions cost, one would expect the volume of trading to shift to the more liquid market, instead of towards home assets.

Thus, it seems unlikely that taxes, transactions costs or other observable costs of investing abroad can explain why investors hold such a large proportion of domestic assets in their portfolios.

CONCLUSION

In this chapter, we examine three factors to see if they can explain the bias towards domestic equities in investors' portfolios. These three factors are: (a) the demand for hedging domestic inflation, (b) institutional controls on foreign investment, and (c) discriminatory taxes and other costs of investing abroad. Our main conclusion is that while these factors may explain some of the bias, the empirical evidence suggests that it is unlikely that the bias observed in investors' portfolios can be explained entirely by these factors.

While the models of Krugman (1981), Sercu (1980), Adler and Dumas (1983), Stulz (1981a, 1983) suggest the demand for hedging home inflation would bias an investor's portfolio towards her home assets, Uppal (1993) shows that this is true only when relative risk aversion is less than one. Cooper and Kaplanis (1991) test the model of Adler and Dumas and strongly reject the hypothesis that the home equity bias is a consequence of investors' attempt to hedge against deviations from purchasing power parity.

Considering direct controls on foreign investment, Halliday (1989) reports that there are few constraints on investing in foreign stock markets today. This is especially true for investing in the markets of developed countries. Even when these controls exist, they are usually not binding. Finally, French and Porterba (1991) and Cooper and Kaplanis (1986, 1991) estimate the level of taxes and other costs needed to explain the home bias observed in portfolios to be between 2 percent and 4 percent. These estimates are much larger than the differences in the transactions costs for trading foreign versus domestic assets (Kemp, 1987).

What other factors may explain the home equity bias puzzle? Bailey and Stulz (1990) suggest that the benefits of international diversification may have been overly optimistic. Jorion (1985) shows that studies that ignore estimation risk seriously overestimate the gains in average returns obtained from international diversification. Glassman and Riddick (1989) discuss the effects of some of the simplifying assumptions often made by models of international portfolio choice. They find, for example, that the effect of assuming that purchasing power parity holds, and that investors maximize nominal wealth, may systematically bias the optimal portfolio weights. Other reasons for not diversifying internationally include the inefficiencies of the smaller stock exchanges, for example, Vienna and Helsinki (Hawawini, 1985). Delays in settling transactions and accounting differences between countries may be also discourage international diversification. Also, it has been suggested by Agmon and Lessard (1977) that investors may diversify internationally by investing in the stock of multinational firms. However, Jacquillat and Solnik (1978) find that the returns of multinational firms are more highly correlated with the return on the domestic market index than with the return on foreign stock markets.

An important factor that may inhibit international diversification is the unfamiliarity with foreign assets. If investors feel that they need to expend greater resources when investigating foreign equities, relative to the cost of analyzing domestic stocks, then this may explain why they do not diversify abroad. These costs may be real or perceived. No direct estimates of these costs are available, and the analysis of portfolio choice with different information gathering costs for domestic and foreign securities merits more serious attention.

NOTES

1. French and Porterba (1991) report that the average pairwise correlations between quarterly returns on the equity markets in Canada, France, Germany, Japan, U.K. and U.S. for the period 1975-89 is 0.502.
2. In a study on the performance of international portfolios, Glen (1989) finds that when sufficiently long periods of time are considered the performance of portfolios hedged against exchange risk may be no better than those unhedged, on a risk adjusted basis.
3. For a review of the literature on the construction of internationally diversified portfolios see Madura (1985).
4. See, for example, the survey article by Singleton (1990).
5. This is a property of the logarithmic function.
6. Note that $\mathbf{1}$ is a vector of ones.
7. To get this result, add and subtract T_i from $1 - T_i\mathbf{1}'\mathbf{V}^{-1}\mathbf{R}$, and rearrange the terms.
8. This, of course, is not the same as an increasing bias towards domestic equity.
9. See also Eldor, Pines, and Schwartz (1988).
10. This model is similar to the one analyzed in Dumas (1992). Black (1973) develops a certainty version of this model.
11. The exchange rate is defined as the relative price of the foreign good, in terms of the domestic good.
12. For other studies on capital market segmentation see, Errunza and Losq (1985), and Jorion and Schwartz (1986).
13. The controls that Hietala (1989) studies were also removed in 1986.

REFERENCES

Adler, M., and B. Dumas. (1983). "International Portfolio Choice and Corporation Finance: A Synthesis." *The Journal of Finance*. 38, no. 3, p. 925.

Agmon, T., and D. Lessard. (1977). "Investor Recognition of Corporate International Diversification." *Journal of Finance*. 32, no. 4, pp. 1049–55.

Bailey, W., and R. Stulz. (1990). "Benefits of International Diversification: The Case of Pacific Basin Stock Markets." *Journal of Portfolio Management*. Summer, pp. 57–61.

Black, F. (1973). "Transportation Costs, Tariffs, and Taxes in a One-sector Model of Trade." M.I.T. working paper.

Black, F. (1974). "International Capital Market Equilibrium with Investment Barriers." *Journal of Financial Economics*. 1, pp. 337–52.

Bonser-Neal, C., G. Brauer, R. Neal, and S. Wheatley. (1990). "International Investment Restrictions and Closed-End Country Fund Prices." *Journal of Finance*. 45, no. 2, pp. 523–47.

Branson, W., and D. Henderson. (1985). "The Specification and Influence of Asset Markets." In R. Jones and P. Kenen (eds.), *Handbook of International Economics*. Vol. II, Elsevier Science Publisher, pp. 749–805.

Cooper, I., and E. Kaplanis. (1986). "Costs to Crossborder Investment and International Equity Market Equilibrium." In J. Edwards et al. (eds.), *Recent Advances in Corporate Finance*. Cambridge University Press.

Cooper, I., and E. Kaplanis. (1991). "What Explains the Home Bias in Portfolio Investment?" London Business School working paper.

Dumas, B. (1992). "Dynamic Equilibrium and the Real Exchange Rate in a Spatially Separated World." *Review of Financial Studies*. 5, no. 2, pp. 153–80.

Dumas, B. (1993). "Partial Equilibrium vs. General Equilibrium Models of International Capital Market Equilibrium." The Wharton School working paper.

Eldor, R., D. Pines, and A. Schwartz. (1988). "Home Asset Preference and Productivity Shocks." *Journal of International Economics*. 25, pp. 165–76.

Errunza, V. (1983). "Emerging Markets: A New Opportunity for Improving Global Portfolio Performance." *Financial Analysts Journal*. pp. 51–58.

Errunza, V., and E. Losq. (1985). "International Asset Pricing Under Mild Segmentation: Theory and Test." *Journal of Finance*. 40, no. 1, pp. 105–24.

Eun, C., and S. Janakiramanan. (1986). "A Model of International Asset Pricing with a Constraint on the Foreign Equity Ownership." *Journal of Finance*. 41, no. 4, pp. 897–914.

Eun, C., and B. Resnick. (1988). "Exchange Rate Uncertainty, Forward Contracts and International Portfolio Selection." *Journal of Finance*. 43, pp. 197–215.

Fairlamb, D. (1989). "The Elusive El Dorado of Spanish Pensions." *Institutional Investor*. April, pp. 177–84.

French, K., and J. Porterba. (1991). "Investor Diversification and International Equity Markets." *American Economic Review*. 81, no. 2, pp. 222–26.

Glassman, D., and L. Riddick. (1989). "A Generalized Model of International Portfolio Diversification: Evaluating Alternative Specifications." Dept. of Economics at UCLA working paper no. 565.

Glassman, D., and L. Riddick. (1990). "A New Method of Testing Models of International Portfolio Choice: Application to International Diversification." University of Washington working paper.

Glen, J. (1989). "Exchange Rate Uncertainty, Forward Contracts, and the Performance of Global Equity Portfolios." University of Pennsylvania Rodney L. White Working Paper 37-89.

Grubel, H. (1968). "Internationally Diversified Portfolios: Welfare Gains and Capital Flows." *American Economic Review*. 58, pp. 1299–1314.

Gultekin, M., B. Gultekin, and A. Penati. (1989). "Capital Controls and International Capital Market Segmentation: The Evidence from the Japanese and American Stock Markets." *Journal of Finance*. 44, no. 4, pp. 849–69.

Halliday, L. (1989). "The International Stock Exchange Directory." *Institutional Investor*. March, pp. 197–204.

Hawawini, G. (1985). *European Equity Markets: Price Behavior and Efficiency*. New York University: Salomon Bothers Center for the Study of Financial

Institutions.

Jacquillat, B., and B. Solnik. (1978). "Multinationals are Poor Tools for International Diversification." *Journal of Portfolio Management*. Winter, pp. 8–12.

Jorion, P. (1985). "International Portfolio Diversification with Estimation Risk." *Journal of Business*. 58, no. 3, pp. 259–78.

Jorion, P., and E. Schwartz. (1986). "Integration Vs. Segmentation In The Canadian Stock Market." *Journal of Finance*. 41, no. 3, pp. 603–13.

Kemp, L. (1987). *The Wardley Guide to World Money and Securities Markets*. London: Euromoney Publication Ltd.

Kirzner, E., and J. Dickinson. (1987). *Guide to International Investing*. Don Mills, Ontario: CCH Canadian Ltd.

Krugman, P. (1981). "Consumption preferences, Asset Demands, and Distribution Effects in International Financial Markets." NBER Working Paper no. 651.

Lessard, D. (1973). "World, National and Industry Factors in Equity Returns." *Journal of Finance*. 29, pp. 379–91.

Levy, H., and M. Sarnat. (1970). "International Diversification of Investment Portfolios." *American Economic Review*. 60, pp. 668–75.

Merton, R. (1971). "Optimum Consumption and Portfolio Rules in a Continuous Time Model." *Journal of Economic Theory*. 3, pp. 373–413.

Sercu, P. (1980). "A Generalization of the International Asset Pricing Model." *Revue de l'Association Francaise de Finance*. 1, pp. 91–135.

Singleton, K. (1990). "Specification and Estimation of Intertemporal Asset Pricing Models." In B. Friedman and F. Hahn (eds.), *Handbook of Monetary Economics*. Amsterdam: North–Holland.

Solnik, B. (1974a). "Why Not Diversify Internationally Rather Than Domestically." *Financial Analysts Journal*. pp. 48–53.

Solnik, B. (1974b). "An Equilibrium Model of the International Capital Market." *Journal of Economic Theory*. 8, pp. 500–24.

Stockman, A., and H. Dellas. (1989). "International Portfolio Nondiversification and Exchange Rate Volatility." *Journal of International Economics*. 26, pp. 271–89.

Stulz, R. (1981a). "A Model of International Asset Pricing." *Journal of Financial Economics*. 9, pp. 383–406.

Stulz, R. (1981b). "On the Effects of Barriers to International Investment." *Journal of Finance*. 36, no. 4, pp. 923–34.

Stulz, R. (1983). "The Demand for Foreign Bonds." *Journal of International Economics*. 15, pp. 225–38.

Stulz, R. (1992). "International Portfolio Choice and Asset Pricing: An Integrative Survey." Ohio State University working paper WPS 92–31.

Uppal, R. (1993). "A General Equilibrium Model of International Portfolio Choice." *Journal of Finance*. 48, pp. 529–53.

CHAPTER 3

A COMPARISON OF RELATIONS BETWEEN SECURITY MARKET PRICES, RETURNS, AND ACCOUNTING MEASURES IN JAPAN AND THE UNITED STATES

Charles Hall
Yasushi Hamao
Trevor S. Harris

INTRODUCTION

Extensive research and discussion has occurred over the last two decades relating to the relevance of accounting differences in the valuation of securities in international capital markets (Choi and Levich, 1990). Yet little empirical evidence exists which evaluates how the accounting measures in Japan are associated with stock prices or returns, especially over periods other than short event windows of a few days, weeks, or months.

The stock prices of companies listed on Japan's securities markets rose at a rapid pace in the 1980s and yielded price-earnings (henceforth P/E) and

The authors thank Clyde Stickney for useful comments. Funding from the Center on Japanese Economy and Business at Columbia University is gratefully acknowledged. Hamao's research was supported in part by the Batterymarch Fellowship; Harris's research was sponsored in part by the Rudolph Schoenheimer Fellowship.

price-to-book value (henceforth P/B) ratios which many observers suggested were high by international standards [Aron (1987, 1989), French and Poterba (1991), Chan, Hamao, and Lokonishok (1991), and Schieneman (1988)]. The last few years have reflected an opposite trend. At the time of writing, the Japanese stock market had lost about 50 percent of its market value since the 1989 high. The accounting measures of the Japanese firms listed on the stock market have not shown the same volatility. We see use of P/E relatives in discussions of cost of capital [for example, McCauley and Zimmer (1991) and Poterba (1991)] and broad international comparisons (for example, Bildersee, Cheh, and Lee (1990), and Dontoh, Livnat, and Todd (1991)]. For such evaluations to be made usefully, we should expect fundamental associations between the accounting and stock market measures to be equivalent across the countries, subject to accounting differences. That is, if equivalent basic associations do not exist, then it is not clear what it means to make such international comparisons.

This chapter evaluates such associations in Japan and compares them to a sample of firms in the United States using a methodology recently developed in Easton and Harris (1991b) and Easton, Harris, and Ohlson (1992), and considered for Germany in Harris and Lang (1992).

Darrough and Harris (1991) and Sakakibara, Yamaji, Sakurai, Shiroshita, and Fukuda (1988) provide evidence that Japanese reported accounting earnings and management forecasts do have information content around earnings announcement dates. Yet, it might be argued that, despite the information content in earnings, the relative returns-earnings associations are different across the United States and Japan, because of both economic factors and accounting differences. For example, expected rates of return might affect the relative coefficients of earnings in returns-earnings association studies and be independent of any accounting differences. However, while such economic differences may affect the coefficient estimates in cross-sectional tests, they should not necessarily affect the degree of association as reflected in the R^2. On the other hand, the garbling of the accounting information may cause differences in both the coefficient estimates and the strength of the association. This would seem to be consistent with the results reported in Chan, Hamao, and Lakonishok (1991). The Easton, Harris, and Ohlson (1992) methodology minimizes the influences of accounting measurement differences so the methods we use should control for much of the garbling effect. Also, Brown, Soybel, and Stickney (1991) find that adjusting Japanese and U.S. financial statement data for differences in accounting principles has only a small impact on average P/Es or rates of return, and Harris and Lang (1992) find equivalent return-earnings associations in Germany and the United States. These results suggest that we might reasonably expect equivalent associations in Japan without any accounting adjustments.

While we do not control for all accounting differences, we do factor in a specific difference by considering both the parent-only and consolidated measures in Japan. Both popular perception in Japan and empirical evidence in Darrough and Harris (1991) suggest that the parent-only earnings appear to be the primary earnings information variable. Until 1991, consolidated data could be, and generally was, reported after the parent data had been presented. The parent data are considered in Aron (1987, 1989), Chan, Hamao, and Lakonishok (1991), and French and Poterba (1991). Yet the international trend is toward increased application of consolidation principles, and there is a perception that consolidation differences are a major factor in explaining differences in Japanese P/E ratios [Aron (1989) and French and Poterba (1991)]. We also consider the role of depreciation, which is presumed to be relevant for explaining international differences in several of the cited studies.

The results suggest that Japanese stock prices were largely unrelated to fundamental values based on accounting measures for most of the 1980s and that, currently, we are seeing a correction towards these fundamentals. Thus, further studies which try to control for other differences in Japanese and U.S. accounting practice in order to explain apparent price differentials are questionable at best.

DEVELOPMENT OF HYPOTHESES

Recently, an advisory body to the Ministries of Finance and of International Trade and Industry

> proposed the standardization of some national financial regulations around the world. They should include standardized methods of international securities settlements, release of information, [and] accounting standards... [The committee] said that standardization was needed to create smoother international financial transactions.[1]

This proposal reflects the common sentiment that different accounting practices impact the international financial markets. Survey analysis (Choi and Levich, 1990) indicates that various participants in the capital markets are influenced by different practices, and yet there are others who seem to be able to cope with the differences. The earlier quote suggests that some Japanese policy advisors believe that differences between Japanese and other countries' accounting practices impact the operation of international financial markets. Yet others have argued that stock prices and fundamental variables, such as accounting earnings and book value of owners' equity, are essentially unrelated in Japan. For example, Zielinski and Holloway (1991) state "share prices have gradually lost touch with the earning power of the companies which they represent" (p. 16), and Viner (1988) suggests that

> the Japanese stock market is only a market of stocks.... Japanese investors will decide what they want and what they wish to discard on the basis of trends and fads which have no Western counterpart.... If the Japanese market will give a kingdom for a horse, then global valuation techniques and internationalization will have no bearing on that decision (p. 124).

Furthermore, anecdotal evidence exists of "ramping" of prices and deals between brokerage firms and important clients who create short-term price movements, which may be unrelated to the earning power of companies.

These two positions are somewhat contradictory. The first suggests that correcting for accounting differences will create a symmetry in the relations of stock prices and accounting fundamentals across countries. This is consistent with the argument made in Aron (1987, 1989). The second position suggests that the basic associations are "structurally" different. We have some evidence that correcting for accounting differences does not explain the relative Japanese and U.S. P/Es or costs of capital [for example, Brown, Soybel, and Stickney (1991), and Poterba (1991)]. Yet there appears to be little empirical evidence analyzing the relative associations between accounting measures and stock prices or returns in Japan.[2] In general, the Japanese accounting system, as prescribed in the Commercial Code, is oriented more toward protection of creditors than to providing information for investors. In addition, there is a tax conformity rule which requires legal entities to include expenses in the reported accounting income if they are to be included as expenses for tax purposes. Together these institutional characteristics suggest that Japanese firms' owners' equity and earnings will be biased downwards and be more conservative than the equivalent measures of their U.S. counterparts. The bias in the reported values will change the expected coefficient (multiple) in cross-sectional tests of the associations between the accounting and stock market measures but need not reduce the strength of the associations themselves. Harris and Ohlson (1987) have shown that U.S. investors rationally discriminate between the relative conservatism of successful efforts and full cost accounting for oil and gas producers. Also, Harris and Lang (1992) have shown that associations between German accounting and stock market measures are associated in a similar way to U.S. firms, despite the potentially strong conservative bias in German accounting practice. In fact, the Japanese accounting system has its early roots (from the time of the Meiji restoration) in German practice. Thus, overall, even if the Japanese accounting system creates some measurement biases, it need not reduce the power of associations with stock market measures if, in fact, Japanese investors consider accounting measures in their pricing decisions in a similar manner to U.S. investors. If Japanese investors largely ignore the accounting measures, then it is harder to argue that effort should be spent on trying to adjust the accounting system to obtain measures which are closer to those provided in the United States, so as to "correct" for apparent differences in valuation.

The major accounting differences are summarized in other papers, including Aron (1987, 1989), Brown, Soybel, and Stickney (1991), French and Poterba (1991), and Viner (1988). Most studies suggest that the large differences relate to the issue of parent versus consolidated reporting and the choice of depreciation method.[3] The understatement of equity and earnings resulting from lack of consolidation varies substantially cross-sectionally, but on average, for our sample, the median ratio of consolidated to parent earnings (owners' equity) ranges from 1.08 (1.02) to 1.12 (1.03) for the years in which consolidation is required. Furthermore, we now have a reasonable period with which to use the consolidated data so that this should not be a concern.[4] The depreciation question is complicated by the fact that it has nothing to do with Japanese accounting per se. Of course, one might argue that the tax conformity rules give Japanese companies an incentive to use accelerated depreciation rules, but these rules are in conformity with U.S. generally accepted accounting practice (GAAP). Thus, we find U.S. firms using equivalent methods (e.g., General Motors and Ford), and the Japanese firms which use U.S. GAAP for their consolidated statements still use accelerated depreciation methods. The accelerated depreciation combined with a growth of investment in capital equipment can depress reported earnings in the short run but should have little impact over longer windows which cover the depreciation cycle. The methodology we employ will therefore largely control for any influence of "excessive" depreciation.

In testing the associations between accounting and stock market measures, we consider two basic approaches. The first simply looks at the basic association between price multiples relative to the fundamental accounting measures. In particular, we focus on the correlation between P/B and return on equity (henceforth, ROE). This can be justified formally using the model outlined in Ohlson (1989, 1991). The model shows price as a weighted average of earnings, book value of owners' equity, and other information, formally:

$$P_{it} = k\theta x_{it} + (1 - k)y_{it} - kd_{it} + v_{it} \tag{3.1}$$

where

P_{it} is the share price of security i at time t,
x_{it} is accounting earnings for firm i at time t,
k is a weight indicating the degree of relevance of earnings,
θ is $R_F / (R_F - 1)$ where R_F is the risk-free rate,
y_{it} is the book value of owners' equity for firm i at time t,
d_{it} is dividends for firm i at time t, and
v_{it} is other information used to price firm i at time t and is orthogonal to earnings and owners' equity.

Dividing through by y_{it} yields the P/B ratio on the left-hand side and the ROE, dividend over owners' equity and (deflated) other information on the right-hand side.[5] Thus, if earnings is considered to be weighted heavily in pricing companies, we should expect a high correlation between P/B and ROE, given the historically small dividends. Alternatively, if book value is weighted heavily in the pricing decision, then we can expect a high negative correlation between P/E and ROE. If other information is being used primarily, that is, accounting measures are being relatively underutilized, then both correlations will be small.[6] Thus, our first test of the relative degree to which accounting measures are used in valuation in Japan is based on the simple correlations outlined above.

The second set of tests considers associations between security returns and measures of accounting earnings. Returns-earnings associations have been the focus of analyzing the value-relevance of accounting information for some time. But the focus has usually been in the form of assessing the information content of unexpected earnings. If one takes the first difference of the variables in equation (3.1), we have returns as a function of deflated earnings and changes in earnings. Therefore, at least for annual return intervals, we consider both earnings variables for explaining returns.[7]

The general model we use to test the returns-earnings associations is derived in Easton and Harris (1991b) and Easton, Harris, and Ohlson (1992) and is represented as follows:

$$R_{iT} = \alpha_0 + \alpha_1 AE_{iT} + \alpha_2 \Delta AE_{iT} + \epsilon_{iT} \tag{3.2}$$

where

R_{iT} is $(P_{iT} - P_{i0} + FVS_{iT}) / P_{i0}$, with T being 1 in an annual window and varying up to $T = 20$ years.

FVS_{iT} is the cumulative dividends from time 1 to T and the earnings on the dividends (d_{it}), assuming a reinvestment at the risk-free rate (R_F), that is

$$FVS(d_{i1}, \cdots, d_{iT}) \equiv d_{i1}(R_F^{T-1}) + d_{i2}(R_F^{T-2}) + \cdots + d_{iT-1}(R_F) + d_{iT} \equiv FVS_{iT},$$

AE_{iT} is $\sum_{t=1}^{T} x_{it} + FVF_{iT}$, with x_{it} being accounting earnings for firm i at time t, and

$$FVF(d_{i1}, \cdots, d_{iT}) \equiv d_{i1}(R_F^{T-1}-1) + d_{i2}(R_F^{T-2}-1) + \cdots + d_{iT-1}(R_F-1) \equiv FVF_{iT},$$

ΔAE_{iT} is $AE_{iT} - AE_{is}$, that is the change in aggregate earnings with respect to the relevant interval with s being equal to some time period prior to T and depending on the definition of change in earnings used,[8] and

ϵ_{iT} is the residual error term.

If accounting data are considered to be valuation relevant, we should expect the earnings variables to be associated with returns. In short windows (up to a year), both the use of other information and potential leads and lags in accounting measurement or recognition of economic events can yield low association metrics. However, as demonstrated in Easton, Harris, and Ohlson (1992), by extending the window length, we minimize accounting measurement problems and, as Easton, Harris, and Ohlson (1992) show, earnings explain more than half the returns over a ten-year window in the

U.S.[9] Hence, if the short window associations using Japanese data are lower than the U.S., this may be partly a result of accounting measurement issues. But, by extending the window length, any measurement problems should largely disappear so that any differences in Japanese and U.S. metrics of returns-earnings associations should converge. On the other hand, if differences remain, it is more likely that Japanese investors are placing more weight on other information (relative to accounting measures) in their pricing of securities.

The analysis of the value-relevance of accounting measures is extended by comparing the returns-earnings associations for Japanese companies across the two reporting options—parent and consolidated. If the consolidated data are considered to be more value-relevant than the parent-only data, then for the comparison using just Japanese companies, we should expect the associations to be higher for the consolidated data. However, previous evidence in Darrough and Harris (1991) and anecdotal evidence suggest that investors focus on the parent report.[10] Hence, simple rule changes to provide superficial conformity of accounting rules will not necessarily create uniformity in the uses of the information.

DATA AND SAMPLE SELECTION

Japan

The Japanese stock-price data are taken from the database described in Hamao (1991), which covers monthly data from January 1970 to December 1992. Parent accounting and dividend data are provided by Daiwa Institute of Research. This is a monthly database which records the accounting information as it is released for all firms in Tokyo Stock Exchange Sections I and II from January 1970 to December 1991. The consolidated statement data are taken from the Nihon Keizai Shimbun Sha (Nikkei) NEEDS database. For each fiscal year we used the month-end price corresponding to the month in which the accounting data was released. The current and lagged prices are then utilized to calculate returns.

While a Japanese firm may choose any month as its accounting cycle end, several firms have changed the end month to March over the years. We drop observations when there is an irregular number of months in an accounting cycle because of the change. We also exclude financial institutions and 12 observations spread over the years with extreme values (e.g., an

ROE of 264,000 percent). This leaves us with a minimum of 935 firms in 1971 and a maximum of 1,277 firms in 1986 in the parent sample.

Since full consolidated reporting became mandatory only after 1983, the consolidated data we have are useful only from 1984. The consolidated data sample consists of 364 firms for which current profit and price data are available for every year from 1984 to 1991. We repeated the tests with the full number of observations with consolidated data. As the results were qualitatively identical, we report only the restricted sample results.

Management forecasts of 364 firms' consolidated current profit are collected from the *Japan Company Handbook*, published by Tokyo Keizai Shimpo Sha. All data are converted to a per-share basis adjusted for stock splits. The Gensaki (bond repo) rate, used as a short-term, risk-free interest rate, is taken from Hamao and Ibbotson (1992).

United States

U.S. accounting data are collected from the 1991 Compustat Industrial database. This was the most recent data available, so U.S. data are only available up to 1990 fiscal year-ends. Price and adjustment factor data are extracted from the Center for Research in Security Prices database for a date three months following the fiscal year end. T-bill rates of return are taken from Ibbotson Associates (1992).

The U.S. sample of 262 firms is selected by matching Japanese firms in the consolidated sample on the basis of the 1990 market value of equity and four-digit SIC code. Japanese firms are assigned an SIC code based on their four-digit Securities Identification Code given by the Japan Securities Identification Code Conference. These codes yield 66 industry classifications. Japanese and U.S. market values of equity are put on a comparable basis by converting the Japanese values at the average 1990 exchange rate extracted from Datastream. U.S. firms are required to have return and earnings data in every year from 1983 to 1990, to ensure that we impose the same survival constraints that we use for the Japanese sample.

Data Summary

Some summary descriptive statistics for the samples are reported in Table 3–1. Panels A, B, and C describe the results for the Japanese parent, consolidated, and U.S. data, respectively.

We report medians to eliminate the impact of a small number of

TABLE 3–1
Summary Statistics

Year	Median Return (%)	Median P/E	Median P/B	Median ROE [a] (%)	Spearman Correlation P/E, ROE [a]	P/B, ROE [a]	Ret., ROE [a]	Int. Rate (%)	N
				Panel A: Japan—Parent					
1971	6.25	10.55	1.31	12.70	−0.20	0.53	0.17	6.61	935
1972	41.18	17.38	1.85	10.05	−0.25	0.40	−0.06	4.83	967
1973	7.00	15.61	1.79	11.14	−0.50	0.21	−0.06	7.40	985
1974	0.47	13.55	1.70	11.83	−0.58	0.15	0.11	13.29	1009
1975	−4.70	17.06	1.65	8.45	−0.23	0.14	0.20	11.21	1012
1976	10.83	21.56	1.86	7.03	−0.16	0.18	0.27	7.20	1050
1977	4.27	20.94	1.90	8.11	−0.27	0.21	0.19	5.94	1141
1978	16.39	23.52	2.22	7.89	−0.17	0.14	0.04	4.94	1158
1979	0.99	20.38	2.12	9.31	−0.39	0.10	−0.05	5.48	1166
1980	−0.56	18.53	2.00	9.99	−0.50	0.19	0.09	10.74	1184
1981	−3.98	19.53	1.86	8.87	−0.35	0.17	0.31	7.54	1194
1982	−3.74	19.67	1.67	7.98	−0.31	0.00	−0.07	6.88	1203
1983	16.11	25.45	1.94	6.95	−0.21	0.06	0.16	6.57	1213
1984	14.46	29.19	2.25	6.83	−0.21	0.09	0.06	6.37	1230
1985	17.95	32.04	2.56	7.01	−0.36	0.14	−0.07	6.55	1245
1986	28.27	45.82	3.20	6.04	−0.29	0.03	0.13	5.19	1277
1987	16.00	56.27	3.61	5.54	−0.26	0.16	0.14	3.93	1260
1988	27.37	59.39	4.22	6.39	−0.38	0.18	−0.05	3.98	1197
1989	12.32	59.24	4.29	6.95	−0.51	0.23	−0.01	4.68	1165
1990	5.89	59.15	3.90	6.25	−0.48	0.32	0.17	7.00	1207
1991	−22.76	45.61	2.99	6.36	−0.47	0.35	0.27	7.38	996
				Panel B: Japan—Consolidated					
1984	15.71	27.90	2.26	7.24	−0.21	0.15	0.07		364
1985	16.73	28.69	2.47	7.97	−0.39	0.22	−0.02		364
1986	30.18	44.17	3.18	6.48	−0.30	0.03	0.15		364
1987	14.20	50.00	3.46	5.48	−0.00	0.04	0.13		364
1988	28.78	55.30	4.31	6.95	−0.28	0.22	−0.04		364
1989	14.96	52.45	4.34	7.66	−0.42	0.34	0.02		364
1990	0.36	53.78	3.86	6.77	−0.52	0.19	0.00		364
1991	−22.82	41.27	2.82	6.61	−0.41	0.24	0.29		364
				Panel C: United States—Consolidated					
1984	6.77	10.76	1.34	12.80	0.03	0.53	0.43	9.85	262
1985	18.53	12.36	1.49	10.97	0.18	0.46	0.43	7.72	262
1986	25.01	15.79	1.83	9.87	0.21	0.52	0.45	6.16	262
1987	−1.78	13.30	1.61	11.86	0.05	0.59	0.33	5.47	262
1988	7.59	11.52	1.60	14.35	−0.15	0.57	0.10	6.35	262
1989	11.52	11.08	1.58	13.34	0.14	0.54	0.38	5.46	262
1990	−2.05	12.73	1.46	11.31	0.21	0.53	0.44	6.34	262

[a] The ROE is defined as earnings divided by book value of equity.

extreme observations. The median returns for Japan are consistent with the market patterns. Notice that the rapid run-up in prices began in 1983 and continued through 1989. While 1989 marked the beginning of the slide in Japan's stock market prices, the 1990 returns still reflect a small average increase with 1991 showing the sharp decline of close to 23 percent for both parent and consolidated samples.

It is also interesting to observe that in 1971 through 1982 the median P/E was around 20, with much lower P/Es in 1971 and 1974. The latter was clearly affected by the high interest rates. From 1983 through 1991 the P/Es have remained at high levels with 1986 to 1991 having P/Es over 40. In contrast, for the U.S. sample, the median P/Es have ranged between 11 and 16. The P/B ratios reflect a similar pattern. For Japan, the P/B based on parent data was below 2.0 up to 1978, as well as from 1981 to 1983. But from 1984 the P/B began moving away from this level based on both parent and consolidated samples. The peak was in 1989 with the median of 4.34 for the consolidated sample. In contrast, the median P/B in the United States never reached 2.0, with a peak of 1.86 in 1986. In principle, we might expect high P/Bs, because of high profitability, but, in fact, the trend was quite the opposite. The peak (median) ROEs in Japan occurred in the early 1970s when multiples were lowest. The median ROEs in Japan were below 8 percent from 1983 onward in Japan, while in the United States during the same periods, the median ROEs were around 11 percent. Some of this difference is related to accelerated depreciation methods and large capital investment in Japan and to the interest differentials between Japan and the United States. But even with these adjustments, it would be hard to argue that Japanese firms were extraordinarily profitable. Next, we consider the tests of associations between accounting and stock market measures.

RESULTS OF PRIMARY TESTS

In most of the reported results we use the maximum number of observations available to ensure robust statistics. All tests were also run on the limited sample of 364 firms used in the long-window analysis of consolidated data for Japanese firms. In all cases the qualitative conclusions are unchanged for all subsets.

Price Ratio Tests

The first set of tests relate primarily to the correlations of P/B and ROE and secondarily to P/E and ROE. As discussed, if investors consider reported earnings to be value-relevant, then we can expect that there is high positive correlation between ROE and P/B. The annual correlations are reported in Table 3–1. We use rank correlations so that large or small observations do not have an undue weighting. The results are reported in panel A for the Japanese parent date, in panel B for the Japanese consolidated data, and in panel C for the U.S. data. For the Japanese data, in all years except 1971 and 1972, we see that the correlation is below 0.40. For the parent reports, the correlations are below 0.30 from 1973 to 1989. The correlations range from 0.03 in 1986 to 0.34 in 1989 for the consolidated data. In comparison the matched sample of U.S. firms has only two years in which the correlation is less than 0.50 and, in both cases, the correlation is greater than 0.45. These results are consistent with the view that, on average, Japanese investors pay less attention to earnings than do U.S. investors.

Similarly, the rank correlations of P/E and ROE are negative and quite high in contrast to the United States, which varies around zero. This is consistent with a greater relative focus on accounting owners' equity than earnings in Japan as compared to the United States, where earnings seem to be more important.

The comparison of parent and consolidated data for Japanese samples is inconclusive. This suggests that the consolidated data are not necessarily superior as we might naively expect from the push towards consolidation around the world.

Returns-Earnings Associations

First, we consider the tests based on annual return windows. These results are reported in Table 3–2, with panels A, B, and C again reporting the Japanese parent, consolidated, and then U.S. samples, respectively. We also report in the last column of panels A and B the adjusted R^2 from the regressions using parent data for the restricted sample of 364 Japanese firms. Beginning with the parent data full sample, we find an R^2 greater than 0.10 in only two years, and in 1982 this appears to be driven by outliers. Furthermore, in several years, particularly in the period from 1983 to 1989, the R^2 is below 0.05. We also find little consistency in the relative importance of the earnings levels versus changes for explaining returns and the size of the

TABLE 3–2
One-Year Window Regressions[a]

Year	α_0 (t-stat)	α_1 (t-stat)	α_2 (t-stat)	Adjusted R^2	Spearman Corr.[b]	N	Adjusted R^2 for 364 firms
			Panel A: Japan—Parent				
1971	0.08	0.62	0.02	0.052	0.41	935	0.042
	(4.9)	(6.6)	(0.6)		0.49		
1972	0.58	−0.01	0.52	0.042	0.35	969	0.074
	(25.8)	(−0.1)	(5.9)		0.33		
1973	0.11	0.42	0.41	0.031	0.31	986	0.050
	(6.1)	(2.1)	(3.7)		0.33		
1974	0.08	−0.60	1.61	0.160	0.34	1009	0.107
	(5.4)	(−3.5)	(10.4)		0.51		
1975	0.01	0.36	0.10	0.021	0.37	1012	0.060
	(0.6)	(3.1)	(1.1)		0.27		
1976	0.23	0.12	0.82	0.070	0.37	1051	0.239
	(15.7)	(0.8)	(6.6)		0.37		
1977	0.09	0.28	0.06	0.034	0.39	1143	0.098
	(9.4)	(3.3)	(0.8)		0.35		
1978	0.27	0.16	0.26	0.025	0.22	1157	0.047
	(19.7)	(1.2)	(3.4)		0.37		
1979	0.10	−0.78	1.51	0.065	0.05	1166	0.016
	(8.3)	(−4.8)	(8.8)		0.25		
1980	0.03	0.39	0.15	0.011	0.19	1184	0.022
	(2.2)	(2.2)	(1.3)		0.29		
1981	0.01	0.62	0.59	0.070	0.41	1194	0.067
	(1.1)	(3.8)	(4.6)		0.39		
1982	0.01	−0.21	1.03	0.164	0.08	1203	0.000
	(0.8)	(−1.8)	(11.6)		0.22		
1983	0.30	−0.23	0.98	0.059	0.13	1214	0.019
	(22.4)	(−1.6)	(8.2)		0.31		
1984	0.24	0.04	0.68	0.019	0.09	1229	0.004
	(17.6)	(0.2)	(4.0)		0.29		
1985	0.25	0.28	0.19	0.003	0.18	1246	0.011
	(15.3)	(1.0)	(1.3)		0.12		
1986	0.43	−0.61	0.94	0.007	0.26	1277	0.023
	(20.7)	(−1.6)	(2.4)		0.31		
1987	0.25	1.30	0.29	0.048	0.23	1260	0.009
	(14.2)	(4.6)	(1.6)		0.28		
1988	0.37	0.50	1.02	0.016	0.16	1197	0.030
	(18.7)	(0.8)	(1.8)		0.22		
1989	0.17	0.39	0.02	0.000	0.16	1165	0.004
	(12.1)	(0.7)	(0.0)		0.17		
1990	−0.02	7.34	−1.4	0.062	0.34	1207	0.023
	(−0.9)	(8.3)	(−2.5)		0.28		
1991	−0.27	3.95	−1.38	0.096	0.43	997	0.102
	(24.5)	(7.0)	(−2.6)		0.37		

[a] The model is $R_{iT} = \alpha_0 + \alpha_1 AE_{iT} + \alpha_2 \Delta AE_{iT} + \epsilon_{iT}$. See text for notations used in the equation.
[b] The first row of Spearman correlation is between R and AE, the second row is between R and ΔAE.

45

TABLE 3–2, concluded
One-Year Window Regressions

Year	α_0 (t-stat)	α_1 (t-stat)	α_2 (t-stat)	Adjusted R^2	Spearman Corr.[b]	N
		Panel B: Japan—Consolidated				
1985	0.23	0.06	0.70	0.015	0.14	364
	(8.4)	(0.1)	(2.2)		0.20	
1986	0.45	0.31	1.14	0.020	0.23	364
	(11.7)	(0.4)	(1.5)		0.30	
1987	0.20	0.36	1.20	0.025	0.16	364
	(10.6)	(0.7)	(2.8)		0.24	
1988	0.37	0.47	1.54	0.009	0.16	364
	(9.7)	(0.3)	(2.1)		0.25	
1989	0.17	–0.15	0.50	0.000	0.09	364
	(7.1)	(–0.1)	(0.5)		0.15	
1990	0.04	2.39	–1.07	0.007	0.16	364
	(1.5)	(2.0)	(–0.8)		0.14	
1991	–0.29	3.93	–0.20	0.140	0.44	364
	(–22.4)	(6.8)	(–0.3)		0.29	
		Panel C: United States—Consolidated				
1983	0.19	0.68	0.46	0.066	0.34	262
	(4.0)	(3.2)	(4.5)		0.28	
1984	–0.08	1.41	–0.92	0.112	0.57	262
	(–2.3)	(5.9)	(–4.1)		0.19	
1985	0.12	0.78	–0.68	0.123	0.46	262
	(3.9)	(4.5)	(–6.2)		0.17	
1986	0.17	0.47	0.44	0.560	0.45	262
	(4.6)	(3.8)	(5.5)		0.19	
1987	–0.14	1.07	0.37	0.223	0.38	262
	(–4.0)	(4.2)	(5.6)		0.36	
1988	0.03	0.23	0.47	0.116	0.43	262
	(1.0)	(1.4)	(3.4)		0.36	
1989	–0.05	1.47	–0.54	0.074	0.28	262
	(–1.3)	(4.7)	(–4.1)		0.29	
1990	–0.06	0.21	–0.12	0.015	0.38	262
	(–2.1)	(2.4)	(–1.1)		0.27	

[a] The model is $R_{iT} = \alpha_0 + \alpha_1 AE_{iT} + \alpha_2 \Delta AE_{iT} + \epsilon_{iT}$. See text for notations used in the equation.
[b] The first row of Spearman correlation is between R and AE, the second row is between R and ΔAE.

coefficients vary from year to year more than one might expect from the interest rate changes reported in Table 3–1. In analyzing the data, we found many extreme observations which had an impact on the parametric analysis, so we also provide rank correlations for returns and each independent variable. One pattern that emerges, which is consistent with the regression results, is a generally poorer correlation in the 1980s, beginning in 1982.

Moving to the consolidated data, we again find very low R^2 (below 0.03) and rank correlations, except for 1991. Use of consolidated data did not affect the associations in any systematic way; in four of the seven years the R^2s are higher for the restricted sample using parent accounting data. Looking at the U.S. sample for a similar period, we find much higher R^2s for every year and a higher rank correlation for the independent variables which are significant in the regression models.[11]

The annual window results are consistent with the interpretation that Japanese investors pay less attention to accounting earnings than U.S. investors, but this could plausibly be a reflection of measurement problems in the accounting process. By extending the window length we attempt to control for this explanation. The results in the annual window also suggest that the period of the 1980s reflect an even greater disregard for fundamental accounting measures in the valuation of Japanese companies.

As explained in "Data and Sample Selections" above, in analyzing the long window results we were constrained by the availability of data. Japanese companies have only been required to prepare full consolidated reports (that is, including equity accounting for their associate companies) since 1983, and 1984 was the first year with large numbers of companies presenting such data. For the parent data we use a similar interval as used for the consolidated data but also consider tests based on the full sample period available, which yields 20 years as a maximum window. We also report results with 1990 and 1991 as the last date. These results should not be considered as independent but the contrast between the two end-periods is quite dramatic for all window lengths and indicates the strength of the adjustment back to fundamentals.

Table 3–3 reports the results for four- and seven-year windows for the Japanese parent, consolidated, and U.S. data in panels A, B, and C, respectively. Panel A also includes the results for 20-year windows ending in 1990 and 1991. To minimize any concerns about independence, we use essentially nonoverlapping years, except for the windows ending 1990 or 1991, for the reasons previously indicated. As large observations can have undue influence on the parametric results, we also report the Spearman rank correlations for the return and aggregate earnings variables described in equation (3.2).

For the seven-year windows, with Japanese parent data, we see that adjusted R^2s range from 0.21 with 1978 as the end-date to 0.08 with 1984 as

TABLE 3–3
Long-Window Regressions[a]

Ending Yr./ Length of Window	α_0 (t-stat)	α_1 (t-stat)	Adjusted R^2	Spearman Corr.	N	Adjusted R^2 for 364 firms
		Panel A: Japan—Parent				
1990 / 20	6.51 (13.7)	1.84 (13.0)	0.211	0.50	647	
1991 / 20	3.35 (8.1)	1.84 (13.0)	0.372	0.56	507	
1978 / 7	1.00 (14.0)	1.22 (15.6)	0.214	0.53	898	0.120
1984 / 7	0.67 (7.8)	1.54 (9.9)	0.080	0.28	1111	0.139
1990 / 7	2.27 (16.7)	3.03 (10.3)	0.102	0.38	923	0.058
1991 / 7	1.36 (15.9)	1.88 (10.4)	0.136	0.49	688	0.167
1975 / 4	0.43 (12.7)	0.88 (15.5)	0.207	0.52	924	0.036
1979 / 4	0.61 (16.6)	0.79 (7.7)	0.054	0.34	1019	0.144
1983 / 4	0.18 (5.4)	0.90 (7.1)	0.041	0.30	1159	0.058
1987 / 4	1.49 (20.2)	1.60 (5.7)	0.026	0.28	1170	0.042
1990 / 4	0.87 (19.2)	1.68 (6.4)	0.038	0.30	990	0.000
1991 / 4	0.00 (0.0)	4.26 (14.7)	0.223	0.52	750	0.195
		Panel B: Japan—Consolidated				
1991 / 8	1.26 (8.9)	2.29 (8.7)	0.170	0.46	364	
1990 / 7	2.48 (13.9)	1.85 (4.7)	0.054	0.32	364	
1991 / 7	0.95 (7.7)	2.43 (8.1)	0.151	0.48	364	
1987 / 4	1.32 (12.4)	1.66 (3.8)	0.035	0.24	364	
1990 / 4	0.91 (11.1)	1.26 (2.1)	0.012	0.29	364	
1991 / 4	−0.04 (−0.8)	3.60 (9.0)	0.183	0.47	364	

[a] The model is $R_{iT} = \alpha_0 + \alpha_1 AE_{iT} + \epsilon_{iT}$. See text for notations used in the equation.

TABLE 3–3, concluded
Long-Window Regressions[a]

Ending Yr./ Length of Window	α_0 (t-stat)	α_1 (t-stat)	Adjusted R^2	Spearman Corr.	N	Adjusted R^2 for 364 firms
			Panel C: United States—Consolidated			
1990 / 7	−0.30 (−2.4)	2.04 (16.5)	0.510	0.80	262	
1987 / 4	0.07 (1.1)	1.91 (15.8)	0.489	0.76	262	
1990 / 4	−0.24 (−3.6)	1.64 (11.2)	0.323	0.55	262	

[a] The model is $R_{iT} = \alpha_0 + \alpha_1 AE_{iT} + \epsilon_{iT}$. See text for notations used in the equation.

the end-date.[12] While 1991 had nothing unusual about its earnings (see Table 3–1), the R^2 increased from 0.10 in 1990 to 0.14 in 1991. The relations among the rank correlations are even more striking. For the seven-year window ending in 1978 the correlation was 0.53, the 1984 end-date correlation was the lowest at 0.28, and the correlation increased from 0.38 to 0.49 when changing the end-date from 1990 to 1991. Although not reported, the R^2 for seven-year windows in the period between 1983 and 1989 were all less than 0.10. Note that even when we extend the window to 20 years, the R^2 increases to only 0.21, when 1990 is the end date, and then jumps to 0.37, when we move the end-date to 1991. The pattern in the rank correlations shows a similar trend.

The four-year window results in panel A are generally lower than those for the seven-year windows, but they are very low with R^2 no greater than 0.06 in any four-year window other than the 1975 and 1991 end-years. While we only report the nonoverlapping years, no other four-year window had an R^2 greater than 0.08. The rank correlations are also below 0.40, except for the first and last end-years.

In general, these long-window results suggest that even when we extend the window to 20 years there seems to be little association between aggregate earnings and stock returns. But it still might be perceived that the results is a function of the use of parent data and the general lack of usefulness of accounting data. To address this, we first look at panel B, which contains the results for the consolidated data. Unfortunately, we only have the period beginning with 1984 which from the parent and annual window results appears to be a period with relatively low use of accounting data in

Japan. The longest window of eight years yields an R^2 of 0.17 and a rank correlation of 0.46. The seven-year window ending in 1991 gives a similar result. But the seven-year window ending in 1990 shows a much lower R^2 of 0.05, and the rank correlation drops from 0.48 to 0.32. The last column in panel A of Table 3–3 presents the R^2 for the parent data for the subset of 364 firms being considered in panel b and reflects similar patterns to those of the larger sample of parent data. The four-year window results show an R^2 of 0.18 for end-date 1991 but 0.01 and 0.04 for 1990 and 1987, respectively, with rank correlations below 0.30 for these two end-dates.

Two points can be made from the long-window results discussed to this point. Using consolidated data does not increase the associations between returns and reported earnings, and lengthening the window has some effect but only a marginal one, unlike the pattern reported in Easton, Harris, and Ohlson (1992) and corroborated in other studies. But perhaps these firms are unusual in some way. The results in panel C report the results of the long-window tests for the matched sample of U.S. firms.

The results for the U.S. firms show that for the seven-year window ending in 1990 we have an R^2 of 0.51 and a rank correlation of 0.80. The four-year windows show similar differences to the Japanese results. The differences in association are quite striking, and it is hard to conceive that these could be a function of accounting differences or even interest rate differentials (see Table 3–1). Thus, once again, the results are consistent with the hypothesis that Japanese investors paid much less attention to the fundamental values reflected in accounting measures. The results also suggest that the price adjustments we have observed reflect a movement back toward the fundamentals, but it would be hard to argue that this process is complete, using only the 1991 data.

However, before drawing these conclusions too strongly, we consider some additional factors, which might be perceived to be omitted variables which would help to explain the results.

THE ROLE OF EARNINGS FORECASTS AND DEPRECIATION

Management's Earnings Forecast

Darrough and Harris (1991) show that while investors do react to earnings announcements, the reaction is affected by the management forecast of earnings issued simultaneously with historic earnings. We would expect rational investors, who use earnings in their valuation of companies, to incorporate the forecast future earnings into the price. Consequently, we use the management forecast of consolidated earnings for 1992 (deflated by beginning price) as an additional variable in the regression model based on equation (3.2) with 1991 as the end-year, for the consolidated sample. These results are reported in Table 3–4.

For the seven- and eight-year windows, we obtain an R^2 of 0.23, as compared to 0.15 and 0.17, respectively, for the aggregate earnings alone. We see some increment in the four-year window, but only a small difference in the one-year window. The results suggest that there is additional information in the earnings forecast but that it still leaves a significant amount of the stock returns unexplained, especially as compared to the U.S. sample.

Depreciation

As discussed in "Development of Hypotheses" above, many studies have argued that depreciation is a cause of differences between the United States and Japan, which affects the relations of accounting and stock market data. While this is spurious as an argument about alternative GAAP, it is conceivable that on average a more conservative depreciation policy may understate earnings in periods of rapid capital expansion as occurred in the 1980s in Japan. We also observe that Chan, Hamao, and Lakonishok (1991) find that net income plus depreciation is more highly correlated with monthly returns than reported earnings.[13] In general, depreciation may be useful as an additional explanatory variable reflecting, or proxying for, the expected growth of a company. In relatively short windows, depreciation may also reflect measurement errors in reported earnings. However, by extending the window we essentially control for such measurement problems. For U.S. companies, Ohlson and Penman (1992) have analyzed components of earnings within the long window framework. Over a ten-year window, they found that depreciation has a negative coefficient approximating the (positive) earnings coefficient in magnitude. This suggests that once we control for measurement problems found in short windows, investors seem to price depreciation like any other expense. Consequently, to evaluate the value-relevance of depreciation in Japan, we rerun the analysis for the parent sample using earnings plus depreciation and depreciation as separate variables.[14]

The results of these tests are reported in Table 3–5. Panels A and B report the results for the Japanese parent and U.S. samples, respectively. The results for the Japanese parent show that depreciation seems to help explain

TABLE 3–4
Japan—Consolidated with Management Forecast[a]

Ending Year/ Length of Window	α_0 (t-stat)	α_1 (t-stat)	α_2 (t-stat)	Adjusted R^2	Spearman Corr. between ret. & forecast	N
1991 / 8	1.16 (8.4)	1.74 (6.4)	2.30 (5.4)	0.229	0.56	364
1991 / 7	0.83 (6.8)	1.55 (4.8)	3.41 (6.1)	0.227	0.55	364
1991 / 1	−0.29 (−23.7)	3.33 (5.8)	0.46 (1.8)	0.146	0.43	364

[a] The model is $R_{iT} = \alpha_0 + \alpha_1 AE_{iT} + \alpha_2 FE_{iT} + \epsilon_{iT}$, where FE is forecast of earnings by management, divided by the beginning stock price.

TABLE 3–5
Regressions with Depreciation[a]

Ending Year/ Length of Window	α_0 (t-stat)	α_1 (t-stat)	α_2 (t-stat)	Adjusted R^2	Spearman Corr.[b]	N
Panel A–1: Japan—Parent (Long Window)[a]						
1978 / 7	0.28 (3.1)	1.48 (15.6)	−1.08 (−8.9)	0.371	0.69 / 0.59	789
1984 / 7	−0.13 (−1.1)	2.53 (12.4)	−2.04 (−8.2)	0.163	0.41 / 0.32	977
1990 / 7	1.79 (9.6)	3.92 (9.5)	−3.51 (−7.0)	0.127	0.41 / 0.29	781
1991 / 7	1.10 (10.4)	2.12 (10.6)	−1.82 (−6.9)	0.170	0.44 / 0.21	631
1983 / 4	0.05 (1.1)	1.28 (8.6)	−1.15 (−6.4)	0.064	0.28 / 0.12	1069
1987 / 4	1.34 (13.0)	1.80 (4.3)	−1.33 (−2.6)	0.024	0.32 / 0.23	1089
1990 / 4	0.70 (12.6)	1.95 (7.3)	−1.12 (−3.0)	0.078	0.32 / 0.19	871
1991 / 4	−0.15 (−3.4)	5.09 (16.7)	−4.85 (−12.9)	0.296	0.49 / 0.24	729

[a] The model is $R_{iT} = \alpha_0 + \alpha_1 (AE_{iT} + D_{iT}) + \alpha_2 D_{iT} + \epsilon_{iT}$, where D_{iT} is cumulative depreciation per share, divided by beginning stock price.
[b] The first row of Spearman correlation is between R and $(AE + D)$, the second row is between R and D. See text for notations used in the equations.

TABLE 3–5, continued
Regressions with Depreciation[a]

Year	α_0 (t-stat)	α_1 (t-stat)	α_2 (t-stat)	α_3 (t-stat)	α_4 (t-stat)	Adjusted R^2	N
			Panel A–2: Japan—Parent (One-Year Window)[b]				
1971	−0.03	1.12	−0.18	−1.05	0.61	0.092	925
	(−1.1)	(7.1)	(−1.3)	(−5.0)	(2.4)		
1972	0.27	0.88	1.12	0.61	−0.48	0.260	945
	(8.3)	(4.5)	(6.0)	(3.0)	(−2.8)		
1973	−0.11	1.09	0.26	0.44	−0.21	0.183	966
	(−4.6)	(5.0)	(1.7)	(1.9)	(−1.7)		
1974	−0.10	0.30	1.25	0.85	−1.10	0.277	993
	(−5.2)	(1.7)	(8.1)	(4.2)	(−5.0)		
1975	0.01	0.57	0.21	−0.55	1.06	0.066	966
	(0.5)	(3.2)	(1.3)	(−2.6)	(4.4)		
1976	0.12	0.55	1.00	0.53	0.30	0.140	977
	(5.0)	(2.7)	(6.2)	(2.1)	(0.9)		
1977	0.05	0.46	−0.02	−0.05	0.22	0.047	1073
	(3.5)	(4.0)	(−0.2)	(−0.3)	(0.6)		
1978	0.17	0.65	0.70	0.36	−1.30	0.070	1089
	(7.9)	(3.1)	(5.0)	(1.3)	(−2.7)		
1979	−0.04	−0.26	1.07	2.14	−4.30	0.141	1113
	(−2.3)	(−1.3)	(6.0)	(8.3)	(−5.4)		
1980	0.04	0.22	0.27	−0.33	0.26	0.004	1146
	(2.0)	(0.9)	(1.5)	(−1.0)	(0.3)		
1981	−0.02	0.95	0.28	−0.73	1.91	0.049	1153
	(−1.2)	(5.1)	(1.8)	(−3.1)	(2.6)		
1982	−0.05	0.16	0.16	0.24	−0.80	0.020	1154
	(−3.9)	(1.2)	(1.8)	(1.4)	(−1.7)		
1983	0.27	0.04	0.85	0.13	−0.53	0.019	1150
	(12.8)	(0.2)	(3.8)	(0.5)	(−0.7)		
1984	0.20	0.10	0.48	0.51	−1.32	0.012	1164
	(9.6)	(0.3)	(.19)	(1.4)	(−3.1)		
1985	0.18	0.29	0.60	0.95	−1.00	0.030	1200
	(8.2)	(0.8)	(2.1)	(2.1)	(−2.5)		
1986	0.47	−1.00	1.22	0.84	−2.10	0.005	1232
	(16.3)	(−2.1)	(2.6)	(1.4)	(−1.3)		
1987	0.16	3.58	0.33	−2.36	−10.93	0.040	1198
	(5.9)	(4.8)	(1.7)	(−2.6)	(−4.0)		
1988	0.17	3.03	0.36	0.85	0.00	0.086	1155
	(6.8)	(3.7)	(0.5)	(0.9)	(0.0)		
1989	0.12	1.89	−0.44	−1.70	−2.98	0.010	1091
	(6.9)	(2.8)	(−2.1)	(−2.1)	(−1.4)		
1990	0.02	5.75	1.18	−5.32	0.91	0.062	1113
	(1.1)	(5.4)	(1.1)	(−4.3)	(0.3)		
1991	−0.27	4.14	−1.27	−4.35	1.7	0.096	994
	(−20.7)	(6.7)	(−2.0)	(−6.2)	(1.0)		

[a] The model is $R_{iT} = \alpha_0 + \alpha_1 (AE_{iT} + D_{iT}) + \alpha_2 \Delta (AE_{iT} + D_{iT}) + \alpha_3 D_{iT} + \alpha_4 \Delta D_{iT} + \epsilon_{iT}$

TABLE 3–5, concluded
Regressions with Depreciation

Ending Year/ Length of Window	α_0 (t-stat)	α_1 (t-stat)	α_2 (t-stat)	Adjusted R^2	Spearman Corr.[b]	N
Panel B: United States—Consolidated (Long-Window)[a]						
1989 / 7	−0.39 (−1.9)	1.94 (12.9)	−1.59 (−5.4)	0.502	0.69 0.26	260
1990 / 7	−0.23 (−1.6)	2.11 (15.0)	−2.28 (−8.7)	0.510	0.69 0.31	260
1987 / 4	0.01 (0.1)	1.85 (14.3)	−1.6 (−6.5)	0.492	0.68 0.20	260
1990 / 4	−0.43 (−5.4)	1.57 (11.0)	−0.95 (−4.4)	0.365	0.46 0.09	260

[a] The model is $R_{iT} = \alpha_0 + \alpha_1(AE_{iT} + D_{iT}) + \alpha_2 D_{iT} + \epsilon_{iT}$, where D_{iT} is cumulative depreciation per share, divided by beginning stock price.
[b] The first row of Spearman correlation is between R and $(AE + D)$, the second row is between R and D. See text for notations used in the equations.

more of the cross-sectional variation in returns. The R^2 for the one-year regressions increase in each year, and the depreciation variable has a significant coefficient in most of the years. But we see that in the U.S. sample, while the impact on the R^2 is not as large, there is an increase in the one-year windows, and the coefficient on depreciation is generally positive. These results suggest that depreciation is probably proxying for some other value-relevant information variable or may be reflecting investors' perceptions of a measurement error. As we increase the window, the increase in R^2 is maintained in the Japanese sample; so, for example, we see the R^2 for the seven-year windows ending 1978, 1984, and 1991 increasing from 0.21, 0.08, and 0.14 (in Table 3–3, panel A) to 0.37, 0.16, and 0.17, respectively. But the coefficients on the depreciation variables are now negative and quite similar in magnitude to the coefficient on aggregate earnings (especially if we adjust for earnings being an after-tax measure). These results are consistent with investors' treating aggregate depreciation similarly to any other expense once we control for periodic measurement issues and also that depreciation may proxy for cross-sectional differences in anticipated growth via capital expenditure. The results for the seven-year window for the U.S. sample show a similar result in terms of the coefficients, but the aggregate depreciation makes no incremental contribution to the R^2. Given the relatively heavy investment in capital equipment in Japan through much of the sample period, it is perhaps not surprising that the depreciation expense proxies for some value-relevant information; however, given the long window results, it is hard to argue that this is purely a consequence of accounting measurement questions. Further analysis of this question is beyond the scope of this particular research.

SUMMARY AND CONCLUSIONS

The debate on the consequences of differences in accounting practices and the effect of these differences on the valuation of securities has frequently considered adjustments to the accounting system with an assumption, at least implicitly, that this would "normalize" the comparative associations between accounting and stock market measures. Yet there has been little systematic evaluation of these associations, particularly where many of the measurement concerns are largely controlled for.

In this chapter we analyze the return-earnings association over varying window lengths and compare the results for sample of Japanese and U.S. firms. Our results are consistent with the perception that Japanese investors utilize accounting information, particularly earnings, less in their pricing of companies than do U.S. investors. The corollary is that Japanese investors place a larger weight on "other information" in their valuations. This conclusion was particularly evident in the "boom" period of the mid-1980s, when the fundamental values inherent in the accounting data appear to have been largely ignored. The increased associations we find with the inclusion of 1991 prices suggest that the current fall in prices is consistent with a return to more emphasis on fundamental values but that this process may not be complete.

We also find results consistent with the notion that depreciation is treated simply as an expense over long windows, but it also appears to act as a proxy for anticipated growth from capital investment. Further research would be needed to test this hypothesis more directly.

A further implication of the research findings is that it is implausible that accounting differences can ever explain differences in the associations between accounting and stock market measures in Japan, relative to other countries. The fact that the associations are so similar for consolidated and parent data itself indicates that using the lack of consolidation as an explanation for past differences is implausible. Rather, investors seeking to make investment decisions in Japan need to reconsider the underlying pricing and institutional practices. Using differences in accounting practice to justify the valuation differentials across countries is essentially using accounting as a scapegoat for more fundamental structural differences.

NOTES

1. This was reported in *The Nikkei Weekly* of the week of June 13, 1992. The advisory body is a subcommittee of the Council on Foreign Exchange and Other Transactions.
2. In a study of the information content of Japanese earnings over short windows, Darrough and Harris (1991) show that there is a market reaction to the announcement of earnings and the management forecast of earnings with a more noticeable reaction occurring for the parent earnings. This suggests that investors do consider earnings as a measure of information about the firm. Also, Chan, Hamao, and Lakonishok (1991) test associations between monthly returns and various fundamental variables, but their tests use 12 return measures for each accounting measure and use various combinations of variables over annual windows without considering the accounting or valuation characteristics of the variables.
3. The issue of cross-holdings is also sometimes considered [Aron (1987, 1989) and French and Poterba (1991)], but we view this as a moot point when evaluating returns-earnings associations as each share owns a portion of the net assets irrespective of who holds the share. To the extent the company owns in itself, there would be a reduction in the net assets as well as the equity. This position is also taken in Brown, Soybel, and Stickney (1991).
4. Of course, this presumes that, in fact, the consolidation rules reflect the notion of capturing the group structure. We would conjecture that in Japan a problem remains because of the nature of the stable shareholdings and the significant influence which exists in the *keiretsu*. This institutional characteristic would argue for equity accounting of these holdings, even though the stakes are below the traditional 20 percent threshold. Thus, in Japan, we might reasonably expect an understatement of earnings and equity based on the as–if equity accounting measures that could be used. This does not presume a mark-to-market measure which would create a circularity in the associations.
5. A similar model derived more heuristically is found in Wilcox (1984). Ohlson's model is found to have empirical validity in Easton and Harris (1991b) and Maydew (1992). Dividend terms have been found to be empirically irrelevant in the studies on U.S. data. Given the relatively low dividend payouts in Japan, this insignificance should be even more true there. Consequently, we ignore dividends in the rest of this chapter.
6. Fairfield and Harris (1991) and Penman (1991) have demonstrated a strong correlation between P/B and ROE for U.S. firms.
7. Ohlson (1989) formally models this relation, and Easton and Harris (1991a) derive and empirically test the relation between earnings levels, earnings changes and

returns, and show that on average the earnings level variable is relevant for explaining returns. Corroborating evidence can be found in Easton and Harris (1991b), Easton, Harris, and Ohlson (1992), Warfield and Wild (1992) for U.S. companies, and Harris and Lang (1992) for German companies.

8. Easton, Harris, and Ohlson (1992) and Ohlson and Penman (1991), and Lys, Ramesh, and Thiagarajan (1992) use alternative definitions of change in earnings. Easton, Harris, and Ohlson use the simple change based on an equivalent time period while the other view change in earnings based on the difference between earnings at the beginning and the end of the relevant window. In general, as one extends the window, the changes variable becomes less well defined and has little relevance in explaining returns. Hence, we do not incorporate the change variable into our long-window analysis.

9. Other studies have corroborated these findings, including Lys, Ramesh, and Thiagarajan (1992) and Warfield and Wild (1992).

10. A report in *The Nikkei Weekly* of January 11, 1992, states:
Sony's stock has been performing poorly in recent months, and stock market observers are critical about the company's consolidated-based management style... Even some Sony officials have begun voicing concern that the emphasis on the consolidation-based management might be wrong.
"That strategy might have resulted in our not paying enough attention to the parent company's profits," said one official (page 8).

11. Comparisons of R^2 must always be interpreted cautiously if the dependent variable changes in any way. The spirit of the comparisons is from the sense of accounting measures being fundamental measures of value or change in value and a standard worldwide valuation model. Thus, *ex ante*, each sample can be considered a random drawing from the same population.

12. Easton, Harris, and Ohlson (1992) note that the choice of a start-date and end-date and the means of choosing the sample had little bearing on the correlations for the ten-year window correlations and R^2 for U.S. data.

13. Chan, Hamao, and Lakonishok (1991) term this variable "cash flow" as is often done in the finance literature, but this is clearly a misnomer, given that depreciation is the only adjustment made to report earnings.

14. In principle, we should adjust the depreciation add-back to earnings for the tax rate. However, Chan, Hamao, and Lakonishok (1991) and others have not done this, and the data are not readily available to us. Thus, the earnings plus depreciation variable is partially misspecified. In addition, we use the parent sample because the consolidated depreciation was only available to us for less than half the 364 firms. Given the lack of difference in consolidated and parent returns-earnings associations, this should have little impact on the interpretation of our results.

REFERENCES

Aron, P. (1987). "Japanese Price Earnings Multiples: Refined and Updated." Daiwa Securities America.

Aron, P. (1989). "Japanese P/E Ratios and Accounting II: Rhetoric and Reality." Daiwa Securities America.

Bildersee, J. J., J. J. Cheh, and C. Lee. (1990). "The International Price-Earnings Ratio Phenomenon: A Partial Explanation." *Japan and the World Economy.* pp. 263–82.

Brown, P. R., V. E. Soybel, and C. P. Stickney. (1991). "Achieving Comparability of U.S. and Japanese Financial Statement Data." New York University working paper.

Chan, L., Y. Hamao, and J. Lakonishok. (1991). "Fundamentals and Stock Prices in Japan." *Journal of Finance.* December, pp. 739–1764.

Choi, F. D. S., and R. M. Levich. (1990). *The Capital Market Effects of International Accounting Diversity.* Homewood, IL: Dow Jones–Irwin.

Darrough, M. N., T. S. Harris. (1991). "Do Management Forecasts of Earnings Affect Stock Prices in Japan?" in W. T. Ziemba, W. Bailey, and Y. Hamao (eds.), *Japanese Financial Market Research.* Amsterdam: North-Holland. pp. 197–229.

Dontoh, A., J. Livnat, and R. Todd. (1991). "International Comparisons of Earnings Price Ratio, Estimation Risk and Growth." New York University working paper.

Easton, P. D., and T. S. Harris. (1991b). "Empirical Evidence on the Relevance of Earnings and Book Value of Owners' Equity in Security Valuation." Columbia University working paper.

Easton, P. D., and T. S. Harris. (1991b). "Earnings as an Explanatory Variable for Returns." *Journal of Accounting Research.* pp. 19–36.

Easton, P. D., R. S. Harris, and J. A. Ohlson. (1992). "Accounting Earnings Can Explain Most of Security Returns: The Case of Long Return Intervals." *Journal of Accounting and Economics.*

Fairfield, P. M., and T. S. Harris. (1991). "An Investigation of Intrinsic Value and Risk as Explanations of the Returns to Price-to-Earnings and Price-to-Book Value Trading Strategies." Columbia University working paper.

French, K., and J. Poterba. (1991). "Were Japanese Stocks Too High?" *Journal of Financial Economics.* 29, pp. 337–63.

Hamao, Y. (1991). "A Standard Data Base for the Analysis of Japanese Security Markets." *Journal of Business.* 64, pp. 87–102.

Hamao, Y., and R. G. Ibbotson. (1992). *SBI - Japan (with updates).* Chicago: Ibbotson Associates.

Harris, T. S., and M. Lang. (1992). "Relations Between Security Market Prices, Returns and Accounting Measures in Germany." Columbia University working paper.

Harris, T. S., and J. A. Ohlson. (1987). "Accounting Disclosures and the Market's Valuation of Oil and Gas Properties." *The Accounting Review.* pp. 651–70.

Ibbotson Associates. (1992). *Stocks, Bills, Bonds and Inflation.* Chicago.

Lys, T., K. Ramesh, and S. Thiagarajan. (1992). "The Role of Earnings Levels vs. Earnings Changes in Explaining Stock Returns: Implications from the Time Series Properties of Earnings." Northwestern University working paper.

Maydew, E. L. (1992). "An Empirical Evaluation of Earnings and Book Values in Security Valuation." University of Iowa working paper.

McCauley, R. N., and S. Zimmer. (1991). "The Cost of Capital for Securities Firms in the United States and Japan." *Federal Reserve Bank of New York Quarterly Reviews*. Fall, pp. 14–27.

Ohlson, J. A. (1989). "Accounting Earnings, Book Value and Dividends: The Theory of the Clean Surplus Equation (Part I)." Columbia University working paper.

Ohlson, J. A. (1991). "Earnings, Book Values, and Dividends in Security Valuation." Columbia University working paper.

Ohlson, J. A., and S. H. Penman. (1992). "Disaggregated Accounting Data as Explanatory Variables for Returns." *Journal of Accounting, Auditing and Finance*.

Penman, S. H. (1991). "An Evaluation of Accounting Rate of Return." *Journal of Accounting, Auditing and Finance*.

Poterba, J. (1991). "Comparing the Cost of Capital in the United States and Japan: A Survey of Methods." *Federal Reserve Bank of New York Quarterly Reviews*. Winter, pp. 20–32.

Sakakibara, S., H. Yamaji, H. Sakurai, K. Shiroshita, and S. Fukuda. (1988). *The Japanese Stock Market: Pricing Systems and Accounting Information*. New York: Praeger.

Schieneman, G. S. (1988). "Japanese P/E Ratios: Are They Overstated by Conservative Accounting Practices?" *International Accounting and Investment Review*. Prudential-Bache Securities.

Tokyo Keizai Shimpo Sha. (1992). *Japan Company Handbook*. Tokyo.

Viner, A. (1988). *Inside Japanese Financial Markets*. Homewood, IL: Dow Jones–Irwin.

Warfield, T. D., and J. Wild. (1992). "Accounting Recognition and the Relevance of Earnings as an Explanatory Variable for Returns." *The Accounting Review*.

Wilcox, J. W. (1984). "The P/B–ROE Valuation Model." *Financial Analysts Journal*. January–February, pp. 58–66.

Zielinski, R., and N. Holloway. (1991). *Unequal Equities: Power and Risk in Japan's Stock Market*. Tokyo: Kodansha International.

COMMENT

Eric B. Lindenberg

DISCUSSION OF CHAPTER 2

As author Raman Uppal clearly states, his chapter limits its discussion of the potential causes of bias to three possible explanations:

- A desire to hedge home country inflation
- Institutional barriers to foreign investment
- Transactions cost and taxes on foreign investments

Professor Uppal concludes, after either reviewing studies done by others or by use of his own model in the case of the hedging explanation, that these reasons do not explain why investors are biased homeward.

At first, I thought that a home country bias was primarily a U.S. phenomenon, consistent with the provinciality and noninternational focus that we Americans have for most other matters. However, I was surprised by the strength of the phenomenon in most other countries, particularly where the local market is small and a bit less liquid (as in Italy) and where economies are supposedly more integrated (as in Europe, at least until recently).

While I agree that these explanations for bias were appropriate to investigate, I am not surprised by the results because in some cases certain assumptions were made that may have oversimplified the problem. For example, the assumption that foreign bond returns and exchange rates are exogenous is not particularly realistic. On the other hand, Prof. Uppal's development of the idea that it is decreasing risk aversion that leads to a home country bias is very neat. The argument that greater risk aversion causes investors to benefit more from balancing capital stocks across countries because they must be concerned with using up domestic consumption capacity too quickly is compelling. There is an assumption here that I might challenge, namely that output (and return) levels are uncorrelated across countries. Relative exchange rates and interest rate changes clearly may favor more production and economic activity shifting in one particular direction.

With respect to institutional constraints on foreign investing, I also might challenge the statement that "there is no segmentation between the U.S. and the Japanese stock markets after the enactment of the Foreign Exchange and Foreign Trade Control law in 1980." This may be true for institutions, but there are still considerable limitations on individual foreign investments in Japan.

The discussion of the lack of importance of foreign taxes in explaining home country bias seems perfectly plausible, but I think there is a difference between reality and the perception by investors on what it will cost them. In my line of work, we talk to issuers of securities and point out to them that borrowing in foreign capital markets makes sense in order to deal with interest allocation rules for U.S. -based multinationals. These rules limit the ability to utilize foreign tax credits in the United States, unless borrowings are done where foreign income is earned. More and more companies are understanding this but the process of getting them to act is slow. There is a clear analog here to the investors' decision-making process.

As far as I can see, there are two major reasons for home country bias that are not fully examined here:

- First, when an investor invests in a home country company, that company often has investments and economic activities located abroad. As such, the investor implicitly invests in foreign markets anyway. Prof. Uppal overlooks this important *implicit* channel of foreign investments.
- Second, investors do not optimally invest abroad because of the high cost of information, monitoring and liquidity costs. There is not much discussion of these matters either.

In summary, I thought this paper was a worthy effort at reviewing some basic reasons for home country bias. I think, however, that ending this paper by saying that the three reasons the author has investigated don't explain the phenomenon is not quite as satisfying as I might have liked.

Nevertheless, there are other avenues to pursue. I've mentioned some and Prof. Uppal has done so as well. Perhaps some will bear fruit.

DISCUSSION OF CHAPTER 3

This chapter confirms my prior beliefs about what drives and does not drive valuations of securities in Japan. Further, it is consistent with the decision-making processes of Japanese issuers of securities who seem to ignore some relevant information when choosing among financing alternatives.

What this chapter says is that after you cut through most of the accounting differences in reported earnings between the United States and Japan in order to put the information on an equal footing, Japanese security prices and investor returns bear far less correlation with earnings information than do corresponding U.S. securities. I agree with this conclusion and I think that the choices made to test these hypothesis, namely use of parent and consolidated data, looking at both P/E and total return data and the use of depreciation data are good choices to make, although I am sure that other specific methods are possible. However, in the end we still are left unsatisfied because we have not answered the question: If Japanese security prices and returns are not related to the same kind of performance data as U.S. prices and returns, then what are they related to?

As I was thinking about this last week while driving in my car, I had tuned the radio to a talk show offering financial advice to people calling in on the phone. The radio expert was asked whether the large drop in the Japanese market suggested real opportunities for buying value. His answer was that the primary drivers of prices in Japan are whim, corruption, and the universal desire for creating investment bubbles that never burst. Further, he stated that value had nothing to do with it. He closed by saying that a pole had not yet been invented that was long enough for him to want to touch the Japanese market with it.

Well, if we accept this view as having a reasonable following, why is it that Japanese investors are willing to participate on a different basis in Japan than U.S. investors?

First, the Japanese have, to this point, been willing to accept a more managed economy either through government oversight or through joint corporate control in the kieretsu. This means that Japanese stock prices less accurately reflect market reality and are much more tied to what the controllers (corporate or government) will or will not do when a problem needs to be solved. Witness the positive and then negative responses, after the Japanese market had fallen precepitously, to the first public statements by key Japanese officials that intervention would occur and then to the lack of follow-up. Put differently, we should only expect strong associations between prices and returns and economic performance data in a free market and not in a managed one.

Second, and related to the first, the U.S. economy is characterized by a much lower marginal cost of information than in Japan. The information market is deeper and more liquid here. This has made the ability to gather data by a broader set of investors far more significant in the United States. Our recent Nobel laureate in economics, Gary Becker, has spent his career arguing that the price structure and competitiveness of information markets will always influence the responses of market participants to new information.

Japan is clearly moving toward the U.S. model in its market for information. Shocks such as the huge decline in the Japanese stock market will accelerate this movement (although in this case, I'm not sure whether the shock is the cause or the effect). The authors of this paper have clearly taken note of the recent changes. In particular, the statistical explanatory power has improved in the most recent years. We shall see where it leads going forward.

Third, and perhaps most important, for some reason which I cannot fully explain, U.S. investors are much more likely to interpret earnings announcements above or below expectations as signals that the net present value of future cash flows is suddenly higher or lower than previously understood. In Japan, in contrast, a longer term view permits a single period's earnings results to have much less weight in estimating future net present values. It is my opinion that U.S. investors are over-reacting and Japanese investors are not acting strongly enough. Again, the recent fall-off in the Japanese market may be evidence of a correction in attitudes. It is the inability to alter the U.S. inferences from earnings that is a major cause of insufficient investment on this side of the Pacific.

Two final points should be made. First, the observations made by Hall, Hamao, and Harris are very much consistent with those made in a Salomon Brothers' publication, "The Cost of Capital in Japan and the U.S.," by my colleagues Niso Abuaf and Kathy Carmody, in which evidence was presented that a clearly lower cost of capital in Japan was present after cutting through accounting and structural differences with the United States. However, that paper points out that expectations for convergence of capital costs are high in light of a movement (we hope) to a single world capital market.

Second, whether the lack of association of market prices and accounting measures in Japan is cultural or not, I am a firm believer in markets and prices ultimately being tied together. This means that as information becomes less expensive and more liquid, the information market in Japan and the United States will have to bear the same relationship to security prices and markets. If this does not happen, the cost to the Japanese investor as well as to the Japanese issuer of securities will be just too high.

COMMENT

Clyde P. Stickney

DISCUSSION OF CHAPTER 2

Professor Uppal addresses the following research question in his chapter: Why do investors weight their portfolios toward domestic assets (debt and equity) when international diversification of their portfolios would reduce their risk by reducing the variance of returns. The author uses analytical modeling and a literature review to address this question.

Professor Uppal suggests three possible reasons for the domestic bias: (1) desire by investors to hedge domestic inflation, (2) existence of institutional barriers to international diversification, and (3) existence of taxes and other transactions costs that inhibit transnational investment. The author concludes that none of these three reasons provide convincing explanations for the domestic investment bias.

Hedge Domestic Inflation

Other researchers have demonstrated that equity returns in the United States have outpaced inflation for most of the twentieth century and therefore serve as an effective domestic inflation hedge. Uppal develops a returns model that incorporates changes in international prices and exchange rates. He demonstrates analytically that an investor desiring to hedge inflation should prefer a mix of domestic and nondomestic investments. His argument rests on the premise that at some point in the future the investor will desire to consume a nondomestic physical asset. The domestic price of that nondomestically-produced asset is subject to price changes in the country of origin and to exchange rate changes. Acquiring equity securities of the producer of that physical product hedges the potential effect of price and exchange rate changes of the physical product. Thus, risk averse investors should weight their investment portfolios more heavily toward nondomestic securities than is now the case.

Uppal's model extends previous research relating inflation and equity returns by factoring in nondomestic prices and exchange rates. One should not view Uppal's results as inconsistent with previous research since he uses a more comprehensive model of risk factors.

Although Uppal's model appears well specified in an analytical sense, the reader is left to wonder why its prescriptions seem to differ from observed reality (i.e., why the domestic bias in investing persists). An empirical test of this model on real world data seems essential at this point. Analytical modeling is an important step in enhancing understanding of economic behavior but the job is only partially completed at this stage.

One issue that Uppal must address in an empirical testing of the model is the definition of a "domestic asset." Most traded U.S. firms have diversified internationally. Acquiring a U.S. equity security may satisfactorily hedge both domestic and nondomestic inflation (and exchange rate changes) so that acquiring nondomestic equity securities is unnecessary.

Existence of Institutional Barriers

Uppal suggests that a lack of access to nondomestic investment opportunities might serve as a constraint on international diversification. For example, countries that impose restrictions on the proportion of foreign ownership may limit investment opportunities abroad. Uppal surveys the limited number of studies addressing this question and concludes that the restrictions are not so severe as to explain the bias toward domestic investments. Research on institutional and cultural differences between countries and their effects on economic decisions is in its infancy. One wonders whether Uppal's conclusion regarding the lack of importance of such factors might be premature.

Existence of Taxes and Other Transactions Costs

Uppal suggests that transactions costs of international investment may be sufficiently high that reductions in returns outweigh reductions in risk. He surveys several studies that have examined *explicit* transactions costs (taxes, commissions). Uppal concludes that such costs are sufficiently low that they should not unduly inhibit international investments.

Having eliminated three potential explanations for the domestic bias in investing, Uppal ponders other possibilities. He suggests that *nonexplicit* transactions costs may be part of the explanation. Differences in language and financial reporting formats and principles, as well as ready access to information about individual companies and countries, may have been a barrier to international investing in the past. Advances in information technology transfer are eroding this barrier at a rapid rate. The theme of this conference is an assessment of how differences in accounting principles may influence financial reports and security returns. A time series study of the extent of international investment would likely show that the domestic bias has decreased in recent years as access to and knowledge of international investment opportunities have improved. One might expect continuing erosion of the domestic bias in the future.

DISCUSSION OF CHAPTER 3

The authors address the following research question: What is the degree of association between accounting measures and stock prices in Japan relative to the U.S.? This exploratory study aims to identify *if* a difference in the degree of association exists rather than to test hypotheses based on institutional, cultural, or other factors that would lead one to expect that differences would exist.

The authors perform three principal correlation analyses:

Correlation 1:   Market Price   ◁——▷   Earnings
                     ─────────────   ────────────
                     Book Value of   *Book Value of*
                     Shareholders'   *Shareholders'*
                     Equity   *Equity*

This correlation relates the market-to-book ratio and the rate of return on shareholders' equity. The authors find positive rank order correlations, with the correlations for U.S. firms exceeding those for Japanese firms.

Correlation 2:   Market Price   ◁——▷   Earnings

                   Earnings   *Book Value of*
                                             Shareholders'
                                             Equity

This correlation relates the price-earnings ratio and the rate of return on shareholders' equity. The authors find a negative rank order correlation for Japanese firms and a positive rank order correlation for U.S. firms. The U.S. correlations exceeded the Japanese correlations.

Correlation 3:   *Market Rate*   ◁——▷   *Earnings +*
                   of Return   *Change in*
                                             Earnings

This correlation relates market rates of return with the levels and changes in earnings. The authors find positive rank order and least squares correlations, with the U.S. correlations exceeding those for Japan. As the returns window increases (i.e., one year versus multiple years), the correlations increase.

Consistent with earlier studies examining the relation between accounting measures and stock prices exclusively in a U.S. setting, the R^2s found in this study tend to be low (rank order correlations generally less than .4 and least squares correlations less than .2).

This study does a commendable job exploring the relation between accounting data and stock prices in a Japanese setting. The study may be viewed as fact finding in nature. The next task is to gain better understanding regarding the reasons for the correlation differences observed. The following comments raise questions or seek elaboration on various aspects of the study.

Sample Selection

The authors use a matched pair sample design of U.S. and Japanese firms. The matching resulted in a sample of 262 U.S. firms and 364 Japanese firms. The chapter needs some discussion of the reasons for the different sample sizes. One suspects that Japanese firms are smaller on average than U.S. firms, requiring more Japanese firms to achieve a matching on size.

Period Studied

The authors examined Japanese data back to 1971 but examined U.S. data only during the 1990s. It would be of interest to extend the period of study for U.S. firms back to 1971 as well. The authors' reason for not studying this earlier period for U.S. firms is that U.S. firms reported consolidated data during these earlier years while Japanese firms reported only nonconsolidated data. Any direct comparison of the correlations is therefore clouded by this difference in accounting principles. However, the authors' finding (consistent with other studies) that stock prices in Japan tend to follow nonconsolidated data more than consolidated data reduces this data comparability concern.

Studying this earlier period for the U.S. firms might shed some light on the authors' finding that the correlations between accounting data and stock prices for Japanese firms were higher in the early 1970s and the late 1990s than in the intervening periods. Does a similar pattern emerge for U.S. firms? Or, were events unique to Japan causing the different correlation results over time?

Interpretation of Results

The authors could improve their paper by exploring more fully possible reasons for the seemingly inconsistent correlation results. U.S. firms experienced higher rank order correlations when the rate of return on shareholders' equity was related to market-to-book ratios (correlation 1), whereas Japanese firms experienced higher rank order correlations when the rate of return on shareholders' equity was related to the price-earnings ratio (correlation 2). The authors' suggest that the difference in correlations is consistent with the greater emphasis on earnings in the U.S. than in Japan. This interpretation of the results is not likely to be obvious to many readers.

PART TWO

INTERNATIONAL GAAP DIFFERENCES AND THEIR EFFECTS ON FIRMS

CHAPTER 4

INTERNATIONAL DIFFERENCES IN GAAP AND THE PRICING OF EARNINGS

Peter F. Pope
William P. Rees

INTRODUCTION

In 1988 Jaguar plc reported net income before extraordinary items of £61.3 million when the income statement was prepared under U.K. generally accepted accounting principles (GAAP). This represented a *decrease* of 26.5 percent compared to the 1987 net income figure. However, when its 1988 income statement was restated under U.S. GAAP, the same firm reported net income of £113.1 million, an *increase* of 89.1 percent on the comparable figure for 1987. At the time, 24 percent of the Jaguar common stock was held in the form of American Depositary Receipts (ADRs) quoted on NASDAQ. The reconciliation between income measures prepared under foreign and U.S. GAAP regimes is mandated under the Securities and Ex-

The authors would like to thank Carol Graham and Donna McDougall for research assistance, and the Chartered Association of Certified Accountants, the Economic and Social Research Council (Research Grant R000233813) and the Research Board of the Institute of Chartered Accountants in England and Wales for financial support. The authors acknowledge helpful comments on earlier drafts received from Ray Ball, Mary Barth, Gary Biddle, Terry O'Rourke, Stephen Penman, Bob Thompson, Ross Watts and seminar participants at Harvard Business School, Lancaster University and University of Maryland. Any remaining errors are the authors' responsibility.

change Commission's 20-F filing requirements covering all U.S. listed foreign corporations. The 20-F disclosure requirements create an almost unique opportunity for market based accounting research to investigate the information content of earnings numbers produced under competing GAAP regimes. As Biddle and Saudagaran (1989) and others have noted, different GAAP regimes lead to significantly different disclosure levels and often require the use of quite different measurement rules for key line items. As a result of measurement differences, significant differences can occur not only in the magnitudes of income numbers, but also in the direction of change of income numbers reported under two GAAP regimes.[1]

The purpose of this chapter is to evaluate the information content of earnings measured under U.K. GAAP and U.S. GAAP by examining the cross-sectional association between returns and earnings for a sample of U.K.-domiciled stocks listed in both the United Kingdom and the United States. Although overall disclosure levels in both the United States and the United Kingdom are high and are oriented towards equity investors (Cairns *et al.*, 1984), there are significant differences in income measurement rules between the two GAAP regimes. Establishing the relative roles played by competing income numbers is potentially interesting for at least three reasons. First, from the perspective of financial statement users such as investors and analysts, it may be useful to establish how the market values the alternative earnings measures on average. Second, it is possible to interpret the information content of earnings measured in different GAAP regimes as a commentary on the relative success of standard-setters in the two regimes in meeting the information needs of equity market investors. And third, the incremental information content of the SEC-mandated disclosures is potentially relevant to the ongoing policy debate currently involving the SEC and the U.S. stock exchanges. It has been argued that the disclosures required by the SEC impose significant costs on reporting firms and that these costs constitute a serious impediment to the growth of New York as a market for international stocks when it is in direct competition with other centers such as London, where no additional reporting requirements are generally imposed on foreign firms seeking a listing.[2] Arguably the case for retaining the 20-F filing requirements would be strengthened should the incremental disclosures involved be found to have information content.

This chapter may also be interpreted as a response to the appeal by Lev (1989) for research on the quality of earnings. Previous studies of the information content of earnings have usually found only weak links between earnings and returns, with R^2 statistics typically ranging from 2 percent to

10 percent, a result that appears to be robust to different testing methodologies. As an alternative to concentrating on refining the methodology used to examine the earnings-return relationship, Lev (1989, p.155) suggests "...a departure in the direction of emphasising accounting issues and in particular the quality of reported information." Implicit in the notion that controlling for quality will enhance the explanatory power of earnings with respect to returns is a belief that market participants adjust reported earnings (or the earnings response coefficient applied to earnings) to allow for the differences in the perceived quality of earnings.[3] Arguably low quality of earnings can be regarded as resulting from measurement error in the earnings variable which in turn causes the R^2 statistic to be lower than it would be if the market's adjustment process could be modeled explicitly.[4]

We believe that it is reasonable to think of earnings quality as a multi-dimensional construct. Potentially each significant dimension will intervene in the returns–earnings relationship. Although a complete discussion of the concept of earnings quality is beyond the scope of this chapter, we suggest that the following accounting characteristics will contribute to perceived earnings quality: (i) measurement rules (involving the selection of accounting policies and discretionary accruals); (ii) the relative magnitudes of various line item earnings components; and (iii) information contained in footnote disclosures that contributes to the interpretation of financial ratios. Arguably by utilizing information on cross-sectional variations in measurement rules, disclosures and earnings components, the market is able to adjust for measurement error in published earnings numbers.

In this chapter we focus on accounting measurement issues. Assuming that quality is relevant to the pricing of earnings, we would expect a higher quality income measure will be more strongly correlated with returns. Thus, conditional on an acceptance of the R^2 criterion as a basis for assessing quality,[5] the GAAP regime that yields earnings with the higher explanatory power can be thought of as the higher quality standard-setting regime. However, it is possible that alternative earnings measures will each possess independent information and that some weighted combination would represent a higher quality measure with lower measurement error. The empirical tests in this paper may be interpreted as tests of the relative quality of earnings based on U.S.- and U.K.-GAAP regimes.

The remainder of the chapter is organized as follows: in the second section we outline the major accounting differences between U.S. and U.K. GAAP and the impact of these differences on earnings; in the third section we briefly review some relevant previous research; in the fourth section we outline the research design; in the fifth section we present the empirical results; and the final section contains our conclusions.

A COMPARISON OF U.S. GAAP AND U.K. GAAP

Despite the progress made towards the international harmonization of accounting standards,[6] significant differences still exist between GAAP in various countries. These differences are due to the definition of acceptable accruals procedures that may have both temporary and permanent impacts upon the income statement and balance sheet. The main differences between U.S. and U.K. GAAP that are relevant to the measurement of earnings are as follows:[7]

a. *Deferred Taxation* is recognised in the United Kingdom only to the extent that it is probable that a liability is expected to arise on timing differences—the partial provision approach (SSAP 15). Over the sample period, U.S. GAAP required firms to account using the deferred method (APB 11) or for all temporary timing differences using the asset/liability method (by voluntary adoption of SFAS 96).

b. *Research and Development* expenditure may be capitalized under U.K. GAAP when the benefit can be assessed with reasonable certainty (SSAP 13), whereas U.S. GAAP requires such expenditure to be expensed as incurred (SFAS 2).

c. *Stocks and Work in Process* are subject to many differences, some major and some minor. Probably the most significant of these is the option available under U.S. GAAP to use LIFO valuation (ARB 43). This option is unavailable under U.K. GAAP (SSAP 9).

d. *Goodwill* arising from acquisitions is normally written off against equity immediately under U.K. GAAP (SSAP 22), whereas U.S. GAAP requires the capitalization of goodwill and the amortization over an appropriate period (ARB 17,18 & SFAS 72).[8]

e. *Asset Revaluations*, normally of properties, are permitted under U.K. GAAP (Companies Act, 1985, Sch. 4) and in addition to causing owners' equity to increase will generally give rise to higher depreciation charges in future years. Asset revaluations are not permitted under U.S. GAAP (APB 6).

f. *Extraordinary Items* are similarly defined in the United Kingdom (SSAP 6) and United States (APB 30), but in practice a more rigorous approach has been adopted in the United States that effectively places more restrictions on the expenses that may be classified as extraordinary. In recent years extraordinary items, particularly losses related to restructuring and discontinued operations, have been quite significant under U.K. GAAP.[9]

g. *Pension Expenses* are quite precisely defined in the United States to include annual actuarial measurement under the projected unit cost method (SFAS 87), whereas U.K. GAAP (SSAP 24) permits a range of methods and actuarial assumptions. While it is not clear that reported pension expenses can be expected to be systematically higher or lower under U.S. GAAP, material differences do arise.

h. *Foreign Currency Translation* practices are similar in the United Kingdom and United States, but income of foreign subsidiaries may be translated only at an average rate in the United States (SFAS 52), whereas U.K. GAAP allows firms the option of using closing rates (SSAP 20).

Weetman and Gray (1991) report the average change in income resulting from the rebasing of income measurement from U.K. GAAP to U.S. GAAP. Based on a sample of 35 dual listed stocks over the period 1985–87 they found that on average U.S. earnings were lower than U.K. earnings by between 9 percent and 25 percent. Goodwill amortization and deferred tax generally accounted for a large proportion of the total adjustment made to earnings after extraordinary items.

Differences between GAAP regimes are capable of generating both permanent differences and timing differences in income recognition. An example of a source of permanent difference would be the U.K. GAAP treatment of goodwill, whereby write-offs are made directly through reserves rather than through the income statement. This will create a "permanent" difference between U.S. earnings and U.K. earnings for the duration of the U.S. GAAP amortization period. Other GAAP differences simply lead to variations in the timing of income recognition. For example, the choice between FIFO and LIFO in accounting for inventory will *ceteris paribus* lead to expected reversals of the GAAP impact in later years. The prospect that GAAP differences will lead to a complex aggregation of permanent and temporary income difference components has implications for the specification of the model used to estimate the returns-earnings relationship, and these will be discussed below.

PREVIOUS EARNINGS DECOMPOSITION RESEARCH

There is very little prior research specifically aimed at examining the information content of accounting accruals under alternative GAAP regimes.
Meek (1984) found that U.S. stock prices react to earnings specified under
foreign GAAP but was unable to differentiate such a reaction from that
observed for U.S. firms reporting under U.S. GAAP. Meek's results confirm
that non-U.S. GAAP accounting disclosures have information content but
the short (three-day) window used precluded an analysis of the information
content of different components of earnings.[10]

Several recent papers have reported components analyses of earnings
measured under U.S. GAAP. Wilson (1986, 1987) assesses the information
content of accruals components of earnings against cash flow and funds
flow components and finds that accruals components do appear to have
incremental information content. Livnat and Zarowin (1990) and Rayburn
(1986) reach similar conclusions. Lipe (1986) and Bublitz *et al.* (1985)
decompose earnings into major components and establish that the decomposition adds marginally to the explanatory power of (cross-sectional) regressions of returns on unexpected earnings, and that the coefficients on
individual components are significantly different from zero and sometimes
significantly different from each other. Recent work by Barth, Beaver, and
Wolfson (1990), Barth (1992) and Barth, Beaver, and Landsman (1992) also
uncover incremental information content in income statement decompositions.

A fundamentally different approach is adopted by Ohlson and Penman
(1992) who show that over long-return windows (e.g., ten years) the response coefficients on income statement line items converge, suggesting the
asymptotic sufficiency of earnings as an explanatory variable for returns.
Thus, in the long run, all earnings components appear to have the same
degree of value-relevance. However, their results also confirm previous
research in showing that over shorter intervals the coefficients on line items
diverge significantly, implying that individual line item disclosures have
information content, independent of the earnings numbers *per se.*[11] The
results of Dechow (1991) also provide insights as to the importance of the
length of the performance measurement interval in determining the appropriate accounting variables for capturing performance and explaining returns. Dechow shows that accounting accruals have advantages over more
primitive cash flow measures of performance in explaining stock returns
over short intervals, particularly for firms experiencing large changes in

their working capital requirements and their investment and financing structures.

In summary, the consensus view emerging from previous research is that earnings decomposition does marginally improve the explanatory power of short-window (e.g., one-year) tests of association between returns and earnings. Although overall the improvement in R^2 statistics attributable to earnings decompositions has been disappointingly low (Lev 1989), there is some evidence supporting the short-run information content of income statement line items. Recent research suggests that the signal-to-noise ratio in earnings improves significantly over long intervals, thus reducing the gains from using information in earnings components to mitigate the effects of measurement error in the earnings.

RESEARCH DESIGN

The Endogeneity of GAAP and U.S. Listing Decisions

In this chapter we analyze the information content of a decomposition of earnings reflecting U.S. GAAP and U.K. GAAP components. If we adopt a purely financial statement analysis perspective and aim to document how the equity market prices earnings components, then sample selection issues may not be too problematic. However, from the perspective of designing an experiment that can be interpreted as a commentary on the comparative success of two bodies of standard setters and that would be capable of informing the disclosure policy debate relating to dual listed stocks, we would ideally like to be able to observe, or be able to compute on the basis of publicly available information, the alternative income measures for a large sample of stocks selected according to criteria that are independent of a company's listing status. Unfortunately because of inadequate and incomplete disclosure, it is difficult to derive reliable estimates of earnings of U.K. (U.S.) companies under U.S. (U.K.) GAAP for the broad cross-section of domestic companies. Consequently we are forced to rely on the population of firms for which sufficient information is generally available, namely the dual listed U.K.-domiciled firms listed in the United States and reporting under the SEC 20-F disclosure provisions.

This approach to sample selection does create a potentially significant problem due to the possible endogeneity of GAAP and of firms' decisions to obtain U.S. listings. GAAP regimes cannot be assumed to differ for entirely random reasons. The evolution of GAAP in different countries will reflect many different influences, including the demands for GAAP from firms, investors, lenders, and other parties involved in contracting with firms. Preferences towards different GAAP alternatives and the weight given to the preferences of different constituencies by GAAP policy makers may vary significantly across regimes. Thus, in equilibrium U.K. GAAP may be interpreted as being efficient for U.K. firms, while U.S. GAAP will be efficient for U.S. firms.

Conceivably there will be U.K.-domiciled firms that have a preference towards using U.S. GAAP in contracting. This might be achieved through voluntary disclosure and through contracting.[12] Dual-listed firms can be thought of as a select group of firms that choose to incur additional disclosure costs and to voluntarily disclose accounting information prepared under U.S. GAAP on a systematic and public basis. These firms might be expected to be party to contracts referencing U.S. GAAP numbers.[13] Assuming that the features of U.S. GAAP relevant to contracts also affect income measurement and that contracts affect the value of the firm, it is possible that the returns-earnings relationship will reflect the indirect influence of GAAP on firm value through the different contracting arrangements that the U.S. GAAP disclosures make possible, rather than information content *per se*. Our empirical tests are conducted under the assumption that such effects are likely to be second order, but clearly the role of foreign GAAP in firm contracting is an area deserving of future research. However, to the extent that the use of U.S. GAAP in contracting is important, it will introduce a bias towards finding incremental information content in U.S. earnings, relative to U.K. earnings.

Because firms self-select through the decision to obtain a dual listing, it is also possible that the sample is biased in other ways. U.K. firms that do not list in the United States can be assumed to expect the incremental costs of listing to exceed the incremental benefits. The benefits are expected to be related to improved contracting opportunities, particularly in relation to raising capital. On the other hand, the incremental costs associated with a U.S. listing will include registration, bookkeeping and compliance costs, and potential negative externalities associated with the additional disclosure requirements. Biddle and Saudagarun (1989) report that the costs of compliance with SEC disclosure requirements can be quite high. Balakrishnan, Harris, and Sen (1988) have observed that firms that are not required to provide segmental disclosures in their domestic markets face a major disincentive to seek a U.S. listing because U.S. segmental disclosure requirements would be a source of competitive disadvantage for those firms. Thus, firms that have chosen not to seek a U.S. listing may either be incapable of absorbing the incremental out-of-pocket costs associated with bookkeeping and compliance, or they may be different from firms that do list in the United States because of the way that incremental disclosures penalize them. In the context of the present study, we believe that this type of self-selection bias is unlikely to be important for at least two reasons. First, although the firms that have U.S. listings are generally large in relation the average market capitalization of U.K. firms, they represent a broad cross-section of industrial sectors. Second, U.K. disclosure requirements (as opposed to GAAP measurement rules) are extensive and very close to U.S. requirements in most important areas, and therefore some of the alleged externalities will be unimportant for U.K. firms.[14]

Although one must be careful to avoid excessive generalizations from results based on the sample of dual listed stocks, we therefore believe that it is interesting to explore the returns–earnings relationship for this group of stocks. A finding of incremental information content will not necessarily imply one GAAP regime is preferable to another in a social welfare context (Gonedes and Dopuch, 1974). However, it would demonstrate that GAAP-specific earnings components or correlated information are important to investors. We should note that the sample selection approach followed here is really the only direct testing option available if we are to explore the comparative information content properties of alternative GAAP income measures within the market-based accounting research paradigm.

The Role of Alternative Income Measures in Security Valuation

In comparing earnings measured under different GAAP regimes our objective is simply to infer, by observing the incremental explanatory power of the earnings components, whether investors appear to revise their estimates of firm value conditional on information captured by the incremental disclosures contained in the decomposition. Revisions of firm value conditional on earnings components could occur for various reasons. One reason would be that the earnings decomposition has information content, for example, that the markets in which stocks are traded are efficient and investors unscramble financial statements and use the information they contain to form unbiased and efficient expectations of future cash flows.[15] An efficient market does not require all investors to be "sophisticated" optimal processors of information. However it is necessary that there exist investors who undertake such analysis and in equilibrium trade on information in their possession until prices (net of marginal transaction costs) are consistent with the expected distribution of future cash flows. Thus, in the context of earnings measured under a particular GAAP regime, earnings will be priced in an efficient market so as to eliminate the effects of any value-irrelevant accruals underlying the earnings numbers. Accounting choices which have no effect on cash flows or risk and have no signalling role will be discounted by the market (Watts and Zimmerman, 1986). By similar reasoning, even where no accounting choice exists for the reporting firm, an efficient market will "undo" the effects of a mandated accounting procedure, if this is expected to enhance assessments of firm value. Similarly, if earnings are perceived as comprising permanent, transitory and noise components, an efficient market will apply different valuation multipliers to each component (Ramakrishnan and Thomas, 1991; Barth, Beaver, and Landsman, 1992).

A contrary explanation of earnings components having significant explanatory power for returns would be that there are marginal investors who are subject to functional fixation in relation to accounting numbers prepared under a particular GAAP regime. One particular specification of functional fixation is the mechanistic hypothesis (MH). Under the MH, prices are set on the basis of reported earnings numbers with no reference to the accounting procedures which underlie the numbers, or to any other value-relevant data. If earnings do not map perfectly into the underlying cash flows, then prices will be inefficient and biased. The existence of investors displaying functional fixation with regard to earnings numbers is necessary for the MH. However, unless either there is a complete absence of sophisticated investors (i.e., every investor is functionally fixated) or, alternatively, the supply of arbitrage capital available to sophisticated investors is limited, in-equilibrium prices can be expected to be set efficiently by the trading activities of sophisticated, well-informed investors (Tinic 1990).

In this chapter we only seek to explore the associations between returns and the alternative earnings definitions. We do not attempt to differentiate between the two competing hypotheses.[16] The main constraint on such analysis is one of data limitations. We recognize from the outset that any statistical associations between earnings measures and returns could have more than one explanation.

If the process of using information on alternative earnings numbers can be summarised by writing "ungarbled" earnings, E, as a linear combination of the two alternative income measures, X_1 and X_2, we have:

$$E = \lambda_0 + \lambda_1 X_1 + \lambda_2 X_2 \qquad (4.1)$$

If we assume that the market is efficient and that the market uses publicly available information optimally, the role of alternative income measures can be summarized within the framework of a linear earnings discount model (Christie 1987). Assuming a constant dividend payout ratio and dividend growth rate, the dividend discount valuation model reduces to price being written as a constant multiple of current earnings and unexpected returns are related to unexpected earnings. If the market is efficient, and if one earnings measure dominates the other as a proxy for the ungarbled earnings number upon which fundamental valuation is based, the regression slope coefficient on the dominated measure will be zero. A comparison of the R^2 statistics from univariate regressions of returns on each earnings number will be a test of *relative* information content. If the market is efficient and both measures contain *incremental* information, after controlling for the information in the alternative measure, then both slope coefficients will be expected to be significant in a regression of returns on the two earnings measures.[17] This should be true even if the market is "segmented" in the sense that some investors give weight to X_1 and some others give weight to X_2. Effectively the stock price acts as a summary statistic for the interaction of heterogeneous beliefs in a market and hence the "consensus" view of the market will be reflected in price.[18]

Prices and GAAP-Specific Information

The sample is based on U.K.-domiciled corporations having ADRs listed on the NYSE, AMEX, or NASDAQ. ADRs entitle the holder to voting rights and dividend entitlements in proportion to the rights attributable to the underlying share entitlement. In the absence of trading frictions we would expect arbitrage to ensure that the U.S. dollar price of ADRs to be identical to the Sterling price of the equivalent shares, converted at the spot exchange rate.[19] If prices differ, arbitrageurs can buy (sell) ADRs in the United States (or indeed in London) and sell (buy) the equivalent shares in London, realizing an arbitrage profit. In practice transaction costs will create a "window" within which arbitrage activity will not be expected to be profitable. Additionally, in practice domestic U.K. investors must pay stamp duty of 50 basis points on all stock purchases made in the London market. For this reason there is generally a systematic difference, equal to the stamp duty, between the prices of ADRs and the equivalent share price. However, since this difference is systematic and affects both bid– and ask–prices, we would expect returns on ADRs only to differ from returns on the underlying shares traded in London by the relevant currency return over the holding period.

Valuation model considerations would also lead us to believe that the prices of ADRs and the equivalent shares will be equal (apart from stamp duty). This can be seen with reference to a simple dividend discount model. U.K. investors will value a share at a price given by

$$P_{UK} = \sum_{t=1}^{\infty} \frac{D_t}{\prod_{\tau=1}^{t}(1 + R_{\tau}^{UK})} \qquad (4.2)$$

In equation (4.2) P_{UK} is the price of a share in the London market, D_t is the expected dividend in U.K. currency at time t, and R_{τ}^{UK} is the relevant (zero coupon) discount rate for a U.K. investor for period τ. Dollar denominated U.S. investors differ from U.K. investors in that dividends paid in U.K. pounds are exposed to currency risk. U.S. investors will also generally use a different interest rate to discount dollar cash flows than U.K. investors will use to discount Sterling cash flows. However, it is possible for U.S. investors to hedge Sterling cash flows through the forward exchange market or by taking offsetting short foreign currency positions. Assume that covered interest rate parity holds, $F_{\tau} / (1 + R_{\tau}^{UK}) = S_0 / (1 + R_{\tau}^{US})$, where F_{τ} is the forward exchange rate for τ periods at time 0, S_0 is the spot exchange rate at time 0 and R_{τ}^{US} is the appropriate U.S. discount rate. It follows that the dollar value of a fully hedged ADR is equal to the Sterling value of the equivalent U.K. share entitlement, converted at the prevailing spot exchange rate.[20] Furthermore, dollar-denominated ADR returns will equal Sterling denominated stock returns plus the currency return.

The evidence of Rosenthal and Young (1990) reveals that ADRs and equivalent shares issued by two U.K./Dutch combines apparently trade at divergent prices on the New York and Amsterdam stock exchanges. However, they are unable to find a similar systematic divergences between share prices quoted in London and their ADR-equivalent package prices and, in any case, price differences do not appear to have been sufficiently large to generate systematic arbitrage opportunities net of transaction costs. Rosenthal and Young (1990) conclude that the law-of-one-price holds.[21] It would appear that it is reasonable to assume that the ADR and the underlying share markets are efficiently integrated and that returns observed in one market (e.g., the London Stock Exchange) fully reflect the information-based trading in both U.K. and U.S. markets.[22] Under the assumption that systematic intermarket arbitrage opportunities do not exist, U.K. stock returns and U.S. ADR returns will only differ by the currency return over the same holding period, and this component of the ADR return can reasonably be assumed to be independent of firm-specific accounting information. Thus tests based on U.K. stock returns should be a satisfactory test of information content of the accounting signals.[23]

Hypotheses

In the empirical tests we examine several related hypotheses. Initially we seek to confirm the value-relevance of U.K.-GAAP earnings and of U.S.-GAAP earnings for our sample of U.K. firms, before controlling for any information contained in the alternative earnings measure. Formally, the first two hypotheses tested, stated in the null form, are:

H_{01}: Earnings measured under U.K. GAAP are uncorrelated with returns.

H_{02}: Earnings measured under U.S. GAAP are uncorrelated with returns.

Tests of these hypotheses take the form of regressions of residual returns metrics on respectively U.K. GAAP earnings measures and U.S. GAAP earnings measures. A comparison of the regression R^2 statistics can be interpreted as a test of relative information content. We subsequently seek to test the incremental information content of one earnings measure conditional on the other by testing the following null hypotheses:

H_{03}: The incremental explanatory power of the U.K. GAAP earnings relative to U.S. GAAP earnings is insignificant.

H_{04}: The incremental explanatory power of U.S. GAAP earnings relative to U.K. GAAP earnings is insignificant.

Rejection of H_{03} and/or H_{04} would occur if either one of the earnings measures (or any of their components) was found to have explanatory power in a multiple regression after controlling for earnings reported under the other GAAP regime.

Design of the Regression Tests

We wish to test whether unexpected changes in earnings and earnings components are associated with returns in a cross-sectional regression. The three accounting numbers of relevance to this study, earnings reported under U.K.

GAAP and U.S. GAAP and the GAAP adjustment are linked by the following identity

$$YUK_{jt} \equiv YUS_{jt} + YADJ_{jt} \qquad (4.3)$$

where YUK_{jt} denotes level of U.K. GAAP earnings per share for firm j in year t, deflated by share price at the beginning of the annual holding period over which returns are calculated, YUS_{jt} denotes deflated U.S. GAAP earnings per share level and $YADJ_{jt}$ denotes the adjustment necessary to restate U.K. GAAP earnings in terms of U.S. GAAP. Changes in earnings are related by a similar identity

$$DUK_{jt} \equiv DUS_{jt} + DADJ_{jt} \qquad (4.4)$$

where DUK_{jt} denotes the deflated change in earnings between years t–1 and t, DUS_{jt} is the deflated change in U.S. GAAP earnings and $DADJ_{jt}$ is the deflated change in the adjustment.

In defining unexpected earnings and earnings components, the research problem is similar to that addressed in the literature concerned with the role of income statement line items in explaining returns. Previous work in this area has often proxied unexpected realizations of earnings components by taking first differences (e.g., Livnat and Zarowin, 1990). This procedure implicitly assumes that each line item follows a martingale process. Alternatively, the expectation of certain components may be assumed to be constant (and often zero) if shocks are expected to be purely transitory (Barth, Beaver, and Wolfson, 1990). In view of the earlier discussion of the transitory nature of certain components of GAAP differences, it is not clear that the martingale assumption is the appropriate time series representation of each component of earnings (or the GAAP adjustment to earnings), even if it is a reasonable approximation of the time series process for aggregate earnings. However, GAAP differences are not expected to be purely transitory either. Therefore it seems preferable to view the GAAP differences as comprising mixed permanent and transitory components.

Several recent papers have examined the appropriate specification of the earnings variables when earnings are expected to contain transitory components. Easton and Harris (1991) show that the explanatory power of a regression of returns on earnings changes is enhanced by the inclusion of an earnings level variable. The notion that the inclusion of scaled earnings levels helps reduce misspecification due to measurement error in unexpected earnings has been suggested by Ohlson and Shroff (1992). They show that the relevance of the earnings change variable will depend upon whether or not earnings changes display positive serial correlation. In the event that earnings are extremely persistent, the levels specification can be expected to be more appropriate. Ali and Zarowin (1992) have subsequently confirmed the predictions of the Ohlson and Shroff (1992) model. They conclude that the assumption that earnings follow a random walk is partially responsible for the low R^2 statistics and earnings response coefficients obtained in regressions of abnormal returns on earnings changes. The main implication of these studies is that if *ex ante* one does not know the average time series properties of the earnings process for the firms in a cross-sectional study, one way of reducing the effects of measurement error is to include both changes and levels variables. This conclusion should apply equally to components of earnings. Effectively one can allow the regression model to extract the optimal combination of two proxy measures for the unexpected earnings components.

In testing the hypotheses we note that equations (4.3) and (4.4) relate the earnings levels variables and the earnings change variables by identities and therefore all regressions containing any pair of variables from one of the identities contain identical information. Thus, for example, a regression involving *DUK* and *DADJ* as regressors is equivalent to a regression employing *DUK* and *DUS*, or alternatively *DUS* and *DADJ*. Consequently, in testing for incremental information content we can rely on estimates of the following regression equations

$$CAR_{jt} = \omega_{01} + \omega_{11} DUK_{jt} + \omega_{21} DADJ_{jt} + v_{1jt} \qquad (4.5)$$

$$CAR_{jt} = \omega_{02} + \omega_{12} YUK_{jt} + \omega_{22} YADJ_{jt} + v_{2jt} \qquad (4.6)$$

$$CAR_{jt} = \omega_{03} + \omega_{13} DUK_{jt} + \omega_{23} YUK_{jt} + \omega_{33} DADJ_{jt} + \omega_{43} YADJ_{jt} + v_{3jt} \qquad (4.7)$$

where CAR_{jt} is the residual return metric defined below, the ω's are regression coefficients and the v's are regression residuals. In equation (4.5), if ω_{21} is different from zero then this would imply that the adjustment, and hence U.S. GAAP earnings changes, has incremental information content after controlling for the information in U.K. GAAP earnings. Exploiting the identity (4.4), rejection of the restriction $\omega_{11} = -\omega_{21}$ would imply that changes in the GAAP adjustment, and hence U.K. GAAP earnings changes, have incremental value-relevance relative to U.S. GAAP earnings changes.[24] Similarly, we can test the incremental information content of the respective earnings level variables using equation (4.6). If ω_{22} is different from zero then this would imply that the adjustment, and hence U.S. GAAP earnings levels, has incremental information content after controlling for the information in U.K. GAAP earnings levels. Exploiting the identity (3), rejection of the restriction $\omega_{12} = -\omega_{22}$ would imply that the adjustment, and hence U.K. GAAP earnings, has incremental information content after controlling for U.S. GAAP earnings. Equation (4.7) represents the comprehensive specification implied by the work of Ohlson and Shroff (1992) and Ali and Zarowin (1992). Rejection of the hypothesis $\omega_{33} = 0$ would imply that changes in GAAP adjustments, and hence U.S. earnings changes, have incremental value-relevance after controling for U.K. GAAP earnings. Conversely, rejection of the restriction $\omega_{13} = -\omega_{33}$ would imply that U.K. GAAP earnings changes have incremental information content, after controlling for U.S. GAAP earnings. Similarly rejection of the hypothesis $\omega_{43} = 0$ would imply that the level of GAAP adjustments, and hence U.S. earnings levels, has incremental information content, after controlling for information in U.K. GAAP earnings levels. Conversely, rejection of the restriction $\omega_{43} = -\omega_{23}$ would imply that U.K. GAAP earnings levels have incremental information content after controlling for U.S. GAAP earnings levels.

In practice, whilst regressions (4.5), (4.6) and (4.7) are comprehensive in the sense that, for a given model specification (changes, levels or both) they capture all the available information across the two GAAP regimes, the clarity of the empirical results is enhanced by repeating the regressions, replacing earnings measures and GAAP adjustments sequentially by the third component from the identities (4.3) and (4.4). Thus, in testing for incremental information content, we supplement equations (4.5), (4.6), and (4.7) by additional regressions that can be reconciled with these equations where the F-tests of restrictions described above are isomorphic with the multivariate regression t-tests.

The empirical tests are based on regressions of one-year cumulative residual returns on the earnings variables. Most previous studies have simply used the market model and have not considered possible measurement bias and the economic interpretation of the metric they are using. However, the derivation of the dependent variable is a potentially important consideration in annual event window studies such as this. The reliance on the market model in previous work has to a very large extent been motivated by the widely cited simulation results of Brown and Warner (1980) showing that event study results appear to be fairly insensitive to the specification of the returns generating model. However, this conclusion may be misleading if there is a significant size effect in stock returns, particularly if the size premium varies over time and if the market capitalization profile of stocks in the treatment sample is substantially different from that of the market index used (Dimson and Marsh, 1986). Under these conditions the calculation of long event window abnormal performance metrics may be biased unless the size effect is controlled for explicitly. Implicitly, the CAPM ignores any size effect and the market model assumes it is constant.[25]

In view of the results of Dimson and Marsh (1986) based on U.K. returns data, but also in the interests of maintaining comparability with previous work, we adopt several alternative specifications of the returns generating process. Residual returns are defined according to one of three general returns generating models: (i) the market model [M-M]; (ii) the capital asset pricing model [CAPM]; and (iii) a size and market adjusted returns model following Dimson and Marsh (1986) [D-M]. The market model is defined in the usual way as follows:

$$R_{jt} = \hat{\alpha}_j + \hat{\beta}_j R_{mt} + \epsilon_{jt} \qquad (4.8)$$

The CAPM is defined as:

$$R_{jt} = (1 - \hat{\beta}_j) R_{ft} + \hat{\beta}_j R_{mt} + \epsilon_{jt} \qquad (4.9)$$

In equations (4.8) and (4.9) the parameters $\hat{\alpha}$ and $\hat{\beta}$ are estimated from OLS regressions over an estimation period of at most sixty months and at least thirty months (depending on the availability of returns data);[26] R_{jt} is the continuously compounded return on stock j in period t and R_{mt} is the return on the relevant market index; and ϵ_{jt} is assumed to be a white noise error term with zero mean and constant time series variance.

In order to address the possibility that the size effect is a confounding influence, we employ two alternative benchmark indices: the broadly-based, capitalization weighted *Financial Times-Actuaries All Share Index* (FTA) and an equally weighted portfolio comprising the stocks belonging to the same size decile, based on year-end market capitalizations. The Dimson and Marsh (1986) methodology involves correcting residual returns for the realized size premium according to the following model:

$$R_{jt} = R_{pt} + (R_{mt} - R_{ft})(\hat{\beta}_j - \hat{\beta}_p) + \epsilon_{jt} \qquad (4.10)$$

where the subscript p refers to the size-based control portfolio and $\hat{\beta}_p$ is the control portfolio's CAPM beta relative to the market index. Dimson and Marsh suggest that this approach is most likely to purge residual return metrics of any size bias.

Residual returns are cumulated for the event window as follows:

$$CAR_{jT} = \sum_{t=1}^{T}[R_{jt} - E(R_{jt})] \tag{4.11}$$

where $E(R_{jt})$ is defined by forming expectations conditional on the realized market return, risk-free rate of interest and decile portfolio return from equations (4.8), (4.9), or (4.10) as appropriate, and T denotes the final month of the 12-month event window.[27] We follow previous work in assuming a fixed three-month offset between the fiscal year end and the end of the event window.[28]

EMPIRICAL RESULTS

The Data and Sample

The results are based on continuously compounded monthly U.K. stock returns data from the *London Business School Share Price Database* (LSPD). Interest rates are the one-month Euro Sterling rates prevailing at the beginning of each month and reported on *Datastream*. Accounting numbers were also obtained from *Datastream*, from corporate annual reports and from copies of 20-F SEC filings made available to the authors by *Disclosure Ltd.*

The sample comprises stocks of nonfinancial corporations satisfying the following criteria:

a. The stock must be a nonfinancial firm listed in ADR form in the United States for at least one year during the period 1987–90 in addition to having a listing on the London Stock Exchange.

b. The stock must have at least 42-months returns data available on the LSPD, including the 12-month event window.

c. Earnings data must be available for the relevant periods from *Datastream.*

d. Earnings reconciliation data must be available for the relevant years either from copies of the 20-F filings obtained from *Disclosure Ltd.* or from company annual reports.

Application of these criteria produced a sample of 85 firm-years.[29]

The earnings measures analyzed are constructed on a per-share basis. The SEC reconciliation requirements relate to net income and often a U.S.-GAAP equivalent earnings per-share number is not reported in a 20-F filing. Thus we estimated U.S. earnings per-share using the following convention:

(i) The basic U.K. earnings variable [YUK] is taken to be the *Datastream* adjusted earnings per share (item #211).[30]

(ii) The U.K. GAAP to U.S. GAAP adjustment per share [YADJ] is calculated as the total income adjustment disclosed in the 20-F filing, excluding extraordinary items, divided by the estimated average number of outstanding shares, defined by dividing the U.K. earned for ordinary shareholders earnings figure (*Datastream* item #210), the numerator of earnings per share, by U.K. earnings per share. We define the GAAP adjustment so as to exclude any adjustment related to extraordinary items.[31] [32]

(iii) The U.S. GAAP earnings per share proxy [YUS] is set equal to the difference between U.K. GAAP earnings and the adjustment.[33]

Results

Table 4–1 contains descriptive statistics relating to the sample. It can be seen that U.S. earnings per share are generally lower than U.K., confirming the results of Weetman and Gray (1991). The magnitude of the adjustment is quite substantial, the mean adjustment [ADJ] being approximately 19 percent of the mean of U.K. GAAP earnings. Even after scaling by beginning of period price, this pattern persists, with the scaled U.S. earnings level being 22 percent below the equivalent U.K. level, on average. The scaled adjustment [YADJ] has a range of between –0.051 and 0.117.

In Table 4–2 we report the cross-correlation between the earnings variables. It is clear that U.K. and U.S. earnings are strongly positively correlated. When the two sets of GAAP numbers are compared, both the changes and the levels variables have correlation coefficients in excess of 0.70. Clearly the two GAAP regimes are capturing a high degree of common information. However, the far from perfect correlation between the alternative earnings numbers also suggest that the alternative measures contain different degrees of noise and/or that the information content of the two variables is different. It is also noteworthy that the adjustment variable [DADJ] is highly correlated with U.S. earnings changes [DUS].

The initial regression tests involve an examination of the association

TABLE 4–1
Descriptive Statistics for Earnings Variables[a]

	Mean	Standard Deviation	Minimum	Maximum
EUK	30.029	21.26	1.370	127.100
ADJ	5.665	9.21	−28.587	34.224
EUS	24.363	22.56	−25.625	121.651
DUK	0.003	0.02	−0.093	0.058
YUK	0.089	0.04	0.008	0.232
DUS	−0.003	0.05	−0.327	0.128
YUS	0.069	0.04	−0.070	0.188
DADJ	0.006	0.03	−0.124	0.235
YADJ	0.020	0.03	−0.051	0.117

[a] The sample is based on 85 firm–years for the period 1987–1990. All earnings figures are expressed in pence per share. Variables are defined as follows:
EUK = U.K. GAAP earnings per share.
ADJ = adjustment from UK to U.S. GAAP earnings per share.
EUS = U.S. GAAP earnings per share.
DUK = change in EUK, scaled by opening share price.
YUK = EUK scaled by opening share price.
DUS = change in EUS, scaled by opening share price.
YUS = EUS scaled by opening share price.
DADJ = change in adjustment, scaled by opening share price.
YADJ = adjustment level, scaled by opening share price.

TABLE 4–2
Correlation Matrix For Earnings Variables[a]

	DUK	YUK	DUS	YUS	DADJ	YADJ
DUK	1.000	–	–	–	–	–
YUK	0.270	1.000	–	–	–	–
DUS	0.703	0.234	1.000	–	–	–
YUS	0.344	0.795	0.534	1.000	–	–
DADJ	−0.007	−0.139	−0.887	−0.494	1.000	–
YADJ	−0.143	−0.117	−0.573	−0.626	0.629	1.000

[a] The sample is based on 85 firm-years for the period 1987–1990. All earnings figures are expressed in pence per share. Variables are defined as follows:
EUK = U.K. GAAP earnings per share.
ADJ = adjustment from U.K. to U.S. GAAP earnings per share.
EUS = U.S. GAAP earnings per share.
DUK = change in EUK, scaled by opening share price.
YUK = EUK scaled by opening share price.
DUS = change in EUS, scaled by opening share price.
YUS = EUS scaled by opening share price.
DADJ = change in adjustment, scaled by opening share price.
YADJ = adjustment level, scaled by opening share price.

between residual returns and earnings measures for each of the two GAAP regimes separately. Table 4–3 reports results based on each of the three returns generating models[34]. The results show that for the CAPM and size/market adjusted D-M returns U.K. earnings changes [DUK] have significant positive coefficients. The U.K. earnings level variable [YUK] is significant in the case of D-M returns and market model returns but not for the CAPM-based regressions. Overall, these results confirm previous evidence that U.K. earnings are value relevant (Strong and Walker, 1992), but suggest that, for this sample at least, the choice of the returns generating model for calculating residual returns is important. The explanatory power of the models is also broadly consistent with previous research, the R^2 statistics being in the order of 6 percent to 8 percent.[35]

The results relating to U.S. GAAP earnings are more mixed. The results in Table 4–3 contain evidence that the U.S. earnings yield variable [YUS] has significant explanatory power when entered alongside changes in U.S. earnings [DUS], although the explanatory power of the regressions is lower than for the comparable U.K. earnings regressions. On the basis of a comparison of the R^2 statistics in Table 4–3 it would appear that the U.S. earnings variables do not explain CAPM and D-M residual returns as effectively as U.K. earnings. However, there is clear evidence in the results that there is information in U.S. earnings relevant to the pricing of stocks. Of course, this may well be due to the common components in both U.K. and U.S. earnings. The market model residual results are again inconsistent with the other two panels in Table 4–3. The negative coefficient on the U.S. earnings change [DUS] suggests that the two earnings variables interact to explain market model residual returns.

The results in Table 4–3 suggest that both U.K. GAAP earnings and U.S. GAAP earnings contain (perhaps common) information that is value-relevant. The question remains as to whether the two earnings measures contain independent information. We test Hypotheses H_{03} and H_{04} using multiple regressions of residual returns on earnings and earnings components.[36] The results reported in Table 4–4 are based on the size and market adjusted D-M returns, although our conclusions are not affected by choosing the CAPM instead.

The panel A of Table 4–4 examines whether the change in adjustment [DADJ] has incremental explantory power relative to U.K. earnings changes [DUK] or U.S. earnings changes [DUS] based on equation (4.5). The results indicate that the coefficient on DADJ is not significantly different from 0 (*t*-value 0.51), suggesting that the GAAP adjustment does not have incremen-

TABLE 4–3
Regressions of Cumulative Abnormal Returns on U.K. and U.S. Earnings Variables[a]

Model	Constant	DUK	YUK	DUS	YUS	$\bar{R}^2$(%)	F
CAPM	−0.081^b (3.13)	2.750^b (2.90)				6.7	7.08^b
CAPM	−0.162^b (2.28)	2.307^b (2.63)	0.966 (1.47)			7.9	4.61^b
CAPM	−0.053^b (2.30)			−0.762 (1.51)		1.3	2.10
CAPM	−0.133^b (2.80)			0.061 (0.13)	1.195^b (2.31)	4.3	2.88
M-M	−0.162˙ (4.73)	1.267 (1.13)				0.0	0.73
M-M	−0.376^b (3.93)	0.092 (0.08)	2.562^b (2.82)			7.0	4.15^b
M-M	−0.148^b (4.67)			0.219 (0.43)		0.1	0.09
M-M	−0.330^b (5.14)			−1.370^b (2.51)	2.715^b (3.91)	9.1	5.18^b
D-M	−0.510 (1.88)	2.723^b (2.76)				5.7	6.05^b
D-M	−0.172^b (2.31)	2.058^b (2.36)	1.449^b (2.02)			9.1	5.21^b
D-M	−0.024 (0.97)			−0.766 (1.55)		1.0	1.86
D-M	−0.134^b (2.70)			−0.201 (0.44)	1.648^b (2.90)	6.9	4.10^b

[a] Regressions are of the form:

$$CAR_{jt} = \omega_0 + \omega_1 \text{(earningslevel)} + \omega_2 \text{(earningsdifference)} + v_{jt}$$

where the earnings variables are computed under U.K. GAAP (level=YUK, difference=DUK) and U.S. GAAP (level=YUS, difference=DUS). t-statistics in parenthesis are White (1980) heteroscedasticity consistent estimates. CAPM denotes capital asset pricing model residuals, M-M denotes market model residuals and D-M denotes size and market adjusted residuals computed as in Dimson and Marsh (1986).
[b] indicate significant test statistics with a p-value ≤ 0.05.

TABLE 4–4
Regressions of Size and Market Adjusted CARs on Earnings Variables and Adjustments[a]

Constant	DUK	YUK	DUS	YUS	DADJ	YADJ	$\bar{R}^2$	F
			Panel A					
-0.055 (1.81)	2.878[b] (2.66)	–	–	–	0.367 (0.51)	–	4.77	3.10[b]
-0.055 (1.81)	–	–	2.877[b] (2.66)	–	3.242[b] (2.00)	–	4.77	3.10[b]
-0.055 (1.81)	3.244[b] (2.00)	–	-0.366 (0.51)	–	–	–	4.77	3.10[b]
			Panel B					
-0.159 (1.88)	–	1.805[b] (2.55)	–	–	–	-1.096 (1.15)	7.22	4.27[b]
-0.159 (1.88)	–	–	–	1.804[b] (2.55)	–	0.708 (0.53)	7.22	4.27[b]
-0.159 (1.88)	–	0.710 (0.53)	–	1.095 (1.15)	–	–	7.22	4.27[b]
			Panel C					
-0.164[b] (2.05)	1.970[b] (2.19)	1.651[b] (2.40)	–	–	1.477[b] (2.24)	-1.835[b] (2.09)	10.06	3.35[b]
-0.164[b] (2.05)	–	–	1.970[b] (2.19)	1.651[b] (2.40)	3.466[b] (2.50)	-0.185 (0.15)	10.06	3.35[b]
-0.164[b] (2.05)	3.45[b] (2.50)	-0.185 (0.16)	-1.477[b] (2.24)	1.835[b] (2.09)	–	–	10.06	3.35[b]

[a] Regressions are of the form:

$$CAR_{jt} = \omega_{03} + \omega_{13}DUK_{jt} + \omega_{23}YUK_{jt} + \omega_{33}DADJ_{jt} + \omega_{43}YADJ_{jt} + v_{3jt}$$

and variations obtained by substituting DUS for DUK and YUS for YUK. The earnings variables are computed under U.K. GAAP (level=YUK, difference=DUK) and U.S. GAAP (level=YUS, difference=DUS). t-statistics in parenthesis are White heteroscedasticity consistent estimates.

[b] indicate significant test statistics with a p-value ≤ 0.05.

tal information content relative to U.K. GAAP earnings. The second regression in panel A of Table 4–4 suggests that the change in GAAP adjustment (and hence U.K. earnings change) has incremental value-relevance relative to the estimated U.S. GAAP earnings change. When both U.K. and U.S. GAAP earnings changes are entered in the same regression the dominance of U.K. earnings changes over U.S. earnings changes is confirmed by the insignificant t-statistic on DUS.

Panel B of Table 4–4 focuses on the value-relevance of the alternative earnings levels variables based on regression equation (4.6). First we regress residual returns on the U.K. earnings level [YUK] and the adjustment level [YADJ]. Consistent with the results in Table 4–3, YUK does have significant explanatory power for returns. The R^2 statistic for the levels specification is higher than for the changes specification in panel A. However, the coefficient on YADJ is insignificant, suggesting that GAAP adjustments do not have incremental value-relevance relative to U.K. GAAP earnings in the levels specification. The second regression in Table 4–4, panel B, substitutes U.S. earnings for U.K. earnings and produces very similar results, suggesting that the level of GAAP adjustments (and hence U.K. GAAP earnings levels) do not have incremental value-relevance when compared to U.S. GAAP earnings levels. This is contrary to the results obtained in the earnings change regression specification in panel A. The third regression in panel B, involving both YUK and YUS as regressors, suffers from multicollinearity and is largely uninformative about the contributions of the two regressors to the overall explanatory power. Essentially, earnings levels appear to be capturing similar information under both GAAP regimes and neither measure appears to dominate the other.

Finally, in panel C of Table 4–4 we examine the comprehensive specification in equation (4.7) and regress residual returns on both changes and levels simultaneously. The adjusted R^2 statistic is approximately 10 percent which is higher than for the changes or levels specifications. When the U.K. earnings variables are entered along with the GAAP adjustment variables we see that all four regressors have significant t-statistics.

With regard to the earnings change variables, whilst the t-statistic on DADJ is significant, an F-test reveals DADJ does not contribue significantly to the explanatory power of the regression (F=2.250, p=0.138). In other words the change in GAAP adjustment (and hence U.S. GAAP earnings changes) do not appear to improve the explanatory power of the regression significantly, consistent with the result in panel A of Table 4–4. An F-test of the restriction that the slope coefficients on DUK and DADJ are equal is strongly rejected ($p = 0.001$), and this again is consistent with U.K. earnings having incremental information content relative to U.S. earnings changes, even after controlling for information that might be captured by U.S. or U.K. earnings level. However, the significant coefficient on YADJ in the first regression of panel C, when taken alongside the insignificant coefficient on YADJ in the second regression in panel C implies that the level of GAAP adjustments, and hence U.S. earnings levels, have some incremental information content relative to U.K. earnings levels and that U.K. earnings levels have no incremental explanatory power over U.S. GAAP earnings levels, after controlling for any information contained in earnings changes. The third regression confirms this interpretation that YUS dominates YUK in information content.

CONCLUSIONS

Lev (1989, p. 155) has suggested that markets show a limited response to earnings changes and considers "...the possibility that the fault lies with the low quality (information content) of reported earnings looms large." This study investigates the information content of two alternative accounting earnings measures constructed under U.K. and U.S. GAAP. The evidence points to U.K. GAAP earnings changes having greater information content than U.S. GAAP earnings changes. In contrast earnings levels measured under U.S. GAAP appear to possess independent value-relevance after controlling for U.K. GAAP earnings. The results are consistent with GAAP adjustments having transitory components, implying that the earnings change specification of the returns-earnings relationship might be inappropriate, at least with respect to the GAAP adjustment component. The empirical results display explanatory power which is still quite low and yet broadly consistent with previous work. However, the inclusion of the earnings levels variables certainly improves the goodness of fit. Additionally, the GAAP earnings adjustments appear to add to explanatory power marginally. The results also show that contrary to the consensus view, care must be taken in studies of information content when specifying the returns generating model used in the computation of residual returns.

Several potential avenues for future research are suggested from by this study. First, with a larger sample it may be possible to examine the value-relevance of components of the GAAP adjustments and attempt to discriminate between those adjustments that might convey information concerning future cash flows and risk and those that do not. Second, it would be of interest to explore the price formation process in relation to the accounting signals in the context of the dual market setting. The intermarket pricing of equivalent assets is still not fully understood. Examination of short-horizon returns data drawn from both foreign and domestic data may reveal insights concerning the role of each market in price discovery, perhaps due to leads and lags in disclosure of similar information in the two markets. Although the assumption of no-arbitrage appears reasonable and is certainly consistent with the tradition of capital markets research in accounting, the process by which globally linked markets are influenced by tax and currency risk differences faced by investors domiciled in different countries is also as yet not understood. The possibility that such factors might interact with accounting measures in determining prices cannot be ruled out. Finally, it will be of interest to broaden the scope of the analysis to examine earnings reported under other GAAP regimes and the possible implications of GAAP reconciliation disclosures for the quality of analysts' forecasts.

NOTES

1. The 20-F filing requirements create an information environment where alternative income numbers are disclosed under the same historic cost valuation convention. Previous research into the information content of simultaneously disclosed alternative income numbers has been concerned with comparisons between income measured under different valuation conventions, e.g., historic cost and replacement cost. See, for example, Beaver, Griffin, and Landsman (1982).
2. It is interesting to note that there are no German stocks listed in the United States at the time of writing, despite the clear demand for many large German stocks from international portfolio managers. The absence of German stock listings in the U.S. is often attributed to the disclosure costs that would be imposed on firms in restating from the ultra-conservative German GAAP into U.S. GAAP. For example, during 1991 BASF, the German chemicals firm, had their application for an NYSE listing stalled by the SEC on the basis that the German GAAP underlying the prospectus numbers were excessively conservative. However, Daimler-Benz has recently reached agreement with the SEC and intends to list in the United States after disclosing hidden reserves of several billion dollars. See *The Economist*, April 3, 1993, p. 76.
3. Anecdotal evidence that professional analysts do pay attention to the quality of earnings can be found in UBS Phillips and Drew (1991).
4. There are good reasons for believing that the R^2 of a regression of returns on earnings variables is not a sufficient statistic for evaluating earnings measurement. For example, from the perspective of evaluating management performance, one would like to exclude the influence of factors beyond management's control. Sloan (1991)

shows that earnings reflect firm-specific changes in value, but are less sensitive to market-wide movements in equity values. Therefore earnings-based contracts serve to shield executives from uncontrollable changes in firm value. Additionally, it is unlikely that the strength of association between returns and earnings will be a good index of the usefulness of earnings for the purposes of debt contracting.

5. This criterion, of course, is a somewhat narrow definition of quality oriented towards equity investors' use of earnings numbers, a limited subset of both accounting information and users.

6. See IASC (1990).

7. This section identifies only some of the more pervasive and significant differences between U.S. and U.K. GAAP relevant to income measurement. Many others exist including lease accounting, the extinguishment of debt, disposals of subsidiaries, interest on receivables and payables, deferred compensation costs, share option and purchase schemes, accounting for futures contracts, oil and gas accounting, capitalizing interest, consolidating subsidiaries, accounting for combinations, and dividend accruals. See Weetman and Gray (1991) for a more comprehensive analysis.

8. U.K. GAAP permits the amortization of goodwill through the income statement, and requires amortization if reserves are unavailable. The accounting standard in this area is currently in the process of being revised.

9. The recent introduction of a new accounting standard FRS 3 *Reporting Financial Performance* (Accounting Standards Board, 1992) will lead to earnings per share being calculated after extraordinary items. At present earnings per share are reported in the U.K. before extraordinary items. FRS 3 will have the effect of bringing reported earnings per share in the U.K. closer to the U.S. GAAP counterpart. In this study, as discussed below, we focus on earnings prior to extraordinary items under both GAAP regimes.

10. The only other unpublished work of direct relevance of which we are aware is Choi *et al.* (1990). According to Choi and Levich (1990) this study concludes that "preliminary evidence... suggests that for a sample of Japanese firms accounting numbers restated to a U.S. GAAP basis do not appear to possess information content. The authors attribute this to the long time period between the release of the original numbers and restated numbers filed with the SEC" (p.105).

11. The Ohlson and Penman (1992) results suggest that it is useful to distinguish between (long run) value-relevance and (short run) information content.

12. For example, the firm might agree with lenders that U.S. GAAP have advantages for the purposes of monitoring debt contract performance.

13. For example, U.K. firms obtaining dual listings in the U.S. are likely to have significant product markets in the United States and are likely to be borrowing in the U.S., for example, through commercial paper programs.

14. Cairns *et al.* (1984) ranked the United Kingdom equal with the United States in terms of mandated disclosures.

15. The prediction of risk characteristics is also relevant in financial statement analysis.

16. Subsequent research will attempt to examine the properties of the GAAP-specific accruals components and their relationships with returns.

17. See Biddle and Seow (1992) for a discussion of the differences between tests of relative information content and incremental information content.

18. As Figlewski (1978) has shown, we would expect the implicit weights attached to different beliefs, or in this case earnings measures, to reflect the dollar weights attached to different investors' trading positions. In the long-run "Darwinism" in the market may be expected to lead to highest weight being given to the most informative information measure. However, in the short-run at least, even if a measure has no real information value, functional fixation could cause it to be given weight in the market.

19. In other words, following Engle and Granger (1987) we would expect the time series of prices of ADR's and the underlying shares to be co-integrated with a co-integrating parameter of unity.

20. The issue of optimal hedging policies from the perspective of the international portfolio investor is beyond the scope of this paper. Similarly, the impact of international differences in the effective tax rates paid by investors on dividends and capital gains is a complex issue to model, although in principle it is not different from the purely domestic market context where tax rates differ across investors. In this paper we follow the spirit of previous capital markets research in accounting by ignoring possible valuation impacts of taxes.

21. In a paper written after the present paper was completed Amir, Harris and Venuti (1993) report correlations above 0.988 for U.K. and currency-adjusted U.S. equivalent stock prices.

22. ADRs are effectively traded in a global market. The proportion of trading volume conducted by official American markets is relatively small in relation to total volume.

23. The information set considered is based on the 20-F SEC filings (specifically the U.S. GAAP earnings reconciliation). This data is also frequently disclosed in U.K. annual reports. However, even if disclosure to U.K.-based shareholders does not occur directly, the 20-F filings are in the public domain and can be obtained in the U.K. at nominal cost from firms such as *Disclosure Ltd*. The absence of any obviously significant costs to acquiring and processing the 20-F information suggests that if the 20-F contains 'value-relevant' information it is likely to be reflected in prices on the London Stock Exchange.

24. Equation (4.5) can be rewritten as

$$CAR_{jt} = \omega_{01} + \omega_{11}DUS_{jt} + (\omega_{11} + \omega_{21})DADJ_{jt} + v_{1jt}.$$

25. The specification of the returns generating model should also be assessed in relation to the economic interpretation of the performance metric adopted. Ohlson (1978) shows that the returns on a zero net investment hedge portfolio is the only valid approach for measuring abnormal returns, and this concept can only be applied in a single factor world if the parameter restrictions implied by the Sharpe (1964), Lintner (1965), Black (1972) capital asset pricing model (CAPM) are imposed. Thus generally, analysis of market model residuals will not lead to a performance metric capable of any simple economic interpretation.

26. This represents a tradeoff between efficiency of estimates and sample size. Privatization stocks with short returns histories were particularly problematic in this regard. Residual returns were also·estimated using the Scholes-Williams (1977) adjustment to correct for the biases associated with non-synchronous trading. The results were not qualitatively different.

27. Alternative specifications of the CAR-statistic based on a multiplicative form and annual rather than monthly residual returns were also tested, without any significant impact on the results.

28. Sensitivity analysis was conducted by moving the event window from months –8 to +3 through to –5 to +6 in monthly steps. The results were strongest and very similar for windows terminating in months +3 and +4. The explanatory power of the regressions fell significantly when the event window terminated in month +6, despite this being the theoretical deadline for SEC filings of 20-F reports. This suggests that generally the information contained in the 20-F's is available well before the six-month deadline date. This is not surprising, given our earlier observation that many firms disclose the 20-F information in their annual reports.

29. *The Quality of Markets Quarterly*, (London Stock Exchange, Winter 1989) reported that 50 U.K. firms have U.S. listings. However, of these, 7 (e.g., BAT, Fisons) do not have to file U.S. GAAP accounting reconciliation statements because of a dispensation for firms listed prior to the introduction of the 20-F disclosure requirements; a further 10 (e.g., Florida Employers Insurance, Unilever) are not genuine U.K.-domiciled firms; 2 are financial stocks; several other stocks have missing data either due to takeover and failure or because they are privatization stocks that have only recently started trading.

30. The adjustment process used by *Datastream* excludes pre-tax extraordinary items, non-operating provisions, exchange gains/losses, transfers to tax exempt reserves and any other items not relating to normal trading activities.

31. There is a lack of standardization in the 20-F disclosures which hampers data analysis. In particular only some of the sample appear to have disclosed the reallocation of extraordinary items, which are generally losses, to above-the-line income when theoretically they are required to do so by U.S. GAAP. The pricing of elements of earnings classified as extraordinary is of interest in itself, but it is not an issue we address directly in this study. It is considered in subsequent sensitivity analysis, however. The U.K. earnings per share calculation in any case excludes extraordinary items.

32. One element of the U.S./U.K. GAAP difference not tested is the different definitions of extraordinary items. As the data regarding the alternative classifications is not available for the full sample, the U.K. extraordinary item per share was included in the models reported in both a difference and yield format. This corresponds to the assumption that U.K. extraordinary items will be reclassified in the U.S.. Throughout the models the estimated coefficients on the extraordinary item variables were clearly insignificant and made no difference to the importance of the other variables. The extraordinary items did not reveal any information content in this sample. This is consistent with other U.K. evidence (Strong and Walker, 1992).

33. Potential differences between U.S. earnings per share, if they are reported, and our proxy could arise because of the standardization of U.K. earnings per share, and because of differences in the U.S. method of computing earnings per share specified in APB 15. This differs marginally from the U.K. methods specified in SSAP 3.

34. The annual subperiods are based on December year ends. The regressions using the pooled sample were also estimated including time dummies. The results were not noticeably different and the time dummies were typically insignificant.

35. Analysis for annual subsamples revealed that there is substantial instability in the explanatory power of the earnings variables for returns over time. Some years, e.g., 1988, display stronger associations between returns and earnings than others. This is consistent with earlier large sample results in Easton and Harris (1991), Strong and Walker (1992), and elsewhere. In view of the small sample sizes involved in annual regressions based on our sample, we report only the full sample results. The issue of why explanatory power varies over time is, however, an issue that is of general concern in cross sectional market based accounting research.
36. I.e., equations (4.8), (4.9), and (4.10) and transformations of these equations.

REFERENCES

Ali, A., and P. Zarowin.(1992). "The Role of Earnings Levels in Annual Earnings-Returns Studies." *Journal of Accounting Research.*

Amir, E., T. S. Harris, and E. K. Venuti. (1993). "A Comparison of the Value-Relevance of U.S. versus Non-U.S. GAAP Accounting Measures Using Form 20-F Reconciliations." Paper presented at Journal of Accounting Research Conference, University of Chicago, May 1993.

Ball, R., and P. Brown. (1968). "An Empirical Evaluation of Accounting Income Numbers." *Journal of Accounting Research.* Autumn, pp. 159–78.

Ball, R., and S. Kothari. (1990). "Security Returns Around Earnings Expectations." University of Rochester working paper.

Beaver, W., R. Clarke, and W. Wright. (1979). "The Association Between Unsystematic Security Returns and the Magnitude of Earnings Forecast Errors." *Journal of Accounting Research.* Autumn, pp. 316–40.

Beaver, W., P. Griffin, and W. Landsman. (1982). "The Incremental Information Content of Replacement Cost Earnings." *Journal of Accounting & Economics.* July, pp. 15–40.

Beaver W., R. Lambert, and D. Morse. (1980). "The Information Content of Security Prices." *Journal of Accounting and Economics.* 2.

Beaver, W. (1981). "Economic Properties of Alternative Security Return Methods." *Journal of Accounting Research.* 19, pp. 163–84.

Biddle, G. C., and S. H. Saudagaran. (1989). "The Effects of Financial Disclosure Levels on Firms' Choices Among Alternatative Foreign Stock Exchange Listings." *Journal of International Financial Management and Accounting.* 1, no. 1, pp. 55–87.

Biddle, G. C., and G. S. Seow. (1992). "Relative versus Incremental Information Content and Cross-Industry Evidence for Net Income, Cash Flows and Sales." University of Washington.

Black, F. (1972). "Capital Market Equilibrium with Restricted Borrowing." *Journal of Business.* 45, pp. 444–55.

Board, J., and M. Walker. (1990). "Intertemporal and Cross-sectional Variation in the Association Between Unexpected Accounting Rates of Return and Abnormal Returns." *Journal of Accounting Research*. Spring, pp. 182–92.

Bowen, R., D. Burgstaler, and L. Daley. (1987). "The Incremental Information Content of Accrual Versus Cash Flow." *Accounting Review*. October, pp. 723–47.

Brown, S., and J. Warner. (1980). "Measuring Security Price Performance." *Journal of Financial Economics*. 8, pp. 205–58.

Bublitz, B., T. Frecka, and J. McKeown. (1985). "Market Association Tests and FASB Statement No 33 Disclosures: A Re-examination." *Journal of Accounting Research*. 1985 Supplement, pp. 1–23.

Cairns, D., M. Lafferty, and P. Mantle. (1984). *Survey of Published Accounts and Accountants 1983-84*. London: Lafferty Publications.

Choi, F. D. S., and R. M. Levich. (1990). *Capital Market Effects of International Accounting Diversity*. Homewood, IL: Dow Jones–Irwin.

Choi, F. D. S., I. K. Joo, and Y. Kim. (1990). "The Information Content of Restated Accounting Numbers." New York University manuscript.

Christie, A. (1987). "On Cross-Sectional Analysis in Accounting Research." *Journal of Accounting and Economics*. 9, pp. 231–58.

Collins, D., and S. Kothari. (1989). "An Analysis of Intertemporal and Cross-sectional Determinants of Earnings Response Coefficients." *Journal of Accounting & Economics*. July, pp. 383–403.

Dechow, P. (1991). "Accounting Earnings and Cash Flows as Measures of Firm Performance: The Role of Accounting Accruals." University of Rochester mimeo.

Dimson, E., and P. Marsh. (1986). "Event Study Methodologies and the Size Effect. The Case of U.K. Press Recommendations." *Journal of Finance*. pp. 113–42.

Easton, P., T. Harris, and J. Ohlson. (1990). "Accounting Earnings Can Explain Most of Security Returns: The Case of Long Event Windows." Columbia University.

Easton, P., and T. Harris. (1991). "Earnings as an Explanatory Variable for Returns." *Journal of Accounting Research*. Spring, pp. 19–36.

Engle, E., and C. Granger. (1988). "Cointegration and Error Correction: Representation Estimation and Testing." *Econometrica*. 55, pp. 251–76.

FASB. (1976). "Statement of Financial Accounting Concepts No 1: Objectives of Financial Reporting by Business Enterprises." Financial Accounting Standards Board.

Figlewski, S. (1978). "Market 'Efficiency' in a Market with Heterogenous Information." *Journal of Political Economy*. 86, pp. 581–97.

Fried, D, and D. Givoly. (1982). "Financial Analysts' Forecasts of Earnings: A Better Surrogate for Market Expectations." *Journal of Accounting and Economics*. October, pp. 85–108.

Gonedes, M., and N. Dopuch. (1974). "Capital Market Equilibrium, Information

Production, and Selecting Accounting Techniques: Theoretical Framework and Review of Empirical Work." *Supplement to Journal of Accounting Research.* 12, pp. 48–130.

Hagerman, R., M. Zmijewski, and R. Shah. (1984). "The Association Between the Magnitude of Quarterly Earnings Forecast Errors and Risk Adjusted Stock Returns." *Journal of Accounting Research.* Autumn, pp. 526–40.

Hoskin, R., J. Hughes, and W. Ricks. (1986). "Evidence on the Incremental Information Content of Additional Firm Disclosures Made Concurrently with Earnings." *Journal of Accounting Research,* Supplement. pp. 1–32.

Hughes, J., and W. Ricks. (1987). "Association Between Forecast Errors and Excess Returns Near to Earnings Announcements." *Accounting Review.* January , pp. 158–67.

IASC. (1990). "Comparability of Financial Statements." International Accounting Standards Committee. E32, January.

Kormandi, R., and R. Lipe. (1987). "Earnings Innovation, Earnings Persistence and Stock Returns." *Journal of Business.* July, pp. 323–45.

Lev, B., and S. Thiagrajan. (1990). "Financial Information Analysis." University of California. October.

Lev, B. (1989). "On the Usefulness of Earning and Earnings Research: Lessons and Directions from Two Decades of Empirical Research." *Journal of Accounting Research Supplement.* pp. 153–92.

Lipe, R. (1986). "The Information Contained in the Components of Earnings." *Journal of Accounting Research Supplement.* pp. 37–64.

Lintner, J. (1965). "The Valuation of Risk Assets and the Selection of Risky Investments in Stock Portfolios and Capital Budgets." *Review of Economics & Statistics.* February, pp. 13–37.

Livnat, J., and P. Zavorin. (1990). "The Incremental Information Content of Cash-Flow Components." *Journal of Accounting & Economics.* 13, pp. 25–46.

Meek, G. (1983). "U.S. Securities Markets Responses to Alternative Earnings Disclosures of Non-U.S. Multinational Corporations." *Accounting Review.* April, pp. 394–402.

Ohlson, J. (1978). "On the Theory of Residual Analyses and Abnormal Perfomance Metrics." *Australian Journal of Management.* October.

Ohlson, J., and P. K. Shroff. (1992). "Changes vs. Levels as Explanatory Variables for Returns." *Journal of Accounting Research.*

Rayburn, J. (1986). "The Association of Operating Cash Flows and Accruals with Security Returns." *Journal of Accounting Research Supplement.* pp. 112–33.

Rosenthal, L., and C. Young. (1990). "The Seemingly Anomalous Price Behaviour of Royal Dutch/Shell and Unilever N.V/Plc." *Journal of Financial Economics.* 26, pp. 123–41.

Scholes, M., and J. Williams. (1977). "Estimating Betas from Non-Synchronous Data." *Journal of Financial Economics.* 5, pp. 309–28.

Sharpe, W. (1964). "Capital Asset Prices: A Theory of Market Equilibrium Under Conditions of Risk." *Journal of Finance*. September, pp. 425–42.

Sloan, R. G. (1991). "Accounting Earnings and Top Executive Compensation." The Wharton School working paper.

Strong, N., and M. Walker. (1992). "The Relation Between Returns and Earnings: A U.K. Panel Data Study." University of Manchester working paper.

Strong, W., and M. Walker. (1991). "The Incremental Information Content of the Exceptional and Extraordinary Components of All-Inclusive Earnings." University of Manchester.

Tinic, S. (1990). "A Perspective on the Stock Markets Fixation on Accounting Numbers." *The Accounting Review*. October, pp. 781–96.

UBS Phillips & Drew. (1991). "Accounting for Growth." London: UBS Phillips and Drew. January.

Watts, R., and J. Zimmerman. (1986). *Positive Accounting Theory*. Englewood Cliffs, NJ: Prentice-Hall.

Weetman, P., and S. Gray. (1991). "International Financial Analysis and Comparative Corporate Performance: The impact of U.K. versus U.S. Accounting Principles on Earnings." *Journal of International Financial Management and Accounting*. 2 & 3, pp. 111–30.

White, H. (1980). "A Heteroscedastic Consistent Covariance Matrix and a Direct Test for Heteroscedaticity." *Econometrica*. 48, pp. 721–46.

Wilson, G. (1986). "The Relative Information Content of Accruals and Cash Flows: Combined Evidence of the Earnings Announcement and Annual Report Release Date." *Journal of Accounting Research Supplement*. pp. 165–200.

Wilson, G. (1987). "The Incremental Information Content of the Accrual and Funds Components of Earnings after Controlling for Earnings." *Accounting Review*. April, pp. 293–322.

)

CHAPTER 5

EFFECTS OF ALTERNATIVE GOODWILL TREATMENTS ON MERGER PREMIA: FURTHER EMPIRICAL EVIDENCE

Changwoo Lee
Frederick D. S. Choi

INTRODUCTION AND BACKGROUND

A recent study by Choi and Lee (1991) documents the impact of international accounting differences on market decisions. They test the conventional belief that non-amortization of goodwill permits U.K. companies to outbid U.S. companies in the acquisition of U.S. targets. They find merger premia associated with U.K acquirors to be consistently higher than for U.S. acquirors. Moreover, premiums paid tend to be more highly associated with goodwill for U.K. than for U.S. acquirors and the higher premiums paid by U.K. acquirors do appear to be associated with not having to amortize goodwill to earnings. A direct implication of the study is that national differences in permitted accounting treatments may produce an unlevel playing field in the market for corporate control.

The authors wish to gratefully acknowledge the financial support of the KPMG Peat Marwick Foundation (Research Opportunities in International Business Information Program). All errors remain our responsibility.

Evidence suggests that British corporates are not the only acquirors offering higher premiums for U.S. target companies. Tandon, Hessel, and Cakici (1989) observed significant premiums paid by Canadian, Japanese and German acquirors as well. In that study, Japanese acquirors were found to pay the highest merger premia, followed by the Canadians, British and Germans, in that order. For sell-offs, the order was just the reverse. A review of merger and acquisition accounting and tax rules across these countries reveals marked contrasts, especially in relation to the United States versus Germany and Japan. Given the juxtaposition of observed premia differentials and differences in national accounting and tax rules, we examine to what extent differences in national accounting and tax treatments are associated with prices paid by Japanese and German companies for U.S. acquisitions.

The competitive significance of this investigation is not confined to the United States. The merger and acquisition movement in Europe has mushroomed (Greenhouse, 1989). This trend, furthermore, is predicted to continue as companies prepare for the more competitive era that will follow the dismantling of international trade barriers by the European Community by the end of 1992. Potential market distortions caused by national differences in M&A accounting would have significant implications for monitoring and enforcing EC directives. The EC has recently put into effect a European Merger Control regulation to control cross-border merger and joint venture activity on a Community-wide basis. As access to markets is no longer determined solely by barriers to trade in physical goods, rules of fair play in matters of cross-border investment and competition have assumed high priority at both the national and international level where they can easily become a source of friction (Montagnon and Riddell, 1990).

The balance of this paper is organized as follows: The second section discusses differential goodwill accounting and tax rules across countries examined in this study. The third section describes our research methodology and data. Empirical results are reported in the fourth section and our conclusions in the final section.

DIFFERENTIAL TREATMENTS OF GOODWILL

In an acquisition accounted for as a purchase, any difference between the purchase price and the fair value (generally market value) of the net assets that are acquired is usually recognized as an intangible asset, goodwill. In the United States, this merger premium must be capitalized and amortized to expense over a period not to exceed 40 years. While a similar methodology can also be employed in the United Kingdom, the accounting treatment preferred by U.K. managers is to write off goodwill immediately against reserves (Weetman and Gray, 1990). This allows British companies to report higher earnings than would be the case if U.S. GAAP were used. As goodwill is not tax deductible either in the United States or United Kingdom, differences in merger premiums offered by U.K. acquirors are attributed largely to reasons associated with performance-based management compensation (Choi and Lee, 1991).

Tax treatments, however, are not the same outside the U.S. –U.K. orbit. Summary accounting and tax practices in Germany and Japan follow.

Accounting Treatments[1]

1. *Japan*: Goodwill is amortized to income over a reasonable period, normally 5 years.
2. *Germany*: Goodwill, if capitalized, may either be amortized to income normally over 4 years or charged to reserves.

Tax Treatments[1]

1. *Japan*: Goodwill is depreciable for tax purposes.
2. *Germany*: Goodwill is depreciable for tax purposes but must be amortized over 15 years.

To summarize, while both Germany and Japan can deduct goodwill for tax purposes, German acquirors have the option of not amortizing goodwill for financial reporting purposes. To what extent are merger premia offered by acquirors in our sample countries associated with differing accounting and/or tax treatments for goodwill? This is the question addressed in this chapter.

RESEARCH METHODOLOGY AND DATA

To answer our research question, we first compare premiums paid by U.S. acquirors with those paid by foreign acquirors of U.S. target companies. Second, we undertake regression analyses on a country-by-country basis to see whether goodwill explains cross-sectional variations in merger premia offered by foreign acquirors. As a final step, we match foreign acquisitions with U.S. acquisitions based on variables identified in our earlier study as having an association with merger premia. For each matched pair, we regress observed premium differences against goodwill differences and a proxy variable for the effect of different accounting treatments for goodwill.

Our sample consists of M&A deals in which the target is a U.S. company and the acquiror either a U.S., or a German or Japanese company, as reported by Automatic Data Processing, Inc.[2] It includes deals announced between 1985 and 1989.

We define merger premia as the difference between the total offering price announced on the deal announcement date and the market value of the acquired firm (purchased portion) prior to the announcement date, standardized by the book value of net assets acquired.[3] While a common measure of goodwill is the difference between the purchase price and the fair market value of net assets acquired, we use as a proxy the difference between the market value and the book value of the net assets acquired.[4] This was necessitated by considerations of data availability and objectivity.[5]

Sample deals selected for inclusion in this investigation were those for which the following information was available:

1. Offering price per share (OFFPRC).
2. Target company's stock price one day, one week, one month, and two months prior to the deal announcement date (TPRC1D, TPRC1W, TPRC1M, and TPRC2M, respectively).
3. Book value of the target company's equity (TEQUIT).
4. Percent of target company's common shares acquired (COMACQ).
5. Target company's common shares outstanding (TSHOUT).

This selection procedure produced a total of 1,217 U.S., 40 Japanese, acquisitions and 15 German acquisitions.

Out of a total of 1,262 sample deals, 13 U.S. acquisitions were identified as outliers and deleted from the sample to avoid the effect of extreme values. A deal was identified as an outlier if the premium paid per dollar of equity (book value) purchased was greater than or equal to 50, or less than or equal to –20, or the goodwill per dollar of equity is greater than 100.[6] In addition, deals with common stock as a mode of payment are deleted to assure that the sample deals used in this study are only those that employ the purchase method of accounting.[7] Accordingly, a total of 1,111 sample deals, 1,056 U.S., 40 Japanese and 15 German acquisitions were used throughout this analysis. Trends in the number of sample deals appear in Panel A of

TABLE 5–1
Description of Sample Deals

Panel A: Number of Sample Deals per Country by Year

Country	1985	1986	1987	1988	1989	Total
Japan	1	6	6	11	16	40
Germany	0	3	3	5	4	15
Total	1	9	9	16	20	55

Panel B: Distributions of Size of Deals by Country (in Million Dollars)

Statistics	U.S.	Japan	Germany
100%	12,635.5	3,477.8	2,723.5
75%	195.9	210.1	116.4
50%	39.6	37.8	41.4
25%	10.0	4.9	10.2
Min.	1.0	1.3	4.4
Mean	337.4	271.5	235.4
N	1,056	40	15

Table 5–1. Panel B of that table discloses the distribution of size-of-deal by country.

EMPIRICAL RESULTS

Mean Difference Tests

Table 5–2 reports the results of our mean difference tests. In this test, we compare merger premia per dollar of a target company's equity (purchased portion) between U.S. and foreign acquisitions. Premium differences were observed at four time points: one day (PREM1D), one week (PREM1W), one month (PREM1M), and two months (PREM2M) prior to the announcement of an M&A deal.[8] Reported p-values of t-statistics are premised on F tests of equal variance.

In the U.S.-Japan comparisons, we observe that Japanese acquirors offer higher merger premia, on average, than their U.S. counterparts, which is statistically significant at conventional levels. Given that goodwill is tax deductible under Japanese tax law, this finding is consistent with the hypothesis that higher merger premia are associated with tax savings opportu-

TABLE 5–2
**Comparisons of Mean Premiums Paid per Dollar of Equity
Purchased (Comparions with U.S. Acquisitions)**

Bidder	N	PREM1D	PREM1W	PREM1M	PREM2M
1. Japan vs. U.S.					
Japan	40	0.7876	0.7575	0.8498	0.9608
United States	1056	0.3876	0.4555	0.5135	0.5423
Prob>|T|:		0.0276	0.1269	0.1028	0.1016
2. Germany vs. U.S.					
Germany	15	0.8383	0.8553	0.9827	0.9180
United States	1056	0.3876	0.4555	0.5135	0.5423
Prob>|T|:		0.1229	0.2024	0.1502	0.3632

nities. We also find German merger premia to be higher, on average, than those offered by U.S. acquirors. Since goodwill can be amortized against reserves and is also tax deductible in Germany, this finding is also consistent with our expectations. Given these findings, we investigate the association of goodwill and merger premia in both countries.

Empirical Model and Regression Analysis

The purpose of this section is to see if goodwill is associated with merger premia and, if that is the case, whether there is any differential impact of goodwill on premia differentials between various countries.

Goodwill represents the ability of a firm to earn an above average rate of return, reflecting the assets that are not recorded on the balance sheet (such as intangibles, R&D, advertising, as well as monopoly profits). Motivating an acquisition is the higher earnings stream made possible by synergies of the combined assets of the target and acquiring firms. This will also translate to a higher earnings stream for managers whose compensation is tied to reported performance. To secure this incremental earnings stream, we theorize that management will be willing to transfer a portion, p^*, of the expected benefits created by the takeover to shareholders of the target company to induce them to sell. From a management's perspective, p^* will be consistent with that level which optimizes the discounted present value of their expected compensation stream. In the case of U.S. acquirors, management's reservation offering price will be constrained by the effects of amortization of any premiums paid on the present value of their performance-based compensation. This logic appears to be the rationale underlying the conventional wisdom which says that foreign companies, by not having to amortize goodwill, are able to offer relatively higher premiums for an acquisition target than their U.S. counterparts. In the case where goodwill is deductible for tax purposes, there will be a real cash savings effect associated with purchased goodwill. Other things the same, acquirors enjoying the favorable tax treatment will be able to offer relatively higher premia than those for which a tax deduction is not available.

We employ the following model[9] to see whether: (a) there is any association between merger premia and goodwill in general, and (b) the strength of the association differs between U.S. and foreign acquisitions.

$$PREM_i = a_0 + b_1 GWQ_i + e_i \qquad (5.1)$$

For each deal i, merger premium (PREM) is defined as the difference between the offering price and the stock price on the date of observation multiplied by the proportionate ownership purchased. This, in turn, is divided by the purchased portion of the target's equity [i.e., PREM1D = (OFFPRC − TPRC1D) × (TSHOUT × COMACQ) / (TEQUIT × COMACQ)]. We compute merger premia at four different time points: one day (PREM1D), one week (PREM1W), one month (PREM1M), and two months (PREM2M) prior to the deal announcement date. Goodwill (GWQ) is defined as the market value of shares purchased minus the book value of net equity purchased[10], divided by the book value of net equity purchased. For example, goodwill one day prior to announcement would be computed as, GWQ = (TPRC1D × TSHOUT × COMACQ − TEQUIT × COMACQ)/ (TEQUIT × COMACQ). The goodwill measures are also observed at four discrete time points corresponding to dates used for our premium measures.

Since goodwill, as we have defined the term, is reflective of a firm's abnormal earning power, we expect, *ceteris paribus*, higher premiums to be paid to a firm with the higher goodwill. Therefore, *a priori*, we would expect the sign of the coefficient of GWQ (b_1) to be positive as the economic effect of a superior earnings potential would presumably dwarf the nominal impact of an accounting effect that has no bearing on firm cash flows.

Table 5–3 reports both Pearson and Spearman Rank correlations between merger premia and goodwill for both Japanese and German

TABLE 5–3
Correlations between Goodwill and Merger Premia

Country	PREM1D & GW1D	PREM1W & GW1W	PREM1M & GW1M	PREM2M & GW2M
Panel A: Pearson Correlations				
Japan	0.4577 (.003)	0.2960 (.064)	0.1590 (.327)	0.1597 (.325)
Germany	0.6727 (.006)	0.6798 (.005)	0.5401 (.038)	0.4852 (.067)
Panel B: Spearman Rank Correlations				
Japan	0.4178 (.007)	0.3751 (.017)	0.3344 (.035)	0.3453 (.029)
Germany	0.2607 (.348)	0.3107 (.260)	0.1393 (.621)	0.0924 (.742)

acquisitions. For both countries, the association is strong and significant. These results indicate that in acquisitions where relatively favorable accounting and/or tax treatments are available, the correlation between goodwill and merger premia are strong and significant. Note also that the German correlation is higher than the Japanese correlation. This may reflect more favorable accounting and tax treatments in Germany vis-à-vis Japan.

Regression results for each sample country are reported in Table 5–4. We observe a strong association between goodwill and merger premia for Japanese and German acquisitions. This result is consistent with our earlier findings(Choi and Lee, 1991). Note also that the coefficient for goodwill is higher for German acquisitions than for Japanese acquisitions. As tax and relatively stronger accounting effects are evidenced in Germany, our findings are consistent with the notion that merger premia are associated with accounting differences among various countries.

Consideration of Confounding Variables

To control for the effects of confounding variables, we obtained additional data that might have some bearing on merger premia. Variables suggested in

TABLE 5–4
Regression Results of Foreign Country Acquisitions (Effect of Goodwill on Merger Premia)

Model: $PREM_i = a_0 + b_1 GWQ_i + e_i$

Variable	PREM1D	PREM1W	PREM1M	PREM2M
Panel A: Japanese Acquisitions (N = 40)				
$\bar{R}^2$	.189	.064	.000	.000
Intercept	0.3506	0.4115	0.6522	0.7457
	(2.539)	(1.552)	(2.159)	(3.511)
GWQ	0.2556	0.1989	0.1199	0.1399
	(2.273)	(1.910)	(0.993)	(0.657)
Model Specification:				
Prob>χ^2	.0891	.1019	.1272	.0438
Panel B: German Acquisitions (N = 15)				
$\bar{R}^2$	.410	.421	.237	.177
Intercept	0.1982	0.2269	0.3823	0.3518
	(0.659)	(0.772)	(0.947)	(0.823)
GWQ	0.9031	0.9093	1.0637	0.9001
	(3.278)	(3.342)	(2.314)	(2.001)
Model Specification:				
Prob>χ^2	.4506	.3830	.3495	.4315

the literature as being associated with merger premia are mode of payment, type of acquisition, tender offers, hostile attitudes, and industrial relationship of the target and acquiring firms, among others [see for example, Huang and Walkling (1987) and Wansley, Lane, and Yang (1983)]. Table 5–5 reports the distribution of these characteristic variables.

Payment mode is dichotomized into two types: cash and other. Foreign acquisitions are also classified into two groups: Acquisition and Other. A sample deal is classified as an Acquisition when a company either acquires 100 percent of the target company, increases its ownership in the target from less than 50 percent to 100 percent, or acquires all of the target's assets.[9] We also classified sample deals by the existence of a public tender offer and the target's attitude toward the deal, whether hostile or not.

TABLE 5–5
**Characteristics of Foreign Acquisitions (Mode of Payment, Type
of Acquisition, Tender Offer, and Hostile Attitude)**

	Class	Japan (N=40)	Germany (N=15)
1. Mode of Payment			
	Cash:	85.0%	80.0%
	Other:	15.0	20.0
2. Type of Acquisition			
	Acquisition:	55.0%	66.7%
	Other Types:	45.0	33.3
3. Public Tender Offer			
	Yes:	40.0%	46.7%
	No :	60.0	53.3
4. Target's Hostile Attitude			
	Yes:	5.0%	0.0%
	No :	95.0	100

Reported statistics show that the majority of deals are based on the cash mode of payment. There is a transfer of ownership from the target to the acquiror in about half of the deals. About half of our sample deals involve a public tender offer, and in most cases, the target's attitude toward the deal is not hostile.

Matched Pair Regressions

Under U.S. GAAP, purchased goodwill recorded on an acquirors' books will affect reported earnings due to amortization. As this may not be the case in our sample countries, foreign acquirors may be able to offer relatively higher premiums for target companies owing to favorable accounting and/or tax treatments for goodwill. In developing a model to test whether differential premiums paid by foreign acquirors are associated with different accounting and/or tax treatments, we postulate the following relationships:

$$\text{PREM}_{US} = f(\text{GW}_{US}, X_2, X_3, \dots) \qquad \text{and}$$

$$\text{PREM}_F = f(\text{GW}_F, \text{GW}^*_F, X_2, X_3, \dots),$$

where $PREM_{US}$ and $PREM_F$ represent premiums paid by U.S. and foreign acquirors, respectively. GW_{US} and GW_F denote the goodwill acquired in U.S. and foreign acquisitions, while X_2 and X_3 denote all factors other than goodwill affecting merger premia. GW^*_F represents the relative financial statement and/or tax effects experienced by foreign acquirors due to their differing goodwill treatments. Suppose X_2, X_3, and other explanatory variables are the same for non-U.S. and U.S. acquisitions. The difference in observed premiums ($PRMDF = PREM_F - PREM_{US}$) would then be:

$$PRMDF = f(GWDF, GW^*_F),$$

where $GWDF = GW_F - GW_{US}$. Based on this relationship, we introduce the following regression form into our analysis:

$$PRMDF_i = a_0 + b_1 GWDF_i + b_2 GWCO_i + e_i, \qquad (5.2)$$

where i denotes each matched pair (matching criteria are explained below) and GWCO is the portion of goodwill common to both foreign and U.S. acquisitions. Note that $GW_F = GWDF + GWCO$. Given that the dependent variable represents the premium difference between matched pairs, the coefficient of GWDF (b_1) is expected to capture both above average earning power of the target company and the advantageous tax and financial statement effects accruing to foreign acquirors arising from the differential treatments of goodwill. The coefficient of GWCO (b_2) captures the accounting and tax effects only.

To control for factors that might impinge on premia differentials other than goodwill, matching is accomplished as follows:
1. All sample deals, including both target and acquiror, are arranged in terms of four-digit SIC industry codes.
2. Each non-U.S. acquisition is then matched with a U.S. acquisition based on type of deal, existence of a tender offer, and industrial relationship between target and acquiring firms.

In our early analyses (Choi and Lee, 1991), type of acquisition (TYPE) and the existence of a tender offer (TENDER) were important variables in explaining merger premia. Therefore, in the matching process, priority is given to these two variables. In addition, an exchange rate parity (XRP) variable is included in the regression based on equation (5.2) to control for foreign exchange rate effects. For example, a strong deutschemark relative to the U.S. dollar might induce German acquirors to offer higher premiums than would otherwise be the case.

Our matched pair regression analysis is conducted on both German and Japanese acquisitions due to the small sample size associated with German acquisitions. To investigate the impact of German accounting treatments which provide reporting entities the option to amortize goodwill against reserves, the following model is used.

$$\text{PRMDF}_i = a_0 + b_1\text{GWDF}_i + b_2\text{GWCO}_i + b_3\text{DFCO}_i + e_i, \quad (5.3)$$

where DFCO = GWCO*D, D is 1 for a German acquisition and 0 for a Japanese acquisition.

Table 5–6 reports the results.

Panel A, provided for comparison purposes, shows that for both German and Japanese acquisitions, there is a positive association between differences in goodwill and merger premiums. This finding is consistent with our earlier investigation. Panel B indicates that, for premia differences measured one day prior to the deal announcement (PRMDF1D), the relative benefit due to differential accounting/tax treatments of goodwill (GWCO) has a positive and significant association with merger premia. The tax advantage of a German acquisition shows up as a positive and significant coefficient on DFCO. Results with the inclusion of exchange rate variable (XRP) are reported in Panel C. While the coefficient on XRP is positive, it is not statistically significant at conventional levels. Accordingly, the results reported in Table 6 are generally consistent with the expectation that merger premia differences are primarily affected by differential accounting and tax treatments for goodwill in Germany and Japan. For German acquisitions there is an additional accounting impact upon merger premia differences.

CONCLUSION

In this chapter, we continue our investigation as to whether or not national differences in the accounting treatment for goodwill affect managerial behavior in the market for corporate control. Specifically, we examine empirically the popular belief that national differences in permitted accounting treatments for purchased goodwill provide non-U.S. acquirors with a bidding advantage when acquiring U.S. target companies.

TABLE 5–6
**Germany and Japan Matched Pair[a] Comparisons (N = 55,
15 Germany & 40 Japan)**

Variable	PRMDF1D	PRMDF1W	PRMDF1M	PRMDF2M
Panel A: $PRMDF_i = a_0 + b_1 GWDF_i + e_i$				
$\bar{R}^2$	.0834	.1004	.0351	.0738
Intercept	0.4576	0.2891	0.3769	0.3912
	(2.739)	(1.608)	(1.888)	(1.996)
GWDF	0.1807	0.2166	0.1540	0.2119
	(2.432)	(2.651)	(1.722)	(2.303)
Model Specification[b]:				
Prob>χ^2	.9470	.4823	.2226	.0963
Panel B: $PRMDF_i = a_0 + b_1 GWDF_i + b_2 GWCO_i + b_3 DFCO_i + e_i$				
$\bar{R}^2$	.2327	.1169	.0139	.0396
Intercept	0.0235	0.0679	0.2974	0.3876
	(0.112)	(0.282)	(1.125)	(1.478)
GWDF	0.3333	0.2883	0.1797	0.2107
	(3.873)	(2.927)	(1.600)	(1.774)
GWCO	0.2872	0.1447	0.0221	–0.0204
	(2.112)	(0.857)	(0.117)	(–0.107)
DFCO	0.5263	0.4091	0.3431	0.1321
	(2.211)	(1.260)	(0.875)	(0.329)
Model Specification[b]:				
Prob>χ^2	.9161	.3039	.7794	.3766

[a] Matching is based on the following priorities: industry relationships based on SIC code groupings of both target and acquiring companies, type of deal, whether the deal involves a public tender offer to shareholders, whether the target's attitude toward the bid is hostile, and mode of payment. The numbers presented in parentheses are t-statistics.
Variable Descriptions:
PRMDF = Differences in premium values between foreign and U.S. acquisitions, computed using the target company's stock prices one day (PRMDF1D), one week (PRMDF1W), one month (PRMDF1M), and two months (PRMDF2M) prior to announcement, respectively.
GWDF = Goodwill differences per dollar of purchased equity between foreign and U.S. acquisitions. These values are computed at four discrete time points: one day, one week, one month, and two months prior to announcement.
GWCO = The portion of goodwill per dollar of purchased equity that is common to both foreign and U.S. acquisitions. This variable is used as a proxy for the possible benefits enjoyed by foreign acquirers due to their advantageous goodwill accounting treatment relative to U.S. acquirers.
DFCO = D*GWCO, where D is 1 for German acquisitions and 0 for Japanese acquisitions.
XRP = Exchange rate parity calculated as dollar per pound exchange rate at the foreign acquisition announcement date divided by the dollar per pound exchange rate at the U.S. acquisition announcement date minus one. The exchange rates are retrieved from CITIBASE.
[b] This is based on White's (1980) model specification tests.

TABLE 5–6, concluded
Germany and Japan Matched Pair[a] Comparisons (N = 55,
15 Germany & 40 Japan)

Variable	PRMDF1D	PRMDF1W	PRMDF1M	PRMDF2M
Panel C: $PRMDF_i = a_0 + b_1 GWDF_i + b_2 GWCO_i + b_3 DFCO_i + b_4 XRP_i + e_i$				
$\bar{R}^2$	.2422	.1223	.0428	.0819
Intercept	–0.0383	0.0021	0.1815	0.2473
	(–0.180)	(0.009)	(0.672)	(0.924)
GWDF	0.3298	0.2855	0.1845	0.2224
	(3.854)	(2.907)	(1.667)	(1.912)
GWCO	0.2851	0.1456	0.0308	–0.0029
	(2.109)	(0.865)	(0.166)	(–0.015)
DFCO	0.5185	0.3974	0.3335	0.1262
	(2.191)	(1.227)	(0.863)	(0.321)
XRP	0.7390	0.7586	1.1885	1.3446
	(1.280)	(1.147)	(1.594)	(1.831)
Model Specification[b]:				
Prob>χ^2	.7121	.4721	.8325	.5732

[a] Matching is based on the following priorities: industry relationships based on SIC code groupings of both target and acquiring companies, type of deal, whether the deal involves a public tender offer to shareholders, whether the target's attitude toward the bid is hostile, and mode of payment. The numbers presented in parentheses are *t*-statistics.
Variable Descriptions:
PRMDF = Differences in premium values between foreign and U.S. acquisitions, computed using the target company's stock prices one day (PRMDF1D), one week (PRMDF1W), one month (PRMDF1M), and two months (PRMDF2M) prior to announcement, respectively.
GWDF = Goodwill differences per dollar of purchased equity between foreign and U.S. acquisitions. These values are computed at four discrete time points: one day, one week, one month, and two months prior to announcement.
GWCO = The portion of goodwill per dollar of purchased equity that is common to both foreign and U.S. acquisitions. This variable is used as a proxy for the possible benefits enjoyed by foreign acquirers due to their advantageous goodwill accounting treatment relative to U.S. acquirers.
DFCO = D*GWCO, where D is 1 for German acquisitions and 0 for Japanese acquisitions.
XRP = Exchange rate parity calculated as dollar per pound exchange rate at the foreign acquisition announcement date divided by the dollar per pound exchange rate at the U.S. acquisition announcement date minus one. The exchange rates are retrieved from CITIBASE.
[b] This is based on White's (1980) model specification tests.

In an earlier investigation, we found merger premia associated with U.K. acquisitions of U.S. targets to be consistently higher than that for U.S. acquisitions. Moreover, these higher premiums appeared to be associated with differences in goodwill accounting treatments. Preliminary evidence on German and Japanese acquisitions in the United States suggests that this phenomenon may not be limited to a single country.

Our findings, however, should be tempered by limitations in our methodology. In measuring the differences in premiums paid, for example, one would ideally like to know the offering prices made by the losing as well as the winning bidder. Unfortunately, data for the former are seldom made public necessitating the use of cross-sectional averaging. Similarly, goodwill is normally defined as the difference between the price paid for an acquisition and the fair market value of the net assets acquired. Owing to data constraints, we defined goodwill as the difference between the market and net book value of the net equity acquired. Measures which take into account differences in asset revaluation increments or decrements would be desirable. Further, owing to resource constraints, data for our analysis was limited to a five year window.

While we attempted to control for as many variables as possible, our controls were not exhaustive. Other variables that might be operationalized and controlled for include such things as strategic considerations and cost of capital differences.[11] Considerations such as these could very well account for the merger premium differences observed. Nevertheless, the evidence marshalled thus far seems to support the conventional notion that national differences in accounting treatments differentially impact on managerial behavior in the market for corporate control. If this is indeed the case, efforts to create a more level playing field have merit. However, they will not be easy. For example, while international accounting standards may appear a logical tack, the evidence presented here suggests that effective harmonization may be difficult in a world characterized by international tax differences. Another implication stemming from this study is that firms capitalizing on an accounting advantage to increase their acquisition bids may do so at the expense of their own shareholders; an interesting study in its own right.

NOTES

1. Coopers & Lybrand, *International Accounting Summaries: A Guide for Interpretation and Comparison,* New York: John Wiley & Sons, 1991; Price Waterhouse, *Information Guide: Doing Business In Series,* New York: 1990; Touche Ross International, *Business Investment and Taxation Handbook,* Chicago, Illinois: Probus Publishing Company, 1989.
2. To be included in the M&A Data Base, a transaction must be valued at $1 million or

more. Real property merger and acquisition activity is not reported.

3. We standardize using book value to avoid the heteroschedasticity problem of cross-sectional data. We could have used market value to standardize our dependent variable. Indeed, we ran the same regression using market value as a deflator and the results were generally consistent with that reported here. One problem in using market value as a deflator, however, is that the dependent variable becomes a return measure. This makes interpretation of the independent variable representing goodwill difficult due to the possibility that the independent variable may be a working proxy for firm size, causing the coefficient to be negative.

4. Market value of net assets acquired is employed in lieu of the total value of the consideration given as the latter includes our measure of the merger premium. This would cause an automatic correlation between the independent and dependent variables due to its inclusion.

5. Commercial data bases generally do not routinely provide a conventional measure of goodwill. One proxy measure would be to estimate the fair market value of the company's net assets. Target firms, however, were not required to provide FAS No. 33 type disclosures during our observation window. Attempts to adjust company specific net assets under these circumstances are extremely subjective. Another alternative would be to obtain goodwill numbers directly from the acquiror's next balance sheet. Multiple acquisitions rendered this alternative unfeasible. Then too, while U.K. companies are encouraged to write off goodwill to retained earnings, the courts have routinely permitted acquiring companies to write off goodwill to other accounts including one or more of the following: revaluation reserves, share premium reserves, merger reserve, discount on acquisition, capital reserve and other/total assets. Tracking goodwill attributable to a given acquisition under these circumstances is practically impossible.

6. Our investigation showed that the inclusion of these outliers does not change the results. However, these deals are deleted from our sample due to their extreme values.

7. 148 U.S. acquisitions were dropped from the sample because of this restriction. In actuality, not all of the 148 deals would necessarily employ the pooling of interests accounting method. However, since the sample size of U.S. acquisitions is large, we decided, in the interest of conservatism, to exclude those acquisitions for which the use of pooling of interests accounting was a possibility.

8. Alternate windows were not available in the data set.

9. While alternative specifications might be possible, in the absence of any constructive theory relating merger premia and goodwill, we believe the linear relationship expressed in equation (1) is reasonable. Plots of merger premia against goodwill suggest that our assumption of linearity is reasonable.

10. Market value of shares purchased is used in lieu of the total value of the consideration given since the latter includes the merger premia.

11. We are in the process of implementing these controls.

REFERENCES

Abel, R. (1969). "A Comparative Simulation of German and U.S. Accounting Principles." *Journal of Accounting Research.* 7, Spring, pp. 1–11.

Agmon, T., and D. R. Lessard. (1977). "Investor Recognition of Corporate International Diversification." *Journal of Finance.* September, pp. 1049–55.

Amit, R., J. Livnat, and P. Zarowin. (1989). "A Classification of Mergers and Acquisitions by Motives: Analysis of Market Responses." *Contemporary Accounting Research.* Vol 6, no. 1, Fall, pp. 143–58.

"An Edge to Foreign Buyers?" *Mergers and Acquisitions.* 22, March/April, pp. 7–8.

Black, F. (1981). "International Capital Market Equilibrium with Investment Barriers." *Journal of Financial and Quantitative Analysis.* March, pp. 113–26.

Choi, F. D. S., and C. Lee. (1991). "Merger Premia and National Differences in Accounting for Goodwill." *Journal of International Financial Management and Accounting.* Autumn, pp. 219–40.

Davidson, S., and J. M. Kohlmeier. (1966). "A Measure of the Impact of Some Foreign Accounting Principles." *Journal of Accounting Research.* 4, Autumn, pp. 183–212.

Dodd, P. (1980). "Merger Proposals, Management Discretion and Stockholder Wealth." *Journal of Financial Economics.* 8. pp. 105–37.

Doukas, J., and N. G. Travalos. (1988). "The Effect of Corporate Multinationalism on Shareholders' Wealth: Evidence from International Acquisitions." *Journal of Finance.* December, pp. 1161–75.

Fitzgerald, R. D., A. D. Sticker, and T. R. Watts. (1979). *International Survey of Accounting Principles and Reporting Practices.* Ontario, Canada: Price Waterhouse International.

Greenhouse, S. (1989). "Europe's Buyout Bulge." *The New York Times.* November 5, pp. D1, D6.

Grubel, H. G. (1968). "Internationally Diversified Portfolios: Welfare Gains and Capital Flows." *American Economic Review.* December, pp. 1299–1314.

Hammer, R. (1990.) "Do Accounting Rules Influence International Business Combination Decisions?" Unpublished manuscript presented at the Price Waterhouse Symposium on Accounting and Auditing, August 7.

Huang, Y. S., and R. A. Walkling. (1987). "Target Abnormal Returns Associated with Acquisition Announcements: Payment, Acquisition Form, and Managerial Resistance." *Journal of Financial Economics.* 19, pp. 329–49.

Jensen, M. C. (1988). "Takeovers: Their Causes and Consequences." *Journal of Economic Perspectives.* Vol. 2, no.1, Winter, pp. 21–48.

Jensen, M. C., and R. Ruback. (1983). "The Market for Corporate Control: The Scientific Evidence." *Journal of Financial Economics.* 11, pp. 5–50.

J. P. Morgan. (1989). *World Financial Markets.* (various issues).

Kogut, B. (1983). "Foreign Direct Investment as a Sequential Process." In C. Kindleberger and D. Andretch (eds.), *The Multinational Corporation in the 1980's.* Cambridge, MA: The MIT Press.

Lev, B., and J. A. Ohlson. (1982). "Market-Based Empirical Research in Accounting: A Review, Interpretation, and Extension." *Journal of Accounting Research.* Supplement, pp. 249–322.

Montagnon, P., and P. Riddell. (1990). "A Delicate Case of Jurisdictions." *Financial Times.* September 20.

Nobes, C., and R. Parker. (1981). *Comparative International Accounting.* Homewood, IL: Richard D. Irwin, Inc.

Riley, V. J., Jr. (1988). "The U.S. on Sale." *Chief Executive.* 48, November/December, pp. 46–51.

Robinson, J. R., and P. B. Shane. (1990). "Acquisition Accounting Method and Bid Premia for Target Firms." *The Accounting Review.* Vol. 65, no. 1, January, pp. 25–48.

Schienman, G. (1988). "The Effect of Accounting Differences on Cross Border Comparisons: A Global Telecommunications Equipment Study." *International Accounting and Investment Review.* April, pp. 1–14.

Stulz, R. (1981). "On the Effects of Barriers to International Investment." *Journal of Finance.* September, pp. 923–34.

Tandon, K., C. Hessel, and N. Cakici. (1991). "International Mergers and Acquisitions: Foreign Ownership in the U.S. and Effects on Shareholder Wealth." *Journal of International Financial Management and Accounting.* Spring, pp. 39–60.

Walkling, R. A., and M. S. Long. (1984). "Agency Theory, Managerial Welfare, and Takeover Bid Resistance." *Rand Journal of Economics.* 15, pp. 54–68.

Wansley, J. W., W. R. Lane, and H. C. Yang. (1983). "Abnormal Returns to Acquired Firms by Type of Acquisition and Method of Payment." *Financial Management.* Autumn, pp. 16–22.

Watts, R. L., and J. L. Zimmerman. (1986). *Positive Accounting Theory.* Englewood Cliffs, NJ: Prentice Hall, Inc.

Weetman, Pauline, and Sidney J. Weetman. (1990). "International Financial Analysis and Comparative Corporate Performance: the Impact of U.K. versus U.S. Accounting Principles on Earnings." *Journal of International Financial Management and Accounting.* Summer& Autumn, pp. 111–30.

White, H. (1980). "A Heteroskedasticity-Consistent Covariance Matrix Estimator and a Direct Test for Heteroskedasticity." *Econometrics.* pp. 817–38.

COMMENT

Terrence O'Rourke

The purpose of this commentary is to discuss Chapter 4, "International Differences in GAAP and the Pricing of Earnings," and Chapter 5, "Effects of Alternative Goodwill Treatments on Merger Premia: Further Empirical Evidence." As both chapters are based primarily on differences between U.S. and U.K. GAAP, it is useful to note a few of the more important differences, particularly the way in which these differences are likely to affect the level and volatility of U.S. GAAP earnings compared to U.K. GAAP earnings.

EXTRAORDINARY ITEMS

Under U.K. GAAP, earnings per share (EPS) are calculated before extraordinary items and a separate EPS after extraordinary items is not reported. In recent years, extraordinary items, particularly extraordinary losses related to restructuring costs and discontinued operations, reported under U.K. GAAP have been quite significant. This has had the effect of reporting higher EPS under U.K. GAAP than under U.S. GAAP. In

Terrence O'Rourke is a manager with Price Waterhouse (Dublin, Ireland). He also serves on the Accounting Review Committee of the Institute of Chartered Accountants in Ireland. His comments are personal and do not necessarily represent the views of Price Waterhouse or the Institute of Chartered Accountants in Ireland.

addition, showing extraordinary losses "below the line" tends to reduce the volatility of EPS under U.K. GAAP.

It is notable that a recent pronouncement by the Urgent Issues Task Force (UITF)—a committee of the U.K. Accounting Standards Baord (ASB)—specified that restructuring costs should not be regarded as extraordinary, thus reducing the incidence of such extraordinary losses. In addition, it is expected that the next Financial Reporting Standard (FRS) to be issued by ASB will prohibit virtually all extraordinary items. This would have the effect of reducing the differences, in the future, of EPS under U.S. GAAP and U.K. GAAP.

GOODWILL

Under U.K. GAAP, goodwil is normally eliminated against equity in the year of acquisition, while under U.S. GAAP, goodwill is capitalized and subject to annual amortization over a period of up to 40 years. As a result, earnings under U.S. GAAP tend to be lower than earning under U.K. GAAP. It is notable that amortization of goodwill is likely to reduce the volatility of U.S. GAAP earnings compared to U.K. GAAP earnings, due to its fairly stable annual level. While ASB has not yet issued an FRS on accounting for goodwil arising on acquisition, it is expected that ASB will consider thoroughly the relative merits of the various possible ways to accounting for goodwill. In particular, ASB is expected to consider the methods of accounting for goodwill alternate to what this commentator regards as "amortization by rote." This is likely to involve an assessment of how firms identify and measure declines in the value of acquired goodwill in order to establish an appropriate method of matching the cost of acquired goodwill with the benefits derived therefrom.

DEFERRED TAX

Under U.K. GAAP, provision is made for deferred tax to the extent that a liability is expected to arise on timing differences. This is regarded as the "partial provision" approach while the U.S. GAAP approach may be regarded as "full provision." Because of the emphasis under U.K. GAAP on the probability factor in relation to the likelihood of a liability crystalizing, complex judgement and scheduling about the pattern of future capital expenditures and other matters is often required. Under FAS 96/109, similar complex scheduling about future reversals of timing differences (including a significant element of judgement), appear likely to be required under U.S. GAAP.

Where substantial timing differences have arisen, I believe it is likely that deferred tax charges have tended to be higher under APB 11 than under U.K. GAAP; however, it may be that U.S. GAAP earnings have been less volatile under APB 11, due to the emphasis on tax equalization rather than probability. It remains to be seen how FAS 96/109 will affect the relative results.

PENSION COSTS

Major differences between pension costs under U.S. GAAP can arise due to:
- the prescriptive nature of FAS 87, including annual actuarial measurement under the projected unit credit method, smoothed by the "corridor" approach.
- the flexibility of U.K. GAAP with regard to the actuarial method adopted, the frequency of actuarial valuation, and the method of amortizing surpluses and deficits.

The flexibility of U.K. GAAP may be expected to reduce the volatility and possibly the level of pension costs. However, this effect is likely to vary substantially in different circumstances.

FAS 106 on Obligation for Postretirement Employment Benefits (OPEB) does not have an equivalent under U.K. GAAP. Postretirement health care costs may not be as significant a factor in the United Kingdom as in the United States. In addition, the UITF is considering introducing disclosure of OPEB costs and may well introduce an accounting requirement similar to U.S. GAAP in due course.

THE PRICING OF EARNINGS PAPER (CHAPTER 4)

This study investigated the information content of earnings reported under U.K. and U.S. GAAP for a sample of U.K.-domiciled stocks. It has three principal conclusions:
- The overall explanatory power of reported earnings is quite low.

- U.K. GAAP earnings changes have greater information content than U.S. GAAP earnings changes.
- U.S. GAAP earnings levels have some independent value-relevance relative to U.K. GAAP earnings.

It is generally recognized that market prices are influenced by many factors, including

- historical earnings,
- projected earnings, including economic trends, industry trends, and profit warnings,
- historical cashflows,
- projected cashflows,
- balance sheet values,
- cost of capital, and
- a multitude of strategic considerations.

However, the most frequently addressed is the price-earnings ratio so the subject of Chapter 4 is important and relevant, particularly in relation to its focus on the U.S. GAAP and U.K. GAAP measurements of earnings.

It is not surprising that the study concludes that U.K.-domicilied stocks are more influenced by U.K. GAAP earnings changes than by U.S. GAAP earnings changes. It is interesting that the U.S. GAAP adjustments provide incremental information.

As a practitioner, I do not intend to attempt to understand or comment on the statistical methodology of Pope and Reese's study. However, I consider that the conclusions of the chapter would have been more persuasive if the body of the chapter had included a number of tables or graphs which could be eye-balled by the nonstatistician in order to provide a link between the regression tables and the conclusions.

The tables might have dealt with such matters as

- an annual comparison of earnings under U.S. GAAP and U.K. GAAP.
- an assessment of the volatility of earnings under U.S. GAAP and U.K. GAAP.
- annual P/E ratios by reference to U.S. GAAP and U.K. GAAP.

The period covered by the sample 1987–1990 is relatively recent. Perhaps inevitably, the sample on which the study is based is quite small—85 firm years in total. It appears likely that relevant financial information for 1991 is now available, and it may well be that the number of firms producing U.S. GAAP reconciliations has increased.

THE CORPORATE CONTROL PAPER (CHAPTER 5)

This study investigated whether U.K. acquirers tend to offer higher merger premia, in respect of U.S. target companies, than U.S. acquirers and tested whether such higher merger premia are associated with U.K. acquirers' not having to amortize goodwill to earnings. The study concluded that U.K. acquirers consistently pay higher merger premia and that these appear to be associated with differences in accounting treatments for goodwill.

As the "conventional wisdom" has been that U.K. acquirers have a competitive advantage over U.S. acquirers in acquisitions, due to their option of not having to amortize goodwill to earnings, the subject of this study is very important in order to establish the validity of the conventional wisdom. This is particularly important as the conventional wisdom may be regarded as indicative of irrational behavior. Ojectively, paying higher merger premia solely because of a different accounting regime appears irrational.

As a practitioner, I would have found the chapter more persuasive if it included additional nonstatistical tables dealing with such matters as

- annual average premia offered by U.S. and U.K. acquirers.
- comparative U.S. and U.K. premia by industry.
- more accessible display of the relationship between higher merger premia and the level of goodwill.

The sample is quite sizable—1,056 U.S. acquisitions and 104 U.K. acquisitions—recognizing that the period covered, 1985–1989, is slightly out of date. (It may be that the study would not have suffered had a representative sample of the U.S. acquirer population been chosen in order to reduce the statistical effort involved.)

The chapter identifies that considerations such as cost of capital differences and other strategic factors may have accounted for the merger premium differences. The endnotes make reference to the implementation of these controls being in process.

BOTH PAPERS

There are number of areas where the models could be used to strengthen and expand the conclusions. In particular, Chapter 4 concentrated on U.K.-domiciled stocks, while Chapter 5 concentrated on acquisitions in the United States. Accordingly, the results of the pricing of earnings paper may be influenced by U.K. investors' having more regard to U.K. GAAP (with which they are more familiar) than U.S. GAAP, while the higher merger premia offered by U.K. acquirers in the United States may be influenced by the need or ability of foreign investors to out-bid domestic investors for nonaccounting reasons.

These possible biases may be tested as follows:

The pricing of earnings study could divide the sample between those firms where there is a higher incidence of U.S. investors and those where there is a higher incidence of U.K. investors. If the possible bias toward more familiar GAAP is present, the results of this division of the sample should show that securities with a higher U.S.-investor content do not have as significant an incremental reaction to U.K. GAAP earnings changes as those with a higher U.K.-investor content.

Similarly, if the corporate control study were repeated in respect of U.K. acquisitions, it would be instructive to assess whether the higher premia offered by U.K. investors are diminished or eliminated.

A further method of testing the conclusions of the corporate control study would be to reperform the pricing of earnings model with the exclusion of the U.S. GAAP adjustment relating to goodwill amortization. If the apparent findings of the corporate control paper are valid, this alternative modeling of the pricing of earnings paper may show a lesser degree of additional value-relevance associated with U.K. GAAP earnings changes and a higher degree of incremental information associated with U.S. GAAP earnings levels.

MAJOR MESSAGES FROM THE TWO PAPERS

There are a number of important messages from the two chapters for investors, acquirers, target companies, and standard setters.

Investors use historical earnings as their major source of information at their peril. The pricing of earnings paper suggests a low level of explanatory power for historical earnings and, accordingly, potential investors should be aware that their investment decisions may be flawed if they do not refer to the various other factors considered by the market in stock pricing.

U.S. acquirers should be aware of the higher premia offered by U.K. acquirers and the apparent association of these higher premia with the U.K. GAAP treatment of goodwill. Perhaps U.S. acquirers should be less concerned with the inevitable negative effect on earnings caused by goodwill amortization and more concerned with the maintainable value of the goodwill acquired. Of course, as the corporate control paper notes, U.K. acquirers may be capitalizing on an accounting advantage to increase their acquisition bids at the expense of their own shareholders.

U.S. target companies, whose stocks may be the subject of a bid by a U.S. acquirer, may be well served by seeking a potential U.K. bidder and perhaps restating their earnings under U.K. GAAP to enable a higher bid from potential U.K. acquirers.

For accounting standards setters around the world, it appears important that they discuss and share the rationale for accounting differences. International accounting differences may well be a barrier to global market efficiency, and efforts to achieve consistency and harmonization should be continued.

COMMENT

Kishore Tandon

We have just seen two important papers, both dealing with international GAAP diversity and their effect on firms. The first paper by Pope and Rees evaluates the informational content of two alternative accounting earnings for the same firm but constructed under different U.S. and U.K. GAAP guidelines. The second paper by Lee and Choi examines the effects of international GAAP diversity (specifically goodwill) on differences in merger premia offered by foreign acquirers to U.S. target firms. The first paper concludes that British firm's earnings tend to be more sensitive to returns under British GAAP than under U.S. GAAP, concluding that GAAP differences may not matter much as far as incremental information content from earnings is concerned. On the other hand, Lee and Choi find that accounting diversity in the treatment of goodwill does affect the merger premia offered by foreign acquirers to U.S. targets. Let me now discuss the two papers separately.

DISCUSSION OF CHAPTER 4

Pope and Rees analyze a sample of British firms that are dually listed in U.K. and in U.S. in the form of ADRs. They examine if the incremental disclosure from the filing of form 20-F with the SEC has any incremental informational content as far as earnings are concerned. If there is no incremental content, they question whether the SEC should really emphasize this additional disclosure in restricting foreign listings on the NYSE (especially German firms). This, as we know, has been a source of contention recently between the NYSE and the SEC. On the presumption that form 20-F is filed simultaneously as the earnings are announced in the United Kingdom, it is hard to distinguish if the stock price reaction is due to British earnings announcement under British GAAP or due to their 20-F earnings, though they are lower when restated under U.S. GAAP. And if there is a lag in time in the filing of 20-F from the moment that earnings are announced in the United Kingdom, one should not expect any incremental information in the U.S. filing of form 20-F.

This study is an interesting one, though the results tend to be as expected a priori: that U.K. earnings announcements tend to affect dually-listed British stock returns in a more sensitive manner than under U.S. GAAP. With a majority of the shares of the dually-listed firms trading in the home country (U.K.), investors there tend to evaluate earnings based on their own GAAP. Four hypotheses are stated here, and two of these are tested under three different return generating models in Table 4–3. Though the results do appear somewhat sensitive to the model used, it is not obvious if we need the three competing models, given that all the firms in the sample are large firms anyway. After all, the paper is researching only large British firms, cross-listed in the United States. The results in Table 4–3 are in line with expectations since, as stated above, prices and information in the United Kingdom should drive British stock prices more than they would in the United States. One problem remains here: it is not clear what the sample size of 85 firm-years really means.

Table 4–4 presents the results of hypotheses H_3 and H_4, testing for the significance of the adjustment factor. The authors find the adjustment factor to be insignificant. All three regressions in each panel of Table 4–4 are equivalent regressions and do not provide any additional information. The authors tend to emphasize the (small) increase in the coefficient of determination, but do not really explain why DUK dominates DUS (i.e., changes in earnings dominate in the United Kingdom), but YUS (levels of earnings) dominate YUK.

Finally, while the Pope and Rees paper does present an interesting hypothesis, an obvious extension of this research would be to see an analysis of the components of earnings. It is only then that one will be able to learn what components of accounting diversity between the United States and the United Kingdom affect stock returns of cross-listed firms. This will also provide a guideline to the SEC as to whether all the additional disclosure sought by it is really relevant for U.S. investors. Overall though, this paper is among the first studies examining international accounting diversity and provides an important contribution relating to earnings announcements.

DISCUSSION OF CHAPTER 5

The second paper by Lee and Choi is amongst the first studies in international accounting diversity, specifically the treatment of goodwill in cross-border acquisitions across the United States, the United Kingdom, Germany, and Japan. It has often been argued by U.S. managers that foreign firms have an unfair advantage in cross-border mergers and acquisitions based on their accounting and tax treatment of goodwill. By not having to amortize goodwill (as in the United Kingdom and Germany) and by making goodwill tax deductible (as in Germany and Japan), foreign bidding firms should be able to offer higher merger premia for their U.S. target firm. On the other hand, foreign firms and critics argue that such goodwill treatment does not affect actual cash flows, and hence it should not make any difference; and even if it does, in a competitive market, there is no reason to expect why foreign firms would offer higher merger premia than they have to.

In this paper, Lee and Choi deal with this issue in a very comprehensive manner, though their measure of goodwill as the difference between market value and net book value of equity may be subject to some criticism. Still, their results may make accounting regulators in the United States uneasy. They find that national differences in the treatment of goodwill affect market decisions and that British, German, and Japanese firms offer higher merger premia to U.S. targets that appear to be positively associated with goodwill. This appears to be related to the fact that foreign GAAP allows British and German firms to write off goodwill immediately and not have to amortize it against future earnings.

Though the results for British acquisitions of U.S. targets have been documented by the authors in an earlier paper, in this paper they document additional evidence for German and Japanese acquisitions in the United States. German GAAP provides favorable accounting and tax treatments, while Japanese acquirers enjoy favorable tax treatment only. The authors find that the merger premia offered by German and Japanese bidders is related to goodwill (Tables 5–8 and 5–9), though it does not appear that the difference is really significant in the case of German firms and appears only marginally significant in Japanese firms. The premia paid by British firms (Table 5–2) is substantially more than that paid by German and Japanese firms (Table 5–6).

A strange result in this study pertains to German acquisitions. Though they realize favorable accounting as well as tax treatment of goodwill, relative to British firms which only realize favorable accounting treatment and Japanese firms which realize only favorable tax treatment, the merger premia offered by German firms is the smallest. Recent research in cross-border acquisitions [e.g., Cakici, Hessel, and Tandon (1991)] has shown that U.S. targets gain substantially more when acquired by British and Japanese firms, but the gains are very small or minimal when acquired by German bidders. In a subsequent paper on foreign bidders, Cakici, Hessel, and Tandon (1992) find that both British and Japanese bidders gain from their acquisitions of U.S. targets, but German bidders lose. Therefore, if German GAAP treatment of goodwill provides both favorable accounting and tax benefit by making it tax-deductible, it needs to be explored why German shareholders offer the least merger premia to U.S. targets and why do German shareholders lose in their U.S. acquisitions.

Overall though, Lee and Choi make a very important contribution by documenting evidence in support of the hypothesis that accounting diversity across countries affects market decisions by firms. A logical extension would be to examine if goodwill is also related to foreign bidding firms' gains.

In conclusion, both Pope–Rees and Choi–Lee document interesting evidence that international GAAP diversity does affect the capital market decisions of firms.

REFERENCES

Cakici, N., C. Hessel, and K. Tandon. (1991). "Foreign Acquisitions in the United States and the Effect on Shareholder Wealth." *Journal of International Financial Management and Accounting.* Vol. 3, no. 2, Spring, pp. 39–60.

Cakici, N., C. Hessel, and K. Tandon. (1992). "Foreign Acquisitions in the United States: Effects on Shareholder Wealth of Foreign Acquiring Firms." Baruch College working paper.

PART THREE

ACCOUNTING DIFFERENCES AND SECURITIES MARKETS REGULATION

CHAPTER 6

COPING WITH INTERNATIONAL ACCOUNTING DIVERSITY: FUND MANAGERS' VIEWS ON DISCLOSURE, RECONCILIATION, AND HARMONIZATION

Ravi Bhushan
Donald R. Lessard

INTRODUCTION

Accounting standards are at the heart of a crucial debate among the Securities and Exchange Commission (SEC), non-U.S. regulatory bodies, major non-U.S. corporations, investment managers, and other parties representing U.S. investor interests. The SEC has taken what some consider the "high road" and others the "head in the sand approach," insisting that in order to list and issue shares in the United States, firms must completely adhere to U.S. standards, either by publishing financial statements prepared according to U.S. GAAP or by issuing a "quantitative reconciliation" of their statements to U.S. GAAP. Those who favor this approach insist that it is the best way to not only ensure the quality of disclosure in U.S. markets, but also to

The financial support of the International Financial Services Research Center at M.I.T. is gratefully acknowledged. The authors thank Gary Bergstrom, Sara Hanks, Richard Levich, Bevis Longstreth, and an anonymous reviewer for their comments and Peter Pavlina for expert research assistance.

influence world standards. Those who disagree see this approach as limiting U.S. influence over global standards. The direct limitation is that by keeping many firms from listing in the U.S., it leaves them outside of any U.S. influence. The indirect limitation arises since this approach amounts to a "take it or leave it" position in international negotiation, a far cry from the movement toward mutual recognition, subject to certain common elements, that has provided so much of the momentum toward harmonization and regulatory reform within Europe. Critics argue that while this stance may have been appropriate when U.S. firms represented more than half of global market capitalization, it is not when its share is one-third or less. Further, they argue, the U.S. accounting-investment management model is no longer the world ideal, with other approaches appearing to yield similar degrees of market efficiency coupled with longer-term perspectives.

This debate over the national disclosure standards in an increasingly interdependent global system has many legal, logical, and pragmatic elements. This paper attempts to contribute to the discussion by examining the practices of a representative sample of U.S.-based international investment managers in order to determine whether and how they are affected by accounting diversity and, therefore, by the presence or absence of quantitative reconciliation, and what their views are towards greater disclosure, reconciliation, or harmonization. While the perspective of investment managers is only one of the many factors that must be taken into account, it is important in establishing the logical basis for a particular set of disclosure requirements.[1]

Determining the optimal level of disclosure would be easy if disclosure was a free good. More is better! However, it is not costless, and it is now generally recognized that a cost-benefit analysis is required, weighing the benefits additional disclosure to investors against the costs, both direct and indirect, to issuers.

In the international context, the problem is even more difficult. In addition to the costs to issuers of meeting any particular set of requirements, one must consider their impact on the total amount and quality of information available to U.S. investors as well as on the world market share and "brand image" of U.S. markets and institutions. The strength and competitiveness of these institutions not only matters from the viewpoint of U.S. income and welfare, it also contributes directly to investors by providing them with a more competent, lower cost infrastructure within which to operate.

Further, given the underlying diversity of institutional contexts, industrial structures, and organizational styles, the benefits of greater or more uniform disclosure and/or presentation are also likely to be more difficult to assess. Finally, these benefits are likely to differ substantially by class of investor. The benefits of additional or more uniform disclosure and/or greater uniformity in presentation are likely to be at best modest, for example, for "worldly-wise" institutional investors who have mastered local principles of accounting and valuation. They may be quite substantial to investors with some world knowledge, but a largely home-biased perspective, but will have very little value, and perhaps even a negative impact, on less sophisticated investors who might misleadingly infer from uniform accounting that there are no significant underlying differences among companies across countries that must be taken into account in valuation.

While we know relatively little about the benefits to investors of more rigorous standards of disclosure or presentation (reconciliation, or harmonization), we know even less regarding the costs of the standards in terms of their impact on the overall quality of information available to U.S. investors. While in earlier periods, this could be taken as synonymous with information available in U.S. securities markets, it clearly no longer is the case, since U.S. investors increasingly participate directly and indirectly in non-U.S. markets, especially when shares from those countries are not listed or traded in the United States.

While rigorous standards in the United States can be expected to result in high quality information for U.S.-listed securities, there is clear evidence that they also deter listings in the United States for non-U.S. firms and perhaps even encourage some domestic firms to delist and, perhaps, go private. Further, if the standards take the form of reconciliation to U.S. accounting principles, they are likely to have less impact on non-U.S. standards than, say efforts to gain mutual recognition via agreement on some minimum level of disclosure or even harmonization. This is especially likely in the current world environment, where the United States is no longer the dominant economic power and where American approaches are no longer necessarily viewed as the ideal. Thus it is probable that there is a substantial trade-off between the rigor, and particularly the U.S. specific nature, of U.S. standards and the worldwide influence of these standards.

The *rationale* behind the quantitative reconciliation requirement of Form 20-F is that in order to make informed investment decisions regarding non-U.S. firms, U.S. investors require financial information in the same form in which it is presented by U.S. firms. The overall conclusion of our review of investor practice is that quantitative reconciliation, while viewed as desirable by most investment managers in an absolute sense, is not necessary to enable them to make informed decisions. Further, to the extent that it comes at a cost in terms of either greater disclosure or harmonization, many managers would choose the alternative. Finally, even with reconciliation, managers would still place greatest reliance on local financial statements than other sources of information because accounting differences are just one among many factors of equal or greater importance that differ across borders and that must be considered in evaluating issues in different countries, and since financial reports can only be understood in the context of such other factors, quantitative reconciliation often conveys an illusion of comparability that in fact does not exist.

Our findings are consistent with the view that reconciliation, harmonization, and more uniform and comparable disclosure are all good if costless, but if there is a trade-off amongst them, then the answer is not so clear. Emphasizing one at the expense of others is unlikely to be optimal.

The chapter is organized in four parts. The second part, which follows this introduction, examines investor practice with respect to investment in shares of non-U.S. issuers to determine whether and how it is affected by accounting diversity. The third part outlines the responses of these investors to changes in disclosure, reconciliation, and harmonization in an international context. The fourth part concludes.

CURRENT PRACTICE OF INTERNATIONAL EQUITY MANAGERS

In this section, we examine the range of investment management styles pursued by investors in foreign equities and their actual practices involving the use of information about foreign equities. In the third part below, we examine their views about the desirability of additional disclosure, reconciliation, and harmonization in an international context.[2]

Since most of the costs of disclosure and presentation are not borne by investors or investment managers, it is not possible to determine optimal levels of disclosure or appropriate presentation formats by simply asking them. On the other hand, by examining the processes that they follow and the information they actually use, and asking them how this process might change with greater disclosure and or more uniform accounting, one can form a clearer view of the benefits of such changes. In order to do this, we examined the investment practices and information usage of a sample of major U.S.-based money managers, with a "control" sample coming from U.K.-based managers. A control sample of the U.K.-based managers is chosen since in addition to the United States, the United Kingdom is the other major country with a well-developed international money management industry. Further, the London Stock Exchange, which has the largest number of foreign listings, requires listed firms to meet international accounting standards.[3] Finally, there is evidence that actual disclosure levels may be influenced by prevailing market conditions. For example, Meek and Gray (1989) find that actual disclosure levels by the firms listed on the London Stock Exchange exceed Exchange requirements through a wide range of voluntary disclosures.

Our goal was to understand the relation between particular investment styles, that is, fundamental stock valuation versus top-down country-based investing, the particular skills associated with each style, the main sources of information required for each style, views regarding the difficulties posed by accounting diversity, mechanisms used to cope with this diversity, and ultimately, views regarding the importance of various proposed changes in accounting across countries.

The Sample

The sample of U.S. managers included in our study is drawn from lists of the top U.S.-based international managers published by Intersec and *Pensions and Investments.*[4] Of the 94 questionnaires sent, 49 firms responded for an overall response rate of 52 percent. Of the 49 responses, 44 were usable.[5] There was no apparent bias in the style of nonrespondent firms. For comparison, we also sent questionnaires to the top 29 U.K.-based managers, and received completed questionnaires from 14 (response rate: 48 percent). All these responses were usable.

The three quartiles for the values of the equities under international management (i.e., invested in non-U.S. securities) by the U.S.-based managers were $130 million, $830 million, and $3 billion. The corresponding figures for the U.K.-based managers were $1.2 billion, $3.1 billion, and $12.6 billion. Thus, the U.K. managers in our sample manage considerably larger amounts of international equity compared to the U.S.-based managers. The larger value of international equity under the control of U.K.-based managers is consistent with the finding that compared to U.S. investors, U.K. investors are much more internationally oriented. For example, U.S. investors have 98 percent of their portfolio in domestic equity, versus 78.5 percent for U.K. investors.[6]

Investment Styles

Investment managers tend to specialize in applying particular styles or approaches.[7] These styles rest on particular skills that the manager claims to have. Each of these styles, in turn, implies particular views of market efficiency and relies on access to particular types of information. Some managers, for example, claim skill at current asset valuation, the so-called value-based approach, while others focus on assessing future prospects, typically referred to as the growth-oriented approach. Others analyze long-term relations between equity prices and particular macroeconomic and/or equity market factors, seeking to identify instances in the short run when a particular security deviates from its "normal" relation to these factors. Still other managers seek to forecast changes in such factors. Some managers emphasize intuition and judgement, while others follow quantitative approaches. Managers further tend to specialize in particular geographic or industry domains, creating a matrix of styles reflecting both the target securities of the manager and the skills/procedures applied.

Our survey thus included questions on whether they pursued a top-down or a bottom-up approach, the extent to which they employed quantitative approaches to risk control, and how much they relied on indexing to allocate investments across countries.[8] We also asked the managers on which skills (e.g., financial and strategic analysis of a company as opposed to a country or a currency analysis) they viewed as critical.

Table 6–1 summarizes our findings on the investment styles and skills employed by the U.S.-based managers, and Table 6–2 presents the corresponding data for the U.K.-based managers. Among the U.S. managers, roughly half view themselves as pursuing fundamental and bottom-up analysis. About one-third follow top-down investment strategies, about a quarter rely on quantitative techniques, and only about ten percent consider themselves as indexers.[9] The results on the skills employed appear consistent with the styles, so that about half of the U.S.-based managers consider skills regarding the financial analysis of a company as critical. Table 6–2 shows that in contrast to the U.S. managers, the U.K.-

TABLE 6–1
Investment Styles and Skills Used—U.S.-Based Managers[a]

Panel A: Investment Styles	Very Much So				Definitely Not
	1	2	3	4	5
Fundamental Value Analysis	52	24	10	12	2
Bottom-Up Manager (Stocks)	52	17	14	0	17
Growth Stock Analysis	36	14	28	10	12
Quantitative Risk Controller	21	14	28	21	16
Quantitative Value Screener	26	23	21	14	16
Top-Down Manager (Countries)	35	12	21	21	11
Indexer	9	5	5	5	76

Panel B: Skills Employed	Critical				Irrelevant
	1	2	3	4	5
Company Analysis—Financial	54	29	5	7	5
Company Analysis—Strategic	35	40	10	8	7
Industry Analysis	20	41	22	10	7
Country Analysis—General, Macro, Political	44	26	19	9	2
Currency Analysis	16	21	37	21	4

[a] The numbers are based on a sample of 44 managers and are reported in percentages.

based managers appear to do more top down investing and less fundamental and quantitative analysis. For example, 57 percent of the U.K.-based managers consider themselves as very much top-down managers versus 35 percent for the U.S.-based managers. As bottom-up managers, only 39 percent of the U.K.-based managers regard themselves very much so versus 52 percent for the U.S.-based managers. There is clearly more emphasis on top-down country allocation in United Kingdom, while U.S.-managers appear to be more bottom-up stock pickers.

A key finding of our survey is that U.S.-based international investment management is an extremely competitive industry characterized by a wide variety of styles and skills employed similar to those observed in the domestic market. Further, these styles do not differ substantially from those practiced by international equity managers based abroad, although a higher proportion of U.S. managers emphasize quantitative techniques for asset allocation, stock selection, and risk control. Corresponding to

TABLE 6–2
Investment Styles and Skills Used—U.K.-Based Managers[a]

Panel A: Investment Styles	Very Much So				Definitely Not
	1	2	3	4	5
Fundamental Value Analysis	36	36	21	7	0
Bottom-Up Manager (Stocks)	39	23	15	8	15
Growth Stock Analysis	15	39	15	31	0
Quantitative Risk Controller	14	0	21	57	7
Quantitative Value Screener	23	23	23	15	15
Top-Down Manager (Countries)	57	21	21	0	0
Indexer	14	0	14	14	58

Panel B: Skills Employed	Critical				Irrelevant
	1	2	3	4	5
Company Analysis—Financial	15	46	39	0	0
Company Analysis—Strategic	46	39	15	0	0
Industry Analysis	7	54	39	0	0
Country Analysis—General, Macro, Political	57	36	7	0	0
Currency Analysis	43	21	36	0	0

[a] The numbers are based on a sample of 14 managers and are reported in percentages.

the wide variety of styles, there is also a great deal of variation in the type of information used and factors employed in asset valuation by these managers. While some take top-down approaches that limit the amount of company information required, others emphasize bottom-up approaches that require extensive company-level information. These bottom-up managers typically emphasize cash to earnings, market to book, or similar comparisons with other firms in the same country as with firms' own histories and all managers who engage in fundamental analysis at the company level tend to put primary emphasis on home country financial reports. Managers pursuing quantitative strategies typically rely on large-scale computer-readable databases for their company information. We discuss the factors employed by the managers in valuing securities and the information sources they rely on more fully in the next section in the context of their views on how to deal with international accounting diversity.

INVESTMENT MANAGERS' VIEWS REGARDING DISCLOSURE, RECONCILIATION, AND HARMONIZATION

From the perspective of investment managers, additional disclosure, reconciliation of foreign accounts to U.S. GAAP, and harmonization are all positive in that they provide additional information, or at least different perspectives on the same information, at no additional cost to the managers. From a regulatory or overall social perspective, of course, it is not nearly so easy since each form of additional disclosure or different presentation costs, not only to the firm that must comply, but also because of the impact of these requirements on listing decisions, etc., which affect the total level of disclosure.

As a result, when examining attitudes of investment managers regarding each of the potential steps toward improved reporting, an attempt must be made to assess the value of this information in order to trade it off against these direct and indirect costs. To get at this value, rather than ask if more disclosure was a "good thing," we sought to determine the extent to which it would change investment practice. Further, since reconciliation to U.S. GAAP implies in most cases greater disclosure, the alternatives are not pure. Therefore, we examined the incremental impact of reconciliation and harmonization relative to greater disclosure. The question we asked managers were:

What impact would the following changes in financial reporting have on your investment practice [5 point scale from big difference (1) to no difference (5)]?

a. More uniform and comparable disclosure across countries.

Assuming there was more uniform and comparable disclosure:

b. Reconciliation of non-U.S. financial statements to U.S. GAAP.

c. Harmonization of local GAAP principles to a single standard.

The distribution of the responses of the U.S.-based managers is presented in Table 6–3.[10] As this table shows, about 60 percent of the managers believe that each of the three strategies—more uniform disclosure, reconciliation, and harmonization would make a considerable difference (a response of 1 or 2) in their investment practices. Based on these descriptive results, we conclude that both reconciliation and harmonization are viewed as having an impact beyond that of more uniform disclosure, but that disclosure by itself is also important. Therefore, policy decisions regarding these should recognize that reconciliation is

TABLE 6–3
Impact of Uniform Disclosure, Reconciliation, and
Harmonization: Views of U.S.-Based Investment Managers[a]

	Big Difference			No Difference	
	1	2	3	4	5
Impact of:					
Disclosure	26	36	24	12	2
Reconciliation	13	51	21	10	5
Harmonization	28	30	32	8	2

[a] The numbers are based on a sample of 44 managers and are reported as percentages.

not an absolute goal, but one that must be traded off against the other two.

A more interesting picture emerges when we compare managers with differing views regarding the impact of accounting changes (greater disclosure, reconciliation, or harmonization) along the dimensions of investment approaches, information sources used, and their views about factors limiting international value comparisons. Table 6–4 presents a comparison of the two groups of managers with differing views on the usefulness of more uniform disclosure. Tables 6–5 and 6–6, respectively, present comparable analyses on reconciliation and harmonization.

Table 6–4 shows that managers who believe more uniformity in disclosure will affect their investment practices considerably rely more heavily on earnings and cash flow information in valuing securities. They also consider very important earnings/cashflows over the next one to three years. They rely much more on the local financial statements than the other group. Between local statements and reconciled statements, managers in the big impact group rely more on local statements. The managers in the big-impact group consider non-comparability of earnings as the biggest factor limiting international value comparisons. Finally, these managers cope with the diversity by mastering local principles and focusing on cashflows and non-financial information.

Looking at Table 6–5, one observes, as expected, that managers who believe reconciliation to U.S. GAAP would make a big impact consider earnings to be a very important factor in valuation. Furthermore, even though these managers consider local statements more useful than U.S. GAAP statements, they rely much more on the U.S. GAAP statements than

TABLE 6–4
Characteristics of Managers Who View that Greater Disclosure Has a Large vs. a Small Impact[a]

Variable	Direction of difference: big vs. small impact	Value: big impact group	Value: small impact group	T-stat for difference
Factors employed in valuation[b]				
Earnings	greater	1.42	2.00	1.71
Cash flows	greater	1.42	2.06	2.20
Assets	greater	2.52	2.86	1.05
Cash flows (1-3 years)	greater	1.54	2.14	2.39
Analysts' recommendations	greater	3.32	3.80	1.40
Importance of information sources[b]				
Local FSA	greater	1.60	2.63	2.46
U.S. FSA	greater	2.52	3.07	1.28
U.S. reports	greater	3.20	3.63	1.32
Country news	less	2.52	2.44	0.20
Company visits	greater	1.92	2.69	1.49
Factors limiting international value comparisons[b]				
Valuation is local	less	2.60	2.53	0.15
Earnings diversity	greater	1.58	2.19	2.44
Coping responses[b]				
Difficulty in coping	greater	2.46	3.08	1.91
Invest top down	less	3.62	3.62	0.00
Master local principles	greater	2.27	3.21	2.36
Rely on recommendations	greater	3.31	3.57	0.58

[a] There were 26 and 16 managers respectively in the big- and small-impact groups.
[b] The responses were on a scale of 1 (very important) to 5 (not important) so that a smaller value of a response corresponds to greater importance of the variable.

managers in the little-impact group. The managers in the two groups do not differ in terms of their views on valuation being locally driven or diversity in accounting for earnings inhibiting international value comparisons.

The results in Table 6–6 are quite similar to those in Table 6–4. Managers who believe more harmonization will make a big impact are similar to those in the disclosure-big-impact group on the dimensions of factors used in valuation, information sources used, and views toward factors limiting global value comparisons. Managers who believe more harmonization will

**TABLE 6–5
Characteristics of Managers who View that Reconciliation Has a
Large vs. a Small Impact[a]**

Variable	Direction of difference: big vs. small impact	Value: big impact group	Value: small impact group	T-stat for difference
Factors employed in valuation[b]				
Earnings	greater	1.24	2.14	3.07
Cash flows	greater	1.52	1.64	0.46
Assets	greater	2.38	2.92	1.83
Cash flows (1-3 years)	greater	1.56	2.08	1.97
Analysts' recommendations	greater	3.38	3.62	0.68
Importance of information sources[b]				
Local FSA	greater	1.67	2.14	1.14
U.S. FSA	greater	2.21	3.31	2.77
U.S. reports	greater	3.21	3.43	0.66
Country news	less	2.50	2.14	0.92
Company visits	greater	1.92	2.36	0.83
Factors limiting international value comparisons[b]				
Valuation is local	less	2.63	2.53	0.18
Earnings diversity	greater	1.84	1.79	0.19
Coping responses[b]				
Difficulty in coping	greater	2.58	2.64	0.19
Invest top down	less	3.63	3.50	0.26
Master local principles	greater	2.33	2.86	1.26
Rely on recommendations	greater	3.25	3.71	1.06

[a] There were 25 and 14 managers respectively in the big- and small-impact groups.
[b] The responses were on a scale of 1 (very important) to 5 (not important) so that a smaller value of a response corresponds to greater importance of the variable.

make a big impact tend to rely more heavily on local analysts' recommendations in coping with international accounting diversity.

The overall picture that emerges from these tables is that managers who believe that either of the three strategies will make a big impact, as opposed to those who do not, do rely more heavily on earnings and cash flow information and on local financial statements. Managers who consider reconciliation very important consider earnings to be a much more important factor than those who consider disclosure and harmonization as having a big impact.

TABLE 6-6
Characteristics of Managers who View that Harmonization Has a Large vs. a Small Impact[a]

Variable	Direction of difference: big vs. small impact	Value: big impact group	Value: small impact group	T-stat for difference
Factors employed in valuation[b]				
Earnings	greater	1.30	1.88	1.94
Cash flows	greater	1.35	1.88	2.25
Assets	greater	2.45	2.75	1.01
Cash flows (1-3 years)	greater	1.43	2.13	2.92
Analysts' recommendations	greater	3.09	3.88	2.47
Importance of information sources[b]				
Local FSA	greater	1.61	2.19	1.47
U.S. FSA	greater	2.57	2.67	0.24
U.S. reports	greater	3.09	3.56	1.53
Country news	less	2.57	2.06	1.38
Company visits	greater	1.78	2.50	1.44
Factors limiting international value comparisons[b]				
Valuation is local	less	2.91	2.25	1.47
Earnings diversity	greater	1.65	2.06	1.53
Coping responses[b]				
Difficulty in coping	greater	2.45	2.81	1.19
Invest top down	less	3.91	3.13	1.74
Master local principles	greater	2.39	2.75	0.89
Rely on recommendations	greater	2.87	4.06	2.99

[a] There were 23 and 17 managers respectively in the big- and small-impact groups.
[b] The responses were on a scale of 1 (very important) to 5 (not important) so that a smaller value of a response corresponds to greater importance of the variable.

As expected, investment managers' views on the impact of more comparable disclosure, reconciliation, and harmonization are positively correlated. Table 6-7, in which we cross-tabulate managers' views regarding the impact of these strategies, documents this positive correlation. In this table, an observation with respect to a variable is classified in the big-impact group if the response on that variable was a 1 or 2. This table shows that the cells representing the two extremes—either all three approaches making a big impact or a little impact—have the two highest concentrations of observations (36 percent and 18 percent, respectively). All other cells, with the

TABLE 6–7
Cross-Tabulation of the Views of U.S.-Based Investment
Managers on the Impact of Uniform Disclosure, Reconciliation,
and Harmonization*

Disclosure		Harmonization	
Big Impact	Reconciliation	Big Impact	Little Impact
	Big Impact	36	15
	Little Impact	10	5
Little Impact	Reconciliation		
	Big Impact	8	5
	Little Impact	3	18

* The numbers are based on a sample of 44 managers and are reported as percentages.

exception of the cell representing disclosure and reconciliation making a big impact and harmonization a little impact, have 10 percent or fewer observations.

Using only the responses of the managers with the most extreme views, that is, those who view more uniform disclosure, reconciliation, and harmonization as having a big impact versus those who view these accounting changes as having little impact, in Table 6–8 we report the differences among the two groups of respondents.

As one would expect, those who place great importance on accounting changes focus much more on company financial variables in their analysis and rely more heavily both on accounting statements and analysts recommendations in their choices. As a group they tend to rely less on country information. Regarding their views of the valuation process itself, they see the difficulty of comparing earnings as the greatest obstacle to cross-border value comparison.

The dimensions in which these two groups do not differ are also interesting.[11] Both adamantly do not avoid international investing due to accounting diversity; they both rely most heavily on comparisons with a firm's own history and with other local firms in the same industry; neither pays much attention to the global industry or global market; both emphasize cash flows to a considerable extent; and so on. With regard to accounting per say, neither group engages in restatement to a great extent, so the value of reconciliation or harmonization, for example, must be more from the information it reveals than from the fact that it provides this information in a common format.

TABLE 6–8
Characteristics of Managers who View that Greater Disclosure, Reconciliation, and Harmonization Have a Large versus A Small Impact*a*

Variable	Direction of difference: big vs. small impact	Value: big impact group	Value: small impact group	T-stat for difference
Factors employed in valuation*b*				
Earnings	greater	1.29	2.57	2.50
Cash flows	greater	1.29	2.14	2.32
Assets	greater	2.31	3.00	1.42
Cash flows (1–3 years)	greater	1.36	2.50	4.57
Analysts' recommendations	greater	3.21	4.00	1.72
Importance of information sources*b*				
Local FSA	greater	1.71	3.14	2.29
U.S. FSA	greater	2.43	3.67	1.89
U.S. reports	greater	3.14	3.85	1.49
Country news	less	2.64	1.71	1.58
Company visits	greater	2.15	3.57	1.91
Factors limiting international value comparisons*b*				
Valuation is local	less	3.00	2.67	0.54
Earnings diversity	greater	1.50	2.29	2.47
Coping responses*b*				
Difficulty in coping	greater	2.42	3.00	1.47
Invest top down	less	4.00	3.00	1.60
Master local principles	greater	2.50	3.71	2.14
Rely on recommendations	greater	2.93	4.00	1.96

a There were 14 and 7 managers respectively in the big- and small-impact groups.
b The responses were on a scale of 1 (very important) to 5 (not important) so that a smaller value of a response corresponds to greater importance of the variable.

CONCLUSIONS

In this chapter we have examined only one part of the cost-benefit equation associated with greater uniformity of disclosure and/or presentation of accounting results in an international context—the benefits of such additional information as inferred from the practices of professional investment managers. What we find is that all three forms of reduced diversity—more uniform disclosure, quantitative reconciliation to U.S. GAAP, and international harmonization are viewed as good things by managers. None, however, appears to be critical in the investment process, as most managers appear to manage quite well with existing information sources. Further, few attempt on their own to restate or otherwise harmonize accounting, stressing that local statements still dominate, for reasons that include but clearly are not limited to accounting diversity. Among the three approaches, reconciliation, if anything, is viewed as being of less importance than more uniform disclosure or harmonization, although the differences are not statistically significant.

Reconciliation is a costly requirement to foreign issuers because it results in a multiple account requirement, but is also especially costly to U.S. investors in that it limits U.S. listing of non-U.S. shares and from a bargaining viewpoint would appear to be the least effective of the three approaches in extending U.S. regulatory and investor influence over all world standards. We, therefore, conclude that the SEC's insistence on reconciliation is not well-founded and that other means, especially greater emphasis on mutual recognition subject to certain minimum standards of disclosure and presentation, would be more effective. This conclusion, however, in large part follows from our view regarding the tradeoff between the rigor and uniqueness of U.S. requirements and the overall influence of U.S. practices on world standards, something on which opinions clearly differ.

NOTES

1. See Choi and Levich (1990) for the impact of accounting diversity on the behavior of other interested parties, such as issuers, underwriters, and regulators.
2. There are at least three data services that provide professional investment managers with company financial and stock market data in computer readable form on thousands of worldwide firms. These are Morgan Stanley Capital International Perspective, Standard and Poor's/Extel GlobalVantage, and CIFAR. In addition, several services including BARRA and Roll and Ross provide risk measurement services for non-U.S. stocks, and IBES provides pooled analyst forecasts for non-U.S., as well as U.S. stocks.
3. See Table 3, Choi and Levich (1990).
4. Intersec (1990), Vosti (1990). See also Welling (1990).
5. For the five non-usable surveys, the respondents indicated that they either managed currency or primarily fixed income securities.
6. See Table 1 in Uppal (1992).
7. For discussions of international investment management styles, see Solnik (1988), Frashure (1989), and Nowakowski (1990).

8. A top-down approach refers to active picking of country markets in which to invest through a top-down valuation process. A bottom-up approach entails picking stocks through traditional security analysis using information primarily in the financial statements.
9. Clearly, these styles are not mutually exclusive.
10. In all of the subsequent analysis, we focus on the U.S. sample, since U.S.-based managers' views are most pertinent to this debate. We, can, however, note that there are no noticeable differences in the views of the U.S.-based and the U.K.-based managers and the analysis on the whole sample produces results almost identical to those on just the U.S. sample.
11. For space considerations, these comparisons have not been tabulated.

REFERENCES

Choi, F. D. S., and R. M. Levich. (1990). *The Capital Market Effects of International Accounting Diversity*. Homewood, IL: Dow Jones-Irwin.

Clarke, R. F. (1985). "The Application of Information Technology in an Investment Management Firm." Massachusetts Institute of Technology unpublished Master's thesis.

Frashure, R. D. (1989). "Investment Styles and Methods." *International Investing*. New York: Institute for Fiduciary Education. pp. 107–12.

Intersec. (1990). *Le Grid: A Comparative Profile of ERISA-Qualified International Investment Managers*. Stamford, CT: Intersec Research Corporation.

Meek, G. K., and S. Gray. (1989). "Globalization of Stock Markets and Foreign Listing Requirements: Voluntary Disclosures by Continental European." *Journal of International Business Studies*. 20, summer, pp. 316–38.

Nowakowski, C. (1990). *Roundtable on International Investment*. Stamford, CT: Intersec Research Corporation.

Solnik, B. (1988). *International Investments*. Reading, MA: Addison-Wesley.

Uppal, R. (1992). "The Economic Determinants of the Home Country Bias in Investors' Portfolios: A Survey." University of British Columbia working paper.

Vosti, C. (1990). "Special Report: International—Global Push Stays Strong." *Pensions and Investments*. June 25.

Welling, K. M. (1990). "On Top of The World: A Survey Rates the Leading Global Money Managers." *Barron's*. April 9.

CHAPTER 7

FINANCIAL DISCLOSURE LEVELS AND FOREIGN STOCK EXCHANGE LISTING DECISIONS

Shahrokh M. Saudagaran
Gary C. Biddle

INTRODUCTION

With the accelerating globalization of capital markets, firms are increasingly listing their shares on foreign stock exchanges. In just six years between 1982 and 1988, trading in foreign stocks by U.S. investors increased 900 percent, to nearly $150 billion per year. During the same period, foreign trades in U.S. stocks increased to nearly $400 billion per year.[1] By year-end 1988, shares worth $640 billion (6.7 percent of the worldwide total) were held by foreign investors.[2] By year-end 1989, foreign stocks accounted for 14 percent of total world stock trading volume.[3] A recent survey lists over 500 companies whose shares trade actively in international markets.[4]

Not all stock exchanges, however, have had equal appeal. By year-

The authors are grateful for comments provided by workshop participants at the University of Oregon, the UBCOW (Universities of British Columbia, Oregon, and Washington) Research Conference, Oklahoma State University, Stanford University, Massey University, the 1991 Annual Congress of the European Accounting Association, the 1991 Asian-Pacific Conference on International Accounting Issues, the 1992 American Accounting Association National Meetings, and the Conference on International Capital Markets in a World of Accounting Differences, sponsored by the New York University Salomon Center. They especially appreciate written comments from Bob Bowen, Linda McDaniel, Gary Meek, and Gim Seow.

end 1987, only 121 foreign firms had listed on one of the two major U.S. exchanges (NYSE and AMEX). In contrast, 584 foreign firms were listed in London, 320 in Amsterdam, and 213 in Zurich, despite the fact that the U.S. exchanges are far larger in terms of market value and volume of shares traded. Between 1981 and 1987, the U.S. exchanges added only 25 new foreign listings, compared with 107 new listings in London, 63 in Amsterdam, and 45 in Zurich. Indeed, one expert recently expressed the fear that "inadequate savings and a surfeit of regulations will combine to diminish the importance of the U.S. in the burgeoning international capital market."[5]

Anecdotal and other evidence suggests that accounting and regulatory disclosure requirements are important considerations in exchange listing decisions. As a result, accounting regulators and policy makers around the globe are facing difficult choices regarding appropriate disclosure standards for foreign firms listing within their jurisdictions.[6] The goal of protecting domestic investors from misleading financial disclosures must be weighed against demands for increased access to foreign capital and investment opportunities. The competitiveness of domestic stock exchanges often hangs in the balance.

In the United States, this debate has become particularly heated, with the Securities and Exchange Commission (SEC) and the New York Stock Exchange (NYSE) on opposite sides of the issue. Several recent articles have commented on the public nature of a dispute between NYSE Chairman William Donaldson and SEC Chairman Richard Breeden over disclosure requirements for foreign listers.[7] Mr. Donaldson would like reporting requirements relaxed for foreign firms listing on the NYSE, while Mr. Breeden is intent on preventing U.S. investors from being misled by financial statements that are not reconciled to U.S. GAAP.

This study provides evidence on a key question in this debate: Whether firms' choices among alternative foreign stock exchange listings are influenced by financial disclosure levels. Biddle and Saudagaran (1989) addressed this question by examining a cross-section of foreign stock exchange listings as of year-end 1981. This study extends that research in three major respects. First, it examines the foreign stock exchange listings of 302 internationally traded firms as of year-end 1987, a date that encompasses dramatic changes in foreign listings and regulatory requirements (see below). Second, by comparing foreign listings in 1981 with those in 1987, it identifies changes in foreign listings between these dates. These listings changes are more likely to have been influenced by the differences across countries in financial disclosure levels during this period. Third, this study employs a financial disclosure index obtained by surveying 142 experts actively involved in the foreign listing process. Financial disclosure levels are interpreted broadly to include mandated accounting, listing, and regulatory requirements, and voluntary disclosures dictated by the expectations of market participants.

Test results based on the cross-section of listings at year-end 1987 are consistent with the hypothesis that exchange choices are influenced by financial disclosure levels. However, they do not lend support to an alternate hypothesis suggesting that this effect should operate only for firms whose domestic disclosure levels are lower than those of a given foreign exchange. Tests based on *changes* in listings between 1981 and 1987 support both hypotheses. Because Hypothesis 2 can be viewed as a refinement of Hypothesis 1 that focuses solely on listings by firms with disclosures levels lower than that of an exchange, it provides a more severe test of associations between disclosure levels and listing decisions. These results for listings changes also hold for two mutually exclusive subsets of firms: (i) firms that had previously listed on one of the nine exchanges examined as of year-end 1981, and (ii) firms that had not listed previously. Listings by this latter sample would not have been influenced by preexisting listings (except possibly by listings on exchanges not examined). Overall, the results lend credence to concerns expressed by regulatory authorities and exchange officials that stringent disclosure levels could reduce access to foreign capital and foreign investment opportunities.

The second section examines previous research on financial disclosure levels, disclosure-related costs associated with foreign stock listings, and recent actions by regulatory authorities in the United States and elsewhere to ease reporting requirements for foreign firms. The third section develops testable hypotheses and describes sample selection procedures. The fourth section presents the empirical findings. The final section provides a summary.

FINANCIAL DISCLOSURE LEVELS AND FOREIGN LISTINGS

Despite recent growth in foreign stock exchange listings, not all foreign exchanges have had equal success in attracting foreign firms. Table 7–1 presents the numbers of firms from various domiciles listing their shares on

TABLE 7-1
Foreign Firm Listings on Nine Major Exchanges by Domicile[a]

Domicile	NYSE/AMEX	Toronto	London	Amsterdam	Paris	Tokyo	Frankfurt	Zurich
				Stock Exchange[b]				
Panel A: Foreign Listings in 1981								
United States	–	58	203	164	42	12	49	92
Canada	58	–	29	13	13	0	2	6
United Kingdom	9	5	–	17	16	0	14	9
Netherlands	2	0	16	–	12	1	15	10
France	0	0	3	4	–	2	10	7
Japan	6	1	8	25	8	–	55	2
Germany	0	0	7	12	11	0	–	23
Switzerland	0	0	1	1	2	0	4	–
Other[c]	21	3	210	21	58	15	28	19
Totals	96	67	477	257	162	15	177	168
Percentage Foreign[d]	4%	8%	17%	59%	22%	1%	28%	60%
Panel B: Foreign Listings in 1987								
United States	–	49	195	141	51	60	56	107
Canada	59	–	26	12	13	6	2	6
United Kingdom	19	8	–	22	17	10	14	11
Netherlands	5	0	16	–	13	1	16	14
France	0	0	5	10	–	0	8	7
Japan	8	1	9	30	18	–	58	8
Germany	0	0	8	16	13	2	–	33
Switzerland	0	0	1	2	2	2	11	–
Other[c]	30	7	324	87	63	7	43	27
Totals	121	65	584	320	190	88	208	213
Percentage Foreign[d]	5%	5%	22%	50%	28%	5%	27%	58%

[a] From fact books of individual stock exchanges.
[b] Exchanges in order of disclosure levels (Table 7-3).
[c] Not included in subsequent empirical tests.
[d] (Number of foreign companies listed / Total companies listed) × 100.

162

the world's nine major stock exchanges at year-end 1981 (panel A) and at year-end 1987 (panel B). Even though it ranks third in total capitalization among the exchanges presented, the London stock exchange has by far the largest number of foreign listings at both dates. In sharp contrast, the stock exchanges in Japan and the United States, the two largest capital markets, have attracted relatively few foreign firms (only Toronto lists fewer foreign stocks).[8] In both years, the Amsterdam and Zurich exchanges have the largest percentages of foreign stocks. All of the exchanges except Toronto increased their foreign listings between 1981 and 1987.[9]

Although many factors are likely to influence patterns of foreign exchange listings, accounting and financial disclosure levels have been cited as key considerations in exchange listing decisions. The next three subsections discuss (i) evidence on differences in disclosure levels across countries, (ii) disclosure-related costs of foreign listings, and (iii) recent actions taken by regulatory agencies to reduce the financial disclosure burden on foreign firms listing within their jurisdictions.

Differences in Disclosure Levels

Differences in national accounting standards reflect the influence of factors such as the structure and sophistication of capital markets, the role of government in the economy, business and tax laws, the organization of the accounting profession, the legal environment, and the country's accounting standard setting process.

Several previous studies have developed indexes measuring disclosure levels in various countries (Barrett, 1976; Lafferty and Cairns, 1980; Choi and Bavishi, 1982; Cairns, Lafferty, and Mantle, 1984; and Tonkin, 1989).[10] Several other studies have classified countries according to common elements and distinctive characteristics of their financial accounting systems (Mueller, 1967; AAA, 1977; Frank, 1979; Nair and Frank, 1980; Nobes, 1983; Nobes and Parker, 1985; Goodrich, 1986; and Gray, 1988). For example, in countries with widespread public ownership of securities such as the United States, United Kingdom, and Canada, there is a greater equity investor orientation in disclosure requirements (Gray, 1980). On the other hand, in countries such as Germany and France, debt financiers, creditors, and bankers dominate shareholders as the major suppliers of capital. Because these parties will in most cases have ready access to company records, there is less pressure for external reporting requirements.[11]

Differences in financial reporting practices between countries and the resulting difficulties in interpreting and comparing financial statements have led to demands for international harmonization or even complete standardization of accounting systems.[12] The analysis and debate over the desirability and feasibility of establishing a set of international accounting standards began in the early 1960s and has continued unabated since (Kraayenhof, 1960; Mueller, 1967; Fantl, 1971; Stamp, 1972; McMonies, 1977; Mason, 1978; McComb, 1979; Daley and Mueller, 1982; Turner, 1983; Gray, McSweeney, and Shaw, 1984; Taylor, 1987; Moulin and Solomon, 1989; Wyatt, 1989; and Choi and Levich, 1990). Over two decades, groups comprised mainly of government representatives and professional accountants[13] have been attempting to harmonize accounting systems with only limited success.[14] Noticeably lacking has been the participation of the firms preparing the financial statements. In fact, many firms have been adept at exploiting ambiguities in the international disclosure standards to continue to use their domestic standards (Evans and Taylor, 1982; Stilling, Norton, and Hopkins 1984; and Tonkin, 1989). This behavior is consistent with the evidence presented below suggesting that differences in financial disclosure levels create costs for firms choosing among alternative foreign stock exchange listings.

Disclosure and Regulatory Costs of a Foreign Listing

A firm considering a foreign stock exchange listing must deal with differences in accounting and auditing practices, financial reporting and registration requirements, and regulatory and legal restrictions between its domicile and the foreign country. Anecdotal and other evidence suggest that these costs can be significant. Provided below is a description of these costs gleaned from the literature on securities listings,[15] articles in the financial press,[16] and from interviews with officials from the SEC, the New York, American and Toronto stock exchanges, investment bankers, securities analysts, legal consultants, public accountants and managers of multinational corporations.[17]

First, regulatory authorities in most countries require foreign firms to prepare financial disclosures in accordance with local reporting requirements. A firm may have to incur substantial costs to bring its financial reporting systems into compliance. In the United States, for example, foreign firms are required to provide financial information substantially similar to that provided by domestic firms in accordance with U.S. generally accepted accounting principles (GAAP).[18] A prominent investment banker recently observed that "the cost of converting to U.S. accounting standards is at least $1 million for a major Japanese or British company. Why do that unless there is availability of capital, or a cost of capital, that you can't get anywhere else in the world?"[19] In contrast, the Amsterdam Exchange accepts "home country" financial statements from foreign listers with very few modifications.

Audit practices in foreign countries may also differ from those in a firm's home country. For instance, auditing standards in certain countries including the United States require that the auditors observe physical inventories and obtain direct confirmation of receivables. This would involve additional costs for firms based in countries where audit standards do not require these steps. Obtaining acceptable audit certification may also increase the time it takes for the firm to list its securities on a foreign stock exchange. For example, local requirements may specify that certification be obtained from a local auditor. Additional auditing and accounting costs may also be incurred to translate the results of foreign operations back into the domestic financial statements.

The greater frequency of financial reporting (e.g., semiannually or quarterly) required by some foreign stock exchanges or regulatory authorities can impose additional costs on companies not required to report as frequently at home. Managements in certain countries such as Germany and Japan strongly oppose quarterly reporting on philosophical grounds, arguing that it adversely affects their ability to take actions that are in the long term interests of their firms.[20]

Significant costs can also arise if a foreign exchange or foreign regulatory authorities require disclosures not required at home. For example, segment reporting (i.e., segmentation of financial information of a business by industry and/or geographic area in which the entity operates) is required in the United States by FASB Statement No. 14, but not under Japanese accounting principles. Japanese firms complain that these disclosures put them at a competitive disadvantage relative to other Japanese companies that are not listed in the United States (Choi and Stonehill, 1982). Tonkin (1989) reports that firms based in countries where segmental disclosures are not required tended not to provide that information. Balakrishnan, Harris, and Sen (1990) argue that segment disclosure requirements have been a major barrier to listings on U.S. stock exchanges by firms from some foreign countries.

Countries with extensive accounting disclosure requirements also tend to have extensive pre-registration requirements. The monetary cost of an initial listing in a foreign country typically includes underwriting and lawyers' fees and translation and printing expenses. The exchange may also require accounting disclosures and historical documentation beyond that required by the accounting regulatory bodies. Cumbersome registration and exchange reporting requirements can cause lengthy delays that may be unacceptable to firms for whom quick access to the stock market is a priority. There may also be recurring monetary and non-monetary costs of complying with periodic re-registration and updating requirements. The experts cited above expressed the view that accounting and regulatory costs are typically considered jointly in exchange listing decisions.

Restrictions imposed by regulatory agencies in foreign countries may also affect stock offerings made concurrently at home and abroad. For instance, in the United States, the Securities Act of 1933 prohibits a publicity campaign advertising a new issue during the period prior to initial filing of the registration statement. These restrictions extend beyond the United States and apply even to the firm's home country if such publicity may reasonably be expected to reach the U.S. market. Given the sophistication of modern telecommunications and the wide media coverage present today, this effectively precludes a campaign anywhere in the world prior to SEC registration and may even influence the nature of an offering in a firm's home country.

Restrictions imposed by regulatory agencies in foreign countries may also affect business practices, not only in those countries, but worldwide. A frequently cited example is the U.S. Foreign Corrupt Practices Act. Many foreign firms believe that these regulations adversely affect their global competitiveness and contradict established business practices. Additional anecdotal evidence of this concern is provided by a study commissioned by the *Keidanren*, Japan's Federation of Economic Organizations. The *Keidanren* engaged Sullivan and Cromwell, a major US law firm, to canvas U.S. regulatory agencies, stock exchange officials and professional organizations regarding the possible relaxation of reporting and regulatory requirements for Japanese firms.[21]

Other factors that may influence decisions to list on a given exchange in addition to accounting, reporting and regulatory practices include geographic and cultural proximity, industry, the relative importance of a country as a market for the company's products, and the relative size of the firm in its domestic capital market. These factors are described in the following section below (p. 171) where they are introduced as control variables in multivariate empirical tests.

The Regulatory Response

Faced with growing numbers of foreign listings, regulatory authorities around the globe are reassessing the relevance of domestic reporting requirements for foreign listers. Goals of disclosure comprehensiveness and comparability are being weighed against demands for increased access to capital and investment opportunities (Thomas 1983). Described below are several relaxations in reporting requirements for foreign listers that were introduced in sample countries during the period 1981–87. Also described are some more recent changes introduced in the U.S. in response to growing pressure for less stringent reporting requirements for foreign listers.

United States[22]   The SEC's mandate to protect investors and ensure that they are well-informed suggests that foreign firms listing securities in the United States provide the same financial information as domestic issuers. However, critics charge that imposing domestic disclosure requirements on foreign issuers makes U.S. listings less attractive, thereby placing U.S. stock exchanges at a competitive disadvantage and depriving U.S. investors of desirable investment opportunities.

Under increasing pressure to make foreign securities more accessible to U.S. investors and to enhance the competitiveness of U.S. exchanges, the SEC adopted the Integrated Disclosure System (IDS) in 1982, after more than three years of deliberation (SEC, 1982). Apart from reducing paperwork by eliminating some of the duplication in registration requirements, these rules also modified other disclosure requirements foreign issuers found burdensome.[23] These include the use of the registrant's domestic GAAP in preparing financial statements, segment reporting, timeliness of the financial statements incorporated in the prospectus, and disclosure of top management's compensation.

Under IDS, foreign firms may now prepare SEC filings (Form 20-F) using foreign, as opposed to U.S., GAAP when the foreign GAAP is part of a comprehensive set of standards. They are required, however, to reconcile material differences, if any, between the amounts determined under the foreign accounting principles and those that would have resulted under SEC Regulation S-X and U.S. GAAP.

Segment reporting under U.S. GAAP requires the disclosure of assets, revenues, and profits by line of business and geographic area. Most other countries do not require this level of detail and many foreign firms are reluctant to provide this information (Tonkin, 1989). Under IDS, firms using foreign GAAP may dispense with segment reporting of profits and assets if they are not required to disclose them under their domestic standards. However, a narrative explanation must be provided if a segment's contribution to total profits is materially different from its share of revenues. Materiality is not defined.

IDS has also relaxed the timeliness requirements for some foreign issuers. Unlike U.S. issuers who must generally provide financial statements no older than 135 days at the date of filing, foreign issuers are now permitted to use financial statements that are up to six months old at the effective date of the registration statement. However, foreign companies' financial statements must include more recent figures if disclosed in compliance with foreign law.

The disclosure of an individual manager's compensation is also perceived as onerous by many foreign issuers. In IDS, the SEC responded to this concern by permitting aggregate disclosure of top managers' and directors' salaries in lieu of individual disclosure, unless information on individual remuneration is routinely disclosed to the shareholders or the public in the issuer's home country.

In IDS the SEC made no concessions with respect to auditing requirements. The objectives of audits differ greatly between countries that rely on statutory audits and those that use private sector audits (i.e., where standards are set by professional accountants' organizations). In the former the auditor attests to the conformity of a company's financial statements with the law while in the latter the emphasis is on a true and fair view and accordance with GAAP (SEC, 1987). In light of these differences, the SEC continues to require foreign listers to obtain audits conducted in accordance with U.S. generally accepted auditing standards.

Thus, while IDS created a precedent for a double standard whereby foreign listers could be exempted from reporting requirements imposed on U.S. firms, its impact on the attractiveness of U.S. listings remains an open question. A full five years after its passage, one critic of U.S. reporting policies observed:[24]

> There's been this huge movement to simplify the rules and procedures for issuing securities in France, Germany, Britain, even Japan. But the U.S. market during this time runs the risk of becoming, in effect, a regional market. No foreign corporation will go to the U.S.market.

I think the SEC should greatly simplify the whole process of registration, disclosure and whether companies need to transform their accounts to American standards. These are all very provincial type rules.

Somehow in the European market we are able to float Japanese companies, Australian companies, Belgian, Finnish, and Swiss companies. Accounting figures, certified by accountants but with different types of national practices, are accepted by the market as legitimate.

If you just looked at interest rates, European firms or governments could have raised money more cheaply in the U.S. So why are they going to the international market? It must be because the price they put on harassment and regulation makes the cheaper cost of the money not worth the effort. That's the only explanation I have.

Under continuing pressure from U.S. stock exchanges and investors, the SEC has more recently loosened reporting requirements for private placements and has proposed modified disclosure rules for Canadian firms. In April 1990, the SEC adopted Rule 144A providing a safe harbor exemption from the registration requirements of the 1933 Securities Act for resales of restricted securities to "qualified institutional buyers".[25] Prior to its passage, traders were unable to resell private-placement securities without registering them with the SEC or holding them for two years. The main implication of Rule 144A is that it permits traders to resell private-placement foreign securities without registration and without a waiting period thereby creating a new market in which institutions will trade securities among themselves. In response to concerns about the potential development of side-by-side public and private markets for the same class of securities, the applicability of Rule 144A is restricted when foreign securities are of the same class as securities listed on a U.S. securities exchange. Some observers expect the "Rule 144A market" to compete with Euromarkets.[26]

In October 1990, the SEC reproposed a multijurisdictional system between the United States and Canada, which had been originally proposed in July 1989 based on a February 1985 conceptual release.[27] The first phase would be limited to prospectuses used in offerings of investment grade nonconvertible debt and preferred stock of "substantial issuers" in Canada.[28] The Canadian regulatory authorities would be responsible for applying their disclosure standards for reviewing the prospectuses. Unless the SEC staff had reason to believe that there was a problem with the filing or offering, the documents would be assigned a "no review" status by the SEC. Canadian issuers would, however, be liable under U.S. civil liability and antifraud laws. They would also be subject to the SEC's authority to stop the issue if it were considered necessary for the protection of U.S. investors. Under the proposed rule, periodic reporting under Canadian rules would satisfy the reporting requirements of the Exchange Act in the U.S. In addition, Canadian issuers would be exempt from U.S. proxy regulations as well as from insider reporting requirements under Section 16 of the Exchange Act. This went into effect in June 1991. [See Part Four of this volume.]

Japan   Regulatory authorities in Japan have also relaxed certain disclosure requirements for foreign companies. In December 1983, amendments to the "Enforcement Order of the Securities and Exchange Law" and to the "Ministerial Ordinance on the Audit Certificate of Financial Statements" eliminated the dual audit requirement for foreign companies listed on the Tokyo Stock Exchange. Previously, listed foreign companies whose financial statements had been audited by a public accountant in their home country were required to file a separate audit report provided by Japanese public accountants. Under the revised regulations, the audit report provided by the foreign company's auditor in its home country is sufficient if the Japanese Ministry of Finance considers it to be adequate protection for Japanese investors. The new regulations became effective for fiscal years ending on or after January 1, 1984. Timeliness requirements for foreign issuers were also relaxed by an amendment of Japan's Securities and Exchange Law in May 1984. The deadline for filing financial statements has been extended from within three months to within six months after the end of the fiscal year.

These changes in Japanese reporting requirements were due largely to the efforts of the Tokyo Stock Exchange, which had been urging the government to relax or eliminate regulatory disclosure burdens on foreign companies. It had argued that this was necessary to attract foreign companies. The Tokyo Stock Exchange had already taken measures in 1983 within its authority to reduce the documents to be filed with the exchange by foreign companies. In addition, it also had simplified and reduced the frequency with which certain other documents were to be submitted to the exchange by foreign companies. Several reports which were previously required on a quarterly basis (and still are for Japanese companies), are now required to be filed only annually by foreign companies.

Other Countries   Between 1981 and 1987, authorities in France and United Kingdom also took steps to increase the competitiveness of the Paris and London stock exchanges respectively.[29] However, their actions related to securities trading procedures rather than to disclosure requirements as was the case in the United States and Japan. Under these provisions, the French government allowed negotiation of discounts on commissions charged by brokers. Previously, all these commission discounts were fixed. With a view to maintaining orderly markets, the French government also introduced a system of using stock jobbers, or specialists, where none had existed before. In 1985, the London Stock Exchange approved plans to open ownership of members to outsiders and usher in deregulated equities trading in London in an effort to make the London market better capitalized and more competitive internationally. The approval allowed foreign banks and stockbrokers, which had been limited to acquiring minority stakes in British brokerage firms, to own 100 percent of such firms. It also did away with fixed commissions.

While no significant changes were identified in the disclosure requirements for foreign firms on the Amsterdam, Frankfurt, Toronto, and Zurich stock exchanges between 1981 and 1987, the changes in the United States, Japan, and the United Kingdom emphasize the importance of the regulatory issues raised by foreign stock listings. The remaining sections of the paper provide empirical evidence on a key question in the ongoing debates: Whether financial disclosure levels have influenced firms' choices among alternative foreign exchange listings.

HYPOTHESES, SAMPLE SELECTION, AND DATA SOURCES

Hypotheses and Design Considerations

If financial disclosure levels are an important consideration to firms choosing among alternative foreign stock exchange listings, there should be an inverse relation between probability that a firm will list on a foreign exchange and the disclosure level of that exchange. This suggests the following hypothesis (in alternative form):

Hypothesis 1:   The probability that a firm will list on a given foreign stock exchange is inversely related to the exchange's disclosure level, *ceteris paribus*.[30]

Hypothesis 1 implies that this inverse relation between likelihood of listing and exchange disclosure levels operates throughout the range of possible exchange choices. An alternate characterization of this relation recognizes that a firm may be much less influenced by disclosure levels if its current disclosure level already exceeds that of a given foreign exchange. If so, an inverse relation will exist only for exchanges with more extensive disclosures than a firm's domicile; for exchanges with disclosure levels that are lower than a firm's current level, exchange choices will be independent of exchange disclosure levels. This suggests Hypothesis 2:

> Hypothesis 2:   The probability that a firm will list on a given foreign stock exchange is inversely related (unrelated) to the exchange's disclosure level when the exchange's disclosure level is higher (lower) than the firm's current level, *ceteris paribus*.

Figure 7–1 illustrates hypotheses 1 and 2 with the slopes indicating the directions of the hypothesized relations.

In order to test hypotheses 1 and 2, some measure of a firm's current disclosure level is required. As a proxy, the disclosure level of a firm's domicile is employed. This choice reflects the reasoning that a firm's accounting and disclosure policies will be influenced primarily by its domestic standards. This reasoning is less compelling for firms that have listed on foreign exchanges with disclosure levels higher than those of their domiciles. However, differences across countries in specific disclosure requirements mean that even in this case, domestic standards remain relevant. In addition, data indicating the order in which firms have listed on various foreign exchanges are not readily available. Tests presented below examine new foreign listings between 1981 and 1987. These data reveal that using the highest disclosure level among a firm's 1981 listings to indicate its disclosure level, rather than its domicile disclosure level, would affect at most 14 out of 275 new listings (Tables 7–7 and 7–8).

Sample Selection and Data Sources

Hypotheses 1 and 2 are tested by examining samples of internationally traded firms that had at least one foreign listing on one of nine major stock exchanges at year-end 1981 or at year-end 1987.[31] Using two cross-sectional samples allows listing changes to be observed, a potentially more powerful design that isolates incremental listing decisions made during a period over which disclosure level ranks obtained from a survey instrument (see below) are representative.

FIGURE 7–1
**The Association Between Financial Disclosure Requirements
and Foreign Exchange Listings**

HYPOTHESIS 1

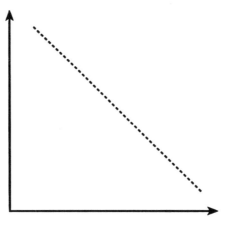

Probability that
a firm will list on
a given foreign
exchange

Financial disclosure levels
on a given foreign exchange

HYPOTHESIS 2

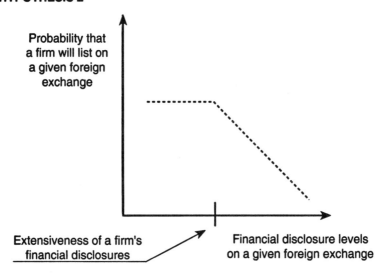

Probability that
a firm will list on
a given foreign
exchange

Extensiveness of a firm's
financial disclosures

Financial disclosure levels
on a given foreign exchange

Exchanges   Nine stock exchanges in eight countries are examined (the NYSE and AMEX are both located in the United States). This choice takes into account exchange size (capitalization and total listings), the economic importance of the countries in which the exchanges are based, and their degree of internationalization (as indicated by the number of foreign firm listings). Since these criteria are correlated, the resulting set of exchanges can be described as the primary stock exchanges of the eight countries with the largest capital markets.

Secondary markets are not included for several reasons. First, secondary markets differ greatly across countries in size, and in the frequency and composition of foreign listings. Second, data on foreign listings and listing requirements are less readily available for secondary markets. Third, this study focuses on the listing decisions of large internationally traded firms. Few large firms list on foreign secondary markets.

Firms   Sample firms were identified using the "Euromoney Corporate List" (*Euromoney*, 1984-88) and fact books from each of the nine exchanges. *Euromoney* was used for two reasons. First, in its March 1985 releases on the internationalization of securities markets, the SEC's Office of International Corporate Finance used the *Euromoney* list to *define* an internationally traded security. Second, *Euromoney* provides a complete set of stock exchanges on which firms' shares are listed. Additional firms with at least one foreign listing were identified using exchange fact books. These data were cross-checked with statistics published by the International Federation of Stock Exchanges (FIBV) and were found to be in agreement. Financial services, real estate, and utilities firms were deleted to ensure that disclosure and control variables were measuring similar attributes. All sample firms exceed the size requirements for listing on all of the exchanges examined. The final 1981 (1987) samples contain internationally traded firms domiciled in one of the eight countries, and with at least one foreign listing in 1981 (1987) on one of the nine exchanges examined in the study.

Table 7–2 presents the foreign listings of the sample firms by domicile (listed in order of disclosure level—see below). The patterns are clearly consistent with the distributions observed in Table 7–1 (which included all foreign firms listed on the exchanges). In 1981 (1987), the U.S. exchanges list fewer foreign firms than all but one (two) of the sample exchanges. No French, German or Swiss firms in the sample are listed on the NYSE or AMEX in either 1981 or 1987. Foreign listings by Japanese firms are concentrated in Frankfurt and those of German firms in Paris and Zurich. Between 1981 and 1987, total foreign listings increased from 475 to 690.

TABLE 7–2
Foreign Listings of Sample Firms by Domicile and Exchange[a]

Domicile	Stock Exchange								Total Foreign Listings	Total Firms Listed	Average Listings per Firm
	NYSE/ AMEX	TOR	LDN	AMS	PAR	TKY	FRA	ZUR			
Panel A: 1981 Sample											
United States	-	28	73	67	32	7	42	66	315	117	2.69
Canada	7	-	6	4	6	0	0	3	26	11	2.36
United Kingdom	8	1	-	8	8	0	7	5	37	24	1.54
Netherlands	2	0	4	-	4	0	3	4	17	5	3.40
France	0	0	1	2	-	1	4	2	10	6	1.67
Japan	5	1	5	8	4	-	17	2	42	27	1.56
Germany	0	0	4	4	8	0	-	8	24	13	1.85
Switzerland	0	0	0	1	1	0	2	-	4	4	1.00
Totals	22	30	93	94	63	8	75	90	475	207	2.29
Panel B: 1987 Sample											
United States	-	31	96	79	37	24	52	81	400	158	2.53
Canada	20	-	14	7	12	1	2	5	61	30	2.03
United Kingdom	11	3	-	11	12	3	13	9	62	29	2.14
Netherlands	3	0	5	-	4	0	5	6	23	7	3.29
France	0	1	3	1	-	1	7	3	16	9	1.78
Japan	8	1	7	19	13	-	31	8	87	46	1.89
Germany	0	0	5	5	9	0	-	17	36	18	2.00
Switzerland	0	0	0	1	1	0	3	-	5	5	1.00
Totals	42	36	130	123	88	29	113	129	690	302	2.28

[a] Exchanges in order of disclosure levels (Table 7–3). Stock Exchange Codes: AMEX American, AMS Amsterdam, FRA Frankfurt, LDN London, NYSE New York, PAR Paris, TKY Tokyo, TOR Toronto, ZUR Zurich.

Indexes of Disclosure Levels   Hypotheses 1 and 2 suggest that foreign exchange listing decisions will be influenced by differences between a firm's current disclosure levels and those in exchange countries. Disclosure levels are interpreted broadly to include both voluntary disclosures and mandated disclosures dictated by accounting, listing, and regulatory requirements. Voluntary disclosures are included because even though foreign firms might be exempt from requirements imposed on domestic companies, they may voluntarily disclose additional information in response to the expectations of market participants. Evidence consistent with this contention is found in Choi (1973b) and Meek and Gray (1989).

Several previous studies have ranked the comprehensiveness of financial disclosures across countries based on inspections of published financial statements (Lafferty and Cairns 1980; Choi and Bavishi 1982; Cairns, Lafferty, and Mantle 1984; and Tonkin 1989). However, these rankings were not designed to measure disclosure levels broadly defined and, as a result, may not reflect fully a manager's perceptions of the accounting, regulatory, and other related costs of listing in a given foreign country.

To measure the reporting and regulatory costs of foreign listings as perceived by managers and their advisors, a survey was conducted of 200 individuals actively involved in the foreign listing process. Survey participants were identified from participants at a roundtable to discuss the IASC's Comparability Project in Washington, D.C., jointly sponsored by the Securities and Exchange Commission, the University of Southern California, and KPMG Peat Marwick. Additional survey participants were identified through local and national partners of the "Big Six" international accounting firms. The survey participants included corporate managers, investment bankers, public accountants, stock exchange officials, attorneys, and academics.

The survey instrument asked participants to rank the eight countries examined in this study on three specific aspects of disclosure and one summary scale: statutory reporting requirements, exchange reporting requirements, capital market expectations, and overall disclosure levels. Mean ranks based on 142 responses (63 U.S. and 79 non-U.S. with a 71 percent overall response rate) are shown in Table 7–3. Because the rankings are highly correlated, subsequent tests are based on rankings of overall disclosure levels (rightmost column). This is termed the "Disclosure Level Rank" (DLR).[32]

Four additional variables are used to control for factors besides disclosure levels which may be influencing foreign listing decisions—geo-

TABLE 7–3
Disclosure Level Survey Results[a] (Based on 142 responses)

	Mean Ranks				
	Statutory Reporting Requirements	Exchange Reporting Requirements	Capital Market Expectations	Overall Disclosure Levels	Disclosure Level Rank (DLR)
United States	7.27	7.29	7.17	7.28	8
Canada	6.48	6.38	5.91	6.41	7
United Kingdom	5.84	5.87	6.09	6.02	6
Netherlands	4.68	4.80	4.50	4.75	5
France	4.11	4.50	4.13	4.17	4
Japan	3.82	4.04	4.22	3.83	3
Germany	3.96	3.90	4.04	3.81	2
Switzerland	2.70	2.78	3.17	2.60	1

Spearman Rank Correlation between Overall Disclosure Levels and:
    Statutory Reporting Requirements   .976
    Exchange Reporting Requirements 1.000
    Capital Market Expectations   .952

[a] Ranks are in descending order with "8" ("1") indicating highest (lowest) disclosure level.

graphic location, industry, product market, and relative size in domestic capital market.

Geographic Location   One reason a firm may be more likely to list its shares on a given foreign exchange is geographic proximity. Geographic proximity may proxy for similarities in language, culture, product markets, factor markets, and familiarity with business practices and conditions. A location dummy variable classifies firms into three geographic areas: (1) North America, including Canada and the United States; (2) Europe, including France, Germany, Netherlands, Switzerland, and the United Kingdom; and (3) Asia, consisting of Japan. Firms from the area of an exchange receive a location score of 1, while those from the other areas are assigned a score of 0.

Industry   Another factor that may affect exchange choices is a firm's industry. These concentrations could be due to location-specific characteristics of the host country, historical links, or to a "follow-the-leader" effect. A zero/one dummy variable is used to indicate whether a firm belongs to a given industry group. Industry classifications were obtained from *Euromoney*.

Product Market   The size of the product market for a firm's goods and services in the country of a foreign stock exchange may also be important in exchange listing decisions. Ideally, we would like to have the proportion of each firm's exports going to a given exchange country. However, these data generally are not disclosed.[33] As a proxy, we use the proportion of exports from a given industry and domicile to a given foreign exchange country; for example, German auto exports to the United States divided by total German auto exports to the other seven exchange countries. Data for these measures were obtained from the *World Trade Annual* prepared by the Statistical Office of the United Nations.

Relative Size in Domestic Capital Market   Because the multivariate tests presented below examine factors influencing decisions to list on *given* foreign exchanges, and because firms can list on more than one exchange, it is also important to control for a firm's motivation to seek a foreign listing. Saudagaran (1988) provides evidence that a firm whose shares account for a larger proportion of the market value of its domestic capital market may be more likely to list on a foreign exchange.

For example, Nestle, which accounted for 11.7 percent of the total market value of all domestic firms listed on the Swiss stock exchanges at the end of 1987, may be more likely to list abroad than Exxon, which accounted for 2.4 percent of the market value of U.S. firms listed on the NYSE. This is despite the fact that Nestle (market value $14.2 billion at year-end 1987) is considerably smaller than Exxon (market value of $54.1 billion).

TEST RESULTS

Two sets of results are presented: (1) univariate and multivariate tests based on the cross-section of listings at year-end 1987, and (2) an analysis of changes in foreign stock exchange listings between 1981 and 1987.[34]

Univariate Tests

Table 7–4 presents the results of univariate tests of association between foreign exchange listings in 1987 and firms' financial disclosure levels (from Table 7–3). Two-by-two contingency tables indicate the numbers of foreign firms with more/less stringent disclosure standards listing/not listing on each of the exchanges. The evidence is consistent with Hypothesis 1. For all but two exchanges (Paris and Frankfurt), a greater propor-

TABLE 7-4

Contingency Tests of Association Between Foreign Listings in 1987 and Financial Disclosure Standards of Domicile Relative to Exchange[a]

Domicile disclosures	NYSE/AMEX		Toronto (TOR)		London (LDN)		Amsterdam (AMS)	
	Listed	Not Listed	Listed	Not Listed	Listed	Not Listed	Listed	Not Listed
More stringent	0	0	31	127	110	78	97	120
Less stringent	42	102	5	109	18	67	26	52
Supports Hypoth. I	N/A[b]		Yes		Yes		Yes	
Chi-square (p-value)	N/A		12.09 (.000)		31.28 (.000)		2.60 (.053)	
Fisher p-value	N/A		(.000)		(.000)		(.053)	

Domicile disclosures	Paris (PAR)		Tokyo (TKY)		Frankfurt (FRA)		Zurich (ZUR)	
	Listed	Not Listed	Listed	Not Listed	Listed	Not Listed	Listed	Not Listed
More stringent	65	159	29	204	110	169	129	168
Less stringent	23	46	0	23	3	2	0	0
Supports Hypoth. I	No		Yes		No		N/A	
Chi-square (p-value)	.285 (.297)		2.11 (.073)		N/A		N/A	
Fisher p-value	(.294)		(.055)		(.313)		N/A	

[a] Based on financial disclosure levels (Table 7–3). p-values are for one-tailed tests.
[b] N/A indicates not applicable.

tion of firms with more stringent domestic requirements than the exchange are listed than with less stringent domestic standards. (This comparison is not applicable to NYSE/AMEX and ZUR since they are the endpoints of the disclosure ranking.) For all exchanges except for Paris and Frankfurt, Chi-squared and Fisher exact tests are statistically significant at conventional levels.[35]

Although these univariate tests are supportive of firms being more (less) likely to list on foreign exchanges with disclosure levels less (more) stringent than their domestic levels, they are subject to several limitations. First, univariate tests do not control for other factors that may influence listing choices such as industry and geographic locale. Second, they do not consider the *degree* to which a firm's domestic disclosure levels differ from those of a foreign exchange. Third, the tests are not independent because firms can list on more than one exchange and thus can appear in more than one contingency table. The following multivariate tests are designed to address the first two of these limitations. Later randomization tests help address the independence limitation.

Multivariate Tests

Two sets of multivariate tests are presented for the 1987 sample. Each is based on a logit model with the dependent variable indicating whether a firm has listed (= 1) or not listed (= 0) on a given foreign exchange as a function of the firm's disclosure level rank (DLR) and other factors that may influence listing decisions. The first set tests Hypothesis 1 which posits an inverse relation between the probability that a firm will list on a foreign exchange and the exchange's DLR. The second set imposes additional structure to allow Hypothesis 1 to be distinguished from Hypothesis 2, which suggests that firms will not be influenced by disclosure levels on exchanges with disclosure levels lower than their domiciles. Both sets of multivariate tests include control variables for industry, geographic location, exports to the exchange market, and firm size relative to the domestic capital market size.

The first set of tests are based on the following model, estimated for each exchange:

$$L_f = \alpha + \Sigma\beta_i \text{IND}_{fi} + \gamma_1 \text{LOC}_f + \gamma_2 \text{EXPMKT}_f + \gamma_3 \text{CAPSIZE}_f + \gamma_4 \text{DLR}_f + \varepsilon_f$$

where

L_f = 1 if firm f is listed on the exchange, 0 otherwise,
α = intercept,
IND_{fi} = 1 if firm f is in industry i and 0 otherwise,
LOC_f = 1 if firm f is domiciled in the same geographical region as the exchange, 0 otherwise,
$EXPMKT_f$ = exports of firm f's industry and domicile to the exchange country as a proportion of industry and domicile exports to all exchange countries in the sample,
$CAPSIZE_f$ = market value of firm f's outstanding common shares as a proportion of the market value of the outstanding common shares of all domestic firms listed on firm f's domestic stock exchange,
DLR_f = financial disclosure level rank for the domicile of firm f, and
β_i, γ_1, γ_2, γ_3, γ_4 are slope coefficients.

Results are reported in Table 7–5. The disclosure level variable (DLR) has a positive sign consistent with Hypothesis 1 for seven of the eight exchanges; six of the seven are statistically significant at p-values < .05. The coefficient for DLR for the eighth exchange (Frankfurt) is negative, inconsistent with Hypothesis 1.

Most industry dummies are not statistically significant. The LOC variable is positive and statistically significant at conventional levels for just two exchanges (NYSE/AMEX and TKY). For four exchanges, LOC is negative, opposite the expected sign, and for two of these (TOR and LDN) the negative coefficient would be statistically significant for a two-tailed test.[36] The EXP variable is positive and statistically significant for six exchanges; those with negative signs would not be significant at conventional levels for two-tailed tests. The CAP variable is positive for all eight exchanges and statistically significant for five.

Overall, the results in Table 7–5 are consistent with Hypothesis 1. After controlling for other factors that may influence listing decisions, the probability that a firm will list on a given foreign exchange appears positively related to the disclosure level of a firm's domicile. Qualitatively identical results were obtained when a continuous disclosure level measure (second to rightmost column in Table 7–3) was substituted for DLR.[37] It may be, however, that the apparent positive relation between listing on an exchange and a firm's DLR operates only for firms with DLRs lower than the exchange, as implied by Hypothesis 2. This is addressed next.

TABLE 7-5
Logit Test of Hypothesis 1 for 1987 Sample[a]

| | Industries | | | | | | | | | | | | % |
	Oil & Gas	Food & Bev	Chem	Drugs & Pharm	Metals	Mach	Elec & Elctm	Auto & Aero	LOC	EXP	CAP	DLR	Pred. sign Q-Indx
									+	+	+	+	
NYSE/AMEX (144 firms)													
Coefficient	.321	-.024	-.158	.045	-.806	.901	.321	.420	1.252	-1.004	15.636	.311	81.3%
t-statistic	.79	-.06	-.31	.06	-1.85	1.89	.77	.82	2.27	-1.76	1.90	2.90	1.17
Significance					(.067)[b]	(.061)[b]			(.012)	(.040)	(.030)	(.002)	
TOR (272 firms)													
Coefficient	.684	-.372	.156	-3.825	.137	-.994	-.124	-.225	-1.280	2.535	1.806	.336	88.5%
t-statistic	2.41	-.90	.45	-.26	.39	-1.79	-.31	-.51	-2.04	3.14	1.61	1.93	1.02
Significance	(.017)[b]					(.075)[b]			(.021)	(.001)	(.055)	(.027)	
LDN (273 firms)													
Coefficient	.435	.192	.267	.349	-.216	.267	.036	.464	-.292	2.635	.993	.166	69.6%
t-statistic	1.68	.78	1.08	.94	-.73	1.12	.15	1.62	-1.37	2.69	.59	4.10	1.33
Significance	(.094)[b]								(.086)	(.004)		(.000)	
AMS (295 firms)													
Coefficient	-.121	.126	.385	-.429	-.212	-.166	.313	.321	-.094	-.032	1.048	.085	68.2%
t-statistic	-.50	.53	1.55	-1.05	-.87	-.76	1.41	1.12	-.36	-.02	1.22	2.17	1.17
Significance												(.015)	
PAR (293 firms)													
Coefficient	-.268	.068	.133	.095	.476	-.556	.230	-.477	.063	2.338	2.412	.023	77.9%
t-statistic	-.92	.27	.54	.26	2.00	-1.80	.97	-1.39	.22	1.78	4.68	.59	1.11
Significance					(.046)[b]	(.073)[b]				(.038)	(.000)		

													% Pred	Q-Indx
TKY (256 firms)														
Coefficient	-.249	.143	-.373	.726	-3.339	-.365	.003	-.331	—	-.806	41.438	.323	92.6%	
t-statistic	-.56	.35	-.80	1.64	-.37	-1.07	.01	-.58	—	-.73	4.85	1.83	1.04	
Significance											(.000)	(.034)		
FRA (284 firms)														
Coefficient	-.227	-.014	.249	-.468	.203	-.254	.095	-.090	-.047	1.412	2.318	-.107	72.3%	
t-statistic	-.90	-.06	1.01	-1.22	.87	-1.07	.43	-.29	-.20	1.81	.12	-2.82	1.20	
Significance										(.035)		(.003)		
ZUR (297 firms)														
Coefficient	.213	.124	.460	.295	.082	-.258	.166	.347	.375	3.220	2.104	.101	69.8%	
t-statistic	.92	.55	2.01	.76	.36	-1.11	.75	1.28	1.90	1.61	1.91	2.55	1.24	
Significance			(.045)[b]						(.029)	(.054)	(.028)	(.005)		

[a] p-values are for one-tailed tests unless otherwise indicated.

LOC   Location dummy variable = 1 if firm in same geographic region as exchange, zero otherwise. For the Tokyo Exchange (TKY), LOC = 0.

EXP   Exports of the firm's domicile industry to a given exchange country as a proportion of the domicile industry's total exports to the eight exchange countries.

CAP   Firm's equity capital as a proportion of the total equity capital of its domestic exchange.

DLR   Financial disclosure level rank of firm's domicile. A higher rank means a higher disclosure level.

% Pred   Percent correct predictions. Predicted value <.5 classified as 0, >.5 as 1.

Q-Indx   Quality of prediction index relative to naive prediction that all firms belong to largest classification. Q-Indx = % Pred / [(Max(listers, nonlisters) / sample size) x 100]. Q-Indx > 1 indicates that prediction model outperforms naive prediction.

[b] Two-tailed probability.

The second set of multivariate tests employ the same logit model except that the DLR variable is replaced by the following two terms:

$$HYP2_f = \min (DLR_f, DLR \text{ of exchange }), \text{ and}$$
$$HYP1_f = DLR_f - \min (DLR_f, DLR \text{ of exchange })$$
$$= (DLR_f - DLR \text{ of exchange })^+,$$

where "+" indicates "non-negative part."

HYP2 tests Hypothesis 2 by assuming an increasing relation between the probability of listing on an exchange and a firm's DLR for firms with DLRs lower than an exchange, and a constant relation for firms with DLRs above that of the exchange. HYP1 allows the relation between listing and DLR to increase throughout the range of DLRs as implied by Hypothesis 1. A positive coefficient for HYP2 combined with an insignificant coefficient for HYP1 would support Hypothesis 2. A positive coefficient on HYP1 but not on HYP2 would be inconsistent with Hypothesis 2. Because Hypothesis 1 operates throughout the range of DLRs, positive coefficients on either HYP1 or HYP2 would be consistent with Hypothesis 1, though stonger support would be provided by positive coefficients on both HYP1 or HYP2.

The results are reported in Table 7–6. The exchanges with the highest and lowest DLRs (NYSE/AMEX and ZUR) are omitted because the variables HYP1 and HYP2 will be useful in distinguishing between Hypotheses 1 and 2 only when there are potential listers with DLRs both higher and lower than the DLR of a given exchange. In Table 7–6, the results for TOR and LDN support Hypothesis 2. The results for AMS and TKY are consistent with Hypothesis 1 only. Neither hypothesis is supported by the results for FRA (the sign on HYP1 is negative). Thus, the evidence in Table 7–6 lends support to the overall implication obtained from Table 7–5 that disclosure levels appear to influence exchange listings. However, the 1987 cross-section of listings does not provide clear support for Hypothesis 2 over Hypothesis 1. A possible explanation is limited power for estimating HYP2 due to the smaller samples of firms with DLRs lower than the exchanges at the bottom of Table 7–6. A potentially more powerful test of the influence of disclosure levels on listing decisions is provided in the following section which examines *changes* in listings between 1981 and 1987.

Tests of Changes in Listings Between 1981 and 1987

Changes in foreign listings between 1981 and 1987 are examined for three sets of firms, the 1987 sample and two mutually exclusive subsets:

TABLE 7-6
Logit Test of Hypothesis 2 for 1987 Sample[a]

| | Industries | | | | | | | | LOC | EXP | CAP | DLR | DLR | % | |
	Oil & Gas	Food & Bev	Chem	Drugs & Pharm	Metals	Mach	Elec & Elctrn	Auto & Aero	LOC +	EXP +	CAP +	DLR H1	DLR H2	Pred.	Q-Indx
TOR (272 firms)															
Coefficient	.878	-.037	.150	-3.781	.238	-.925	.033	.096	.421	1.832	-.001	-.174	1.377	87.4%	
t-statistic	2.92	-.10	.43	-.25	.66	-1.67	.09	.22	1.39	2.58	-1.44	-.35	2.70	1.01	
Significance	(.004)[b]					(.096)[b]			(.083)	(.005)	(.076)		(.004)		
LDN (273 firms)															
Coefficient	.266	.189	.258	.492	.048	.548	.354	.651	.729	-.613	2.062	.118	.333	68.3%	
t-statistic	1.12	.75	1.05	1.20	.21	2.34	1.44	2.10	2.33	-.54	1.08	.70	3.11	1.30	
Significance						(.020)[b]		(.037)[b]	(.010)				(.001)		
AMS (295 firms)															
Coefficient	-.250	.145	.212	-.585	-.115	-.204	.248	.327	-.300	1.199	1.079	.171	-.038	68.5%	
t-statistic	-1.06	.64	.91	-1.49	-.49	-.94	1.15	1.19	-1.23	1.43	3.43	1.59	-.32	1.18	
Significance										(.077)	(.000)	(.056)			
PAR (293 firms)															
Coefficient	-.294	.068	.175	.138	.437	-.493	.301	-.409	.377	1.789	2.543	-.012	.165	70.7%	
t-statistic	-1.00	.27	.70	.37	1.82	-1.59	1.25	-1.19	2.01	1.76	4.75	-.16	.97	1.01	
Significance					(.070)[b]				(.023)	(.040)	(.000)				
TKY (256 firms)															
Coefficient	-.266	.122	-.355	.714	-3.141	-.622	.012	-.300	—	-.686	41.256	.289	1.807	89.4%	
t-statistic	-.59	.29	-.76	1.60	-.37	-1.05	.03	-.51	—	-.59	4.82	1.41	.30	1.01	
Significance											(.000)	(.080)			

TABLE 7-6
Logit Test of Hypothesis 2 for 1987 Sample[a]

	Industries								LOC	EXP	CAP	DLR H1	DLR H2	% Pred. Q-Indx
	Oil & Gas	Food & Bev	Chem	Drugs & Pharm	Metals	Mach	Elec & Elctrm	Auto & Aero	+	+	+			
FRA (284 firms)														
Coefficient	-.185	.006	.206	-.411	.246	-.337	.006	-.150	-.369	1.785	2.087	-.128	.406	67.5%
t-statistic	-.73	.03	.82	-1.08	1.03	-1.39	.02	-.48	-2.11	2.55	2.85	-3.23	.73	1.12
Significance									(.018)	(.006)	(.002)	(.001)		

[a] p-values are for one–tailed tests unless otherwise indicated.

LOC   Location dummy variable = 1 if firm in same geographic region as exchange, zero otherwise. For the Tokyo Exchange (TKY), LOC = 0.

EXP   Exports of the firm's domicile industry to a given exchange country as a proportion of the domicile industry's total exports to the eight exchange countries.

CAP   Firm's equity capital as a proportion of the total equity capital of its domestic exchange.

DLR   Financial disclosure level rank of firm's domicile. A higher rank means a higher disclosure level.

% Pred   Percent correct predictions. Predicted value <.5 classified as 0, ≥.5 as 1.

Q-Indx   Quality of prediction index relative to naive prediction that all firms belong to largest classification. Q–Indx = % Pred / [(Max(listers, nonlisters) / sample size) x 100]. Q–Indx > 1 indicates that prediction model outperforms naive prediction.

[b] Two–tailed probability.

1. 1987 Sample — 302 firms that had foreign listings as of year-end 1987,
2. Previous Listers — 191 firms in the 1987 sample that also had foreign listings in 1981,[38] and
3. New Listers — 111 firms in the 1987 sample that did not have foreign listings in 1981.

As suggested above, new foreign listings by the Previous Listers may have been influenced by disclosures prepared for the prior listings. Because the New Listers subset reveals exchange choices by firms making initial foreign listings, these choices would be less influenced by prior listings.

Panel A of Table 7–7 presents by domicile and exchange the locations of 275 foreign stock exchange listings made between 1981 and 1987 by the 1987 sample. To control for possible differences across domiciles in the frequency of listings, Panel B presents the percentages of new listings on given exchanges by firms from each domicile. Hypothesis 1 suggests that across each domicile row, the percentages of new listings should be concentrated on exchanges with lower disclosure level ranks (DLRs). Because Table 7–7 lists exchanges in descending DLR order, this means larger percentages of new listings towards the right ends of domicile rows. Panel B appears to support this pattern. To provide a formal statistical test, a randomization procedure is employed (Noreen, 1989).

The inverse relation suggested by Hypothesis 1 between listing probability and exchange DLR can be captured by a statistic equal to the sum across domiciles of differences between a domicile's disclosure level and that of an exchange, multiplied by the proportion of listings made on that exchange by firms from the domicile. Thus, the difference between the DLR of the U.S. (8) and that of TOR (7) multiplied by .079 is added to the difference between the DLR of the U.S. (8) and that of LDN (6) multiplied by .262, and so on, which sums to 7.092. Formally, this statistic can be expressed as:

$$\text{STAT1} = \sum_{ij} [(\text{DLR}_i - \text{DLR}_j) (L_{ij} / \sum_k L_{ik})]$$

where L_{ij} is the number of foreign listings by firms in domicile i on foreign exchange j in panel A of Table 7–7 (notice that $L_{ij} = 0$ when $i = j$). The larger the value of STAT1, the more consistent are the data with Hypothesis 1. Randomization allows statistical significance to be determined by comparing the original value of STAT1 with values obtained

TABLE 7-7
Foreign Listings between 1981 and 1987 by Firms with Foreign Listings in 1987[a]

Domicile	Stock Exchange								Total New Foreign Listings	Firms in Sample	Average New Listings per Firm
	NYSE/ AMEX	TOR	LDN	AMS	PAR	TKY	FRA	ZUR			
Panel A: Numbers of New Listings											
United States	–	10	33	20	9	19	12	23	126	158	.80
Canada	14	–	10	5	6	1	2	2	40	45	.90
United Kingdom	3	2	–	3	4	3	6	4	25	10	2.50
Netherlands	2	0	2	–	1	0	3	3	11	11	1.00
France	0	1	2	0	–	0	3	1	7	9	.78
Japan	6	0	3	13	10	–	16	5	53	46	1.15
Germany	0	0	1	1	1	0	–	9	12	18	.67
Switzerland	0	0	0	0	0	0	1	–	1	5	.20
Totals	25	13	51	42	31	23	43	47	275	302	.91
Panel B: Percentages of New Listings by Domicile											
United States	–	7.9	26.2	15.9	7.1	15.1	9.5	18.3	100.0		
Canada	35.0	–	25.0	12.5	15.0	2.5	5.0	5.0	100.0		
United Kingdom	12.0	8.0	–	12.0	16.0	12.0	24.0	16.0	100.0		
Netherlands	18.2	0.0	18.2	–	9.1	0.0	27.3	27.3	100.0		
France	0.0	0.0	28.6	0.0	–	0.0	42.8	14.3	100.0		
Japan	11.3	14.3	5.7	24.5	18.9	0.0	30.2	9.4	100.0		
Germany	0.0	0.0	8.3	8.3	8.3	0.0	–	75.0	100.0		
Switzerland	0.0	0.0	0.0	0.0	0.0	0.0	100.0	–	100.0		

[a] Exchanges in order of disclosure levels (Table 7–3). Stock Exchange Codes: AMEX American, AMS Amsterdam, FRA Frankfurt, LDN London, NYSE New York, PAR Paris, TKY Tokyo, TOR Toronto, ZUR Zurich.

when DLRs are assigned to exchanges randomly (without replacement). Based on 1,000 random shufflings of DLR, the statistical significance of the original value of 7.092 is $p < .060$, thus lending support to Hypothesis 1.[39]

A randomization test for Hypothesis 2 is obtained by modifying slightly the statistic described above. Because Hypothesis 2 suggests that foreign listing decisions will be unaffected by disclosure levels for firms whose domestic levels exceeds that of a given exchange, the difference in disclosure levels is set to a constant (= 1) whenever $DLR_i > DLR_j$. Thus,

$$STAT2 = \sum_j [(DLR_i - DLR_j) (L_{ij} / \sum_k L_{ik})],$$

with $(DLR_i - DLR_j) = 1$ for $DLR_i > DLR_j$. Once again, data more consistent with Hypothesis 2 will provide a larger value for this statistic. Based on the data in Panel A of Table 7–7, STAT2 equals –0.758. Based on 1,000 random shufflings of DLR, the statistical significance of this original value is $p < .012$. Thus, the data in Table 7–7 also lend support to Hypothesis 2.[40]

Table 7–8 presents by domicile and exchange the 65 new foreign listings made between 1981 and 1987 by the subset of 191 previous listers. The data once again support both hypotheses. STAT1 based on panel A of Table 7–8 equals 8.014, with a randomization $p < .003$. STAT2 for panel A of table 8 is -2.141, with a randomization $p < .046$.

Table 7–9 presents by domicile and exchange the 210 foreign listings made by the subset of 111 firms listing for the first time between 1981 and 1987 on one of the nine exchanges examined. The pattern of listings in table 9 is also supportive of both hypotheses, with STAT1 equal to 7.474 ($p < .077$) and STAT2 equal to 0.056 ($p < .014$).

Overall, the listings in Tables 7–7, 7–8, and 7–9 suggest that foreign exchange listing decisions are being influenced by financial disclosure levels. Because these data focus on new listings between 1981 and 1987, they are more likely to reflect the disclosure rankings provided by the survey respondents, rather than rankings that may have been applicable in prior periods. Examining separately the subset of first-time foreign listers (Table 7–9) reduces the influence of prior listings on current listing decisions. That the randomization tests for Tables 7–7, 7–8, and 7–9 support Hypothesis 2 as well as Hypothesis 1 lends additional credence to a relation between disclosure levels and foreign stock exchange listing

TABLE 7-8
Foreign Listings between 1981 and 1987 by Firms with Foreign Listings in Both 1981 and 1987[a]

Domicile	Stock Exchange								Total New Foreign Listings	Firms in Sample	Average New Listings per Firm
	NYSE/ AMEX	TOR	LDN	AMS	PAR	TKY	FRA	ZUR			
Panel A: Numbers of New Listings											
United States	–	0	1	1	4	15	3	4	28	104	.27
Canada	0	–	0	1	0	1	2	0	4	24	.17
United Kingdom	0	2	–	1	2	3	2	3	13	5	2.60
Netherlands	1	0	0	–	0	0	1	0	2	9	.22
France	0	1	1	0	–	0	0	0	2	6	.33
Japan	2	0	1	2	3	–	3	1	12	27	.44
Germany	0	0	0	1	0	0	–	3	4	12	.33
Switzerland	0	0	0	0	0	0	0	–	0	4	.00
Totals	3	3	3	6	9	19	11	11	65	191	.34
Panel B: Percentages of New Listings by Domicile											
United States	–	0.0	3.6	3.6	14.3	53.6	10.6	14.3	100.0		
Canada	0.0	–	0.0	25.0	0.0	25.0	50.0	0.0	100.0		
United Kingdom	0.0	15.4	–	7.6	15.4	23.1	15.4	23.1	100.0		
Netherlands	50.0	0.0	0.0	–	0.0	0.0	50.0	0.0	100.0		
France	0.0	50.0	50.0	0.0	–	0.0	0.0	0.0	100.0		
Japan	16.7	0.0	8.3	16.7	25.0	–	25.0	8.3	100.0		
Germany	0.0	0.0	0.0	25.0	0.0	0.0	–	75.0	100.0		
Switzerland	0.0	0.0	0.0	0.0	0.0	0.0	0.0	–	100.0		

[a] Exchanges in order of disclosure levels (Table 7-3). Stock Exchange Codes: AMEX American, AMS Amsterdam, FRA Frankfurt, LDN London, NYSE New York, PAR Paris, TKY Tokyo, TOR Toronto, ZUR Zurich.

TABLE 7-9
Foreign Listings between 1981 and 1987 by Firms with Foreign Listings in 1987 but Not in 1981ᵃ

Domicile	Stock Exchange								Total New Foreign Listings	Firms in Sample	Average New Listings per Firm
	NYSE/ AMEX	TOR	LDN	AMS	PAR	TKY	FRA	ZUR			
Panel A: Numbers of New Listings											
United States	–	10	32	19	5	4	9	19	98	54	1.82
Canada	14	–	10	4	6	0	0	2	36	21	1.71
United Kingsom	3	0	–	2	2	0	4	1	12	5	2.40
Netherlands	1	0	2	–	1	0	2	3	9	2	4.50
France	0	0	1	0	–	0	3	1	5	3	1.67
Japan	4	0	2	11	7	–	13	4	41	19	2.16
Germany	0	0	1	0	1	0	–	6	8	6	1.33
Switzerland	0	0	0	0	0	0	1	–	1	1	1.00
Totals	22	10	48	36	22	4	32	36	210	111	1.89
Panel B: Percentages of New Listings by Domicile											
United States	–	10.2	32.6	19.4	5.1	4.1	9.2	19.4	100.0		
Canada	38.9	–	27.8	11.1	16.7	0.0	0.0	5.5	100.0		
United Kingdom	25.0	0.0	–	16.7	16.7	0.0	33.3	8.3	100.0		
Netherlands	11.1	0.0	22.2	–	11.1	0.0	22.2	33.4	100.0		
France	0.0	0.0	20.0	0.0	–	0.0	60.0	20.0	100.0		
Japan	9.8	0.0	4.9	26.8	17.1	–	31.7	9.7	100.0		
Germany	0.0	0.0	12.5	0.0	12.5	0.0	–	75.0	100.0		
Switzerland	0.0	0.0	0.0	0.0	0.0	0.0	100.0	–	100.0		

ᵃ Exchanges in order of disclosure levels (Table 7–3). Stock Exchange Codes: AMEX American, AMS Amsterdam, FRA Frankfurt, LDN London, NYSE New York, PAR Paris, TKY Tokyo, TOR Toronto, ZUR Zurich.

decisions since tests of Hypothesis 2 rely solely on listings by firms whose disclosure levels are below that of an exchange.

SUMMARY

With firms increasingly listing their shares on foreign stock exchanges, regulatory authorities worldwide are grappling with the question of whether to loosen financial reporting requirements for foreign firms. The goal of protecting domestic investors from misleading financial disclosures is being weighed against charges that imposing domestic requirements on foreign firms denies domestic investors access to desirable investment opportunities and places domestic stock exchanges at a competitive disadvantage.

Nowhere is this debate more heated than in the United States. Under headlines reading "NYSE's New Chief Seeks to Make Big Board More International"[41] and "Big Board Facing Serious Erosion as Market for Stocks, Chief Warns,"[42] incoming NYSE Chairman William Donaldson has vowed to "tackle the major issue that has impeded the trading of large numbers of foreign stocks on the Big Board—the fact that most big foreign corporations don't meet stringent U.S. financial disclosure and accounting rules."[43] In May 1991, SEC Chairman Richard Breeden rejected a NYSE proposal to relax reporting requirements for foreign firms, arguing that without adequate protection, U.S. investors "might select a foreign company's stock [...] only to discover later that differences in accounting or auditing standards made the foreign stock look better." More lenient standards for foreign firms, he also argued, "would seriously disadvantage U.S. firms in their home market."[44] Even more recently, SEC resistance appears to have softened. Admitting "a growing worry [...] that we drove companies and investors to settle outside the U.S.,"[45] the SEC in June 1991 proposed new rules exempting certain foreign rights offerings from SEC disclosure and reporting requirements and indicated that more changes may be imminent.[46]

This study provides empirical evidence on an important question in this debate: Whether firms' choices among alternative foreign stock exchange listings are influenced by financial disclosure requirements. Two possible relations were considered, one suggesting that the probability that a firm will list on a given foreign exchange is inversely related to the exchange's disclosure level, and the other suggesting that this relation applies only when a firm's disclosure level is lower than that of an exchange.

Two sets of tests were conducted. The first examined possible determinants of foreign listings as of year-end 1987. The second examined whether financial disclosure levels could account for changes in listings between 1981 and 1987. The sample was limited to firms that have actually made exchange choices; all are internationally traded with at least one foreign listing on one of nine major stock exchanges as of year-end 1987. Financial disclosure levels were obtained from survey responses provided by 142 experts actively involved in the foreign listing process.

Cross-sectional univariate and multivariate tests based on foreign exchange listings at year-end 1987 lend support to the hypothesis that exchange choices have been influenced by financial disclosure levels (Hypothesis 1). However, the cross-sectional evidence does not support strongly the hypothesis that this effect operates only for firms with disclosure levels lower than that of a given foreign exchange (Hypothesis 2).

Changes in listings between 1981 and 1987 provide potentially more powerful tests since these incremental listing decisions are more likely to have been influenced by the cross-country differences in disclosure levels reflected in the survey disclosure index. Randomization tests based on all listings changes between 1981 and 1987 support both Hypotheses 1 and 2. Because Hypothesis 2 can be viewed as a refinement of Hypothesis 1 that focuses solely on listings by firms with disclosures levels lower than that of an exchange, it provides a more severe test of associations between disclosure levels and listing decisions. Hypotheses 1 and 2 also are supported for two mutually exclusive subsets of firms with new foreign listings between 1981 and 1987: (i) firms that had previously listed on one of the eight exchanges examined as of year-end 1981, and (ii) firms that had not listed previously. Listings for this latter sample would not have been influenced by preexisting listings (except possibly by listings on exchanges not examined). Overall, these findings lend support to the view expressed by regulators and stock exchange officials that financial disclosure levels influence foreign stock exchange listing decisions.

NOTES

1. U.S. Government Accounting Office, *International Finance: Regulation of International Securities Markets*. Washington D.C.: GAO, 1989, pp. 9–10.
2. M.R. Sesit, Foreign investing makes a comeback. *Wall Street Journal*, September 1, 1989, pp. C1, C11.
3. M.R. Sesit and B. Donnelly, Global stock trading develops own haves, have-nots. *Wall Street Journal*, May 8, 1991, pp. C1, C8.

4. The Corporate List. *Euromoney*, May 1988, pp. 127–143.
5. John Hennessy, Chairman of Credit Suisse First Boston Limited, *Forbes*, March 9, 1987, p. 64.
6. For example, in recent years financial disclosure requirements for foreign firms have been the subject of regulatory debate in Australia, Canada, Italy, Japan, the United Kingdom, and the United States (see below).
7. Torres, C., "NYSE's New Chief Seeks to Make Big Board More International," *Wall Street Journal*, December 21, 1990; Torres, C., "Big Board Facing Serious Erosion as Market for Stocks, Chief Warns," *Wall Street Journal*, March 13, 1991; Power, W. and K. G. Salwen, "Big Board's Donaldson Says SEC Rules Could Cost Exchange Its Global Standing," *Wall Street Journal*, December 31, 1991, p. C1; Siconolfi, C. and K. G. Salwen, "Big Board, SEC Fight Over Foreign Stocks," *Wall Street Journal*, May 13, 1992, p. C1; Jarrell, G., "SEC Crimps Big Board's Future," *Wall Street Journal*, June 19, 1992, p. A10.
8. In April 1987, the Tokyo Stock Exchange surpassed the New York Stock Exchange in size as measured by the total capitalization of listed equity securities ($2.688 versus $2.672 trillion) (*Wall Street Journal*, April 13, 1987). With a recent and dramatic decline in the market values of Japanese equities, the Tokyo Stock Exchange has dropped below the New York Stock Exchange in total capitalization.
9. The foreign listings of Japanese firms are particularly striking. By year-end 1987, only eight Japanese firms were listed in New York and only nine were listed in London. However, 58 were listed in Frankfurt, 30 in Amsterdam, and 18 in Paris. Japanese firms often cite U.S. and U.K. disclosure requirements as being stringent.
10. For example, Lafferty and Cairns (1980) assigned weights as follows:

Financial statements	65%
Non-financial statement data	25%
Timeliness	10%
Total	100%

For the financial statement component, fifteen points each were available for consolidation, disclosure of acceptable accounting policies, segmental data and inflation accounting data. A further five points were available if the financial statements were audited. In the nonfinancial component, ten points were available for employment data, and five points each were available for value added statements, statements about future prospects and other items deemed useful by the authors.
11. Barrett (1976), Choi (1973a; 1973b) and Cairns, Lafferty, and Mantle (1984) have characterized these differences in disclosure requirements as reflecting the "level of development or sophistication" of a capital market. An alternate characterization is that more extensive financial disclosure requirements reduce the moral hazard problems facing individual investors, thereby making widespread public ownership of securities possible. In other words, more extensive disclosure requirements may be the price paid for greater "democratization" of securities markets.
12. In policy debates, a distinction has been drawn between "harmonization" and "standardization." Harmonization implies a reconciliation of different points of view and permits different standards in individual countries so long as there is no logical

conflict. Standardization would dictate a uniform standard in all countries.

13. These include the International Accounting Standards Committee (IASC), International Federation of Accountants (IFAC), United Nations (UN), European Community (EC), Union Europeenne des Expertes Comptables Economiques et Financiers (UEC), Federation des Experts Comptables Europeens (FEE), African Accounting Council (AAC), ASEAN Federation of Accountants (AFA), Asociacion Interamericana de Contabilidad (AIC), Confederation of Asian and Pacific Accountants (CAPA), and the Nordic Federation of Accountants (NFA).

14. For a historical perspective on these attempts, see Choi and Mueller (1984) and Meek and Saudagaran (1990). Earlier, some hoped that the increasing internationalization of capital markets would lead to increasing harmonization of financial disclosures. As the title of an article in the *Wall Street Journal* suggested "Where boards and governments have failed, the market could internationalize accounting" (May 8, 1985), p. 38. However, the current sentiment is that the enforcement power of the national regulatory agencies is required in order to achieve global harmonization. There are signs that these agencies may be willing to provide the necessary support (Moulin and Solomon 1989).

15. See for example, Stapleton and Subrahmanyam (1977), Stonehill and Dullum (1982), Adler and Dumas (1983), Howe and Kelm (1987), Saudagaran (1988), and Eiteman and Stonehill (1989).

16. See, for example, Leach, R., "Who Lists Abroad—and Why," *Euromoney*, October 1973; McNish, J., "Why Toronto-Dominion Went to London," *Euromoney*, May 1984; Lim, Q.P., "Why Wall Street Was Shunned," *Euromoney*, May 1984; Sesit, M. R., "More U.S. Concerns Seek to be Listed Overseas," *Wall Street Journal*, June 10, 1985; Cox, M., "American Express Plans to List, Issue Shares in Tokyo," *Wall Street Journal*, July 16, 1985; Browning, E.S., "Tokyo Exchange: To Join or Not to Join?," *Wall Street Journal*, September 27, 1985; Freeman, A., "Montreal Exchange Plans Bid to Attract U.S. Investors by Listing Overseas Stocks," *Wall Street Journal*, September 30, 1985; Sesit M.R. and A. Monroe, "Small U.S. Companies Go Public in London," *Wall Street Journal*, October 28, 1985; Tanzer, A., "Listing for Success," *Forbes*, December 15, 1986; Freund, W. C., "Stock Exchange Rivalry Yields Dividends," *Wall Street Journal*, October 5, 1987; Winkler, M., "Rule on Private Placements Seen Altering Market," *Wall Street Journal*, January 19, 1989; Newman, A., "New Electronic Bulletin Board Promises to Make Trading Foreign Stocks Easier," *Wall Street Journal*, June 11, 1990; Torres, C., "NYSE's New Chief Seeks to Make Big Board More International," *Wall Street Journal*, December 21, 1990; Torres, C., "Big Board Facing Serious Erosion as Market for Stocks, Chief Warns," *Wall Street Journal*, March 13, 1991; Fuhrman, P., "Esperanto for Accountants," *Forbes*, March 18, 1991; Tanzer, A., "How Apple Stormed Japan," *Forbes*, May 27, 1991; Block, S., "SEC Proposal Aids Investors in Foreign Issues," *Wall Street Journal*, June 5, 1991; Labaton, S., "U.S. May Ease Rules Affecting Foreign Stocks," *New York Times*, June 5, 1991.

17. The following individuals, all of whom are actively involved in foreign stock listings, were interviewed by the first author: Edmund Lukas, V. P. International Business Development, New York Stock Exchange; Bernard H. Maas, Consultant, American Stock Exchange; Robert G. Cook, Director, Original Listings, Toronto Stock Ex-

change; Mark J. Lerner, V.P. Investment Banking Division, Merrill Lynch Capital Markets; Tetsuo Kadowaki, V.P. Investment Banking, Nomura Securities International; Martin J. Siegel, V.P.-Manager International Arbitrage Department, Salomon Brothers; Albert K. Woo, Sr. V.P. and Controller of International Operations, Shearson Lehman Brothers; Richard Watkins, Managing Director, Phillips & Drew International; Stephen A. Grant, Partner, Sullivan & Cromwell; Morton B. Solomon, Partner, KPMG Peat Marwick; Robert M. Tarola, Partner, Price Waterhouse; Richard P. Miller, Manager, Ernst & Whinney; Peter Aslet, U.S. Investor Relations Manager, Imperial Chemical Industries; Yoichi Aoki, Manager, Financial Public Relations Office, American Honda Motor Co.; Yuji Ikeo, Manager, New York Financial Liaison Office, Kubota; Yukio Ozawa, Manager, Corporate Financial Communications, Sony.

18. If a foreign firm's financial statements are prepared in compliance with any other body of accounting rules then the firm is required to discuss the nature of the differences from U.S. GAAP. It is also required to quantify material variations and to reconcile the income statement with the earnings as they would appear under U.S. GAAP.

19. John Hennessy, *op cit.*

20. For example, in recent negotiations regarding the standardization of international accounting standards, Gerhard Liener, Chief Financial Officer of Daimler-Benz, was quoted as saying that "it is inconceivable for us to accept the sort of quarterly reporting rules that lead to companies like General Motors showing a profit of $700 million in the first quarter of 1990 and a loss of $2 billion in the third quarter." The article continues, "the Germans are insisting that they will not provide profit figures more than twice a year." P. Fuhrman, "Esperanto for Accountants," *Forbes*, March 18, 1991, p. 72.

21. The study concluded that, for the time being, Japanese firms raising capital in the U.S. would be held to virtually the same reporting and regulatory requirements as U.S.-domiciled firms. Sullivan and Cromwell, Attorneys at Law, "Report to the Keidanren on segment reporting by Japanese companies," New York, June 7, 1985.

22. The following discussion highlights main features of recent changes in U.S. disclosure policy for foreign private issuers. For a more detailed discussion see Saudagaran (1991).

23. SEC commissioner Barbara Thomas characterized IDS as "the most significant change in foreign issuer registration requirements since the original passage of the Securities Act in 1933" (Thomas 1983, p. 130). Under IDS, certain foreign private issuers can satisfy the registration requirements of the Securities Act of 1933 (Securities Act) by attaching supplements (Forms F-1, F-2 or F-3) to the Form 20-F already filed with the SEC in accordance with the Securities Exchange Act of 1934 (Exchange Act). These issuers must file a Form 20-F, under the Exchange Act, if they have previously offered securities in the U.S., have securities listed on a U.S. exchange, or have more than 500 shareholders and more than $5 million in total assets. The information to be provided on the supplementary forms varies depending on the nature of the securities being registered, the market value of the stock being held by non-affiliates ("float") and the length of time that the company has been an SEC registrant.

24. John Hennessy, *op cit.*

25. Rule 144A defines qualified institutional buyers as institutions that own and invest on a discretionary basis at least $100 million in securities of issuers that are not affiliated with that qualified institutional buyer. Securities Act of 1933 Release No. 6862.
26. S. Hanks, SEC ruling creates a new market, *Wall Street Journal*, May 16, 1990, p. A20.
27. In February 1985, the SEC issued a concept release (Securities Act of 1933 Release No. 6568) soliciting public comment on two approaches—reciprocal and common prospectus, aimed at facilitating multinational securities offerings by non-governmental issuers. The intent was to harmonize disclosure and distribution practices among the United States, Canada and the United Kingdom. The reciprocal approach would require agreement that a prospectus of an issuer in its own domicile would be accepted *as is* for offerings in the other participating countries, providing that certain minimum requirements were met. Under the common prospectus approach, agreement would be required on common disclosure standards for a prospectus that could be used in all the participating countries. Under both approaches, a foreign issuer would be subject to the liability provisions of the U.S. securities laws applicable to domestic issuers for false or misleading statements contained in a prospectus. The 1989 multijurisdictional system was proposed in Securities Act of 1933 Release Nos. 6841 and 6879.
28. As relates to investment grade debt and preferred stock, a "substantial issuer" is defined as one that has a market value of at least Canadian $180 million.
29. France announces steps to deregulate financial markets, *Wall Street Journal*, April 2, 1985, p. 32; London Stock Exchange members pass plans to deregulate equities trading, *Wall Street Journal*, June 5, 1985, p. 35.
30. As suggested above, higher disclosure levels mean more extensive financial disclosures due to either regulatory or reporting requirements or in response to competitive market expectations.
31. An examination of the firms listed on the nine stock exchanges at the end of 1989 did not reveal any major changes in exchange listings which would affect the generalizability of the results. This is not surprising. A listing on a foreign stock exchange is a major step that can take years of preparation. For this reason, firms are unlikely to delist in the short term except in cases of mergers and acquisitions.
32. The overall disclosure ranking provided by this survey is very similar to a disclosure ranking used in Biddle and Saudagaran (1989), which was based on measures developed by Lafferty and Cairns (1980), Choi and Bavishi (1982), Cairns, Lafferty, and Mantle (1984). The only difference is that Canada's rank is 7 rather than 5.
33. Firms typically do not disclose a country-by-country breakdown of revenues. In the United States, under SFAS 14, foreign revenue has to be reported if revenue generated by foreign operations from sales to unaffiliated customers is 10 percent or more of consolidated revenue. However, management has discretion as to the level of aggregation in reporting geographical segments within the framework of the 10 percent rule. Thus information on foreign revenues can be reported as a single segment distinct from domestic revenues or as a number of segments disaggregated by country, or groups of countries or even by continents. Other countries have even less specific rules on segment disclosure.
34. Biddle and Saudagaran (1989) examined the cross-section of listings as of year-end 1981.

35. Fisher exact tests are more appropriate than Chi-squared tests when the number of observations in a row or column becomes very small (Siegel 1956, chapter 6).

36. A possible explanation is that the LOC variable classifies the United Kingdom with other European countries. However, cultural links and commonalities of language and business practices may cause U.K. firms to view markets in the United States and Canada as more readily accessible. A recent SEC release multinational securities offerings grouped the United States, Canada, and the United Kingdom together when discussing harmonization, reciprocity arrangements, and listing requirements (SEC Release No. 33-6568; File No. S7-9-85, March 1985).

37. These results are contained in an addendum available on request from the authors.

38. Sixteen firms in the 1981 sample do not appear in the 1987 sample. All are U.S. firms that delisted on foreign exchanges due to mergers and acquisitions. They are: American Motors, Baker International, Beatrice Foods, Burroughs, Crown-Zellerbach, Esmark, Freuhauf, General Foods, Getty Oil, Gulf Oil, Rexnord, Signal, Standard Oil of California, Standard Oil of Ohio, Sperry Rand, and Uniroyal. These firms account for a loss of 57 foreign listings.

39. As it turns out, there are 8! or 40,320 possible permutations of the ranks one through eight. In other words, the disclosure level ranking of exchange countries provided by the experts (Table 7–3) is only one of 40,320 possible rankings. The randomization tests assess whether the score provided by the expert ranking yields a statistic value that is unusual compared to scores obtained from other possible rankings.

40. An alternate statistic for testing Hypothesis 1 that takes into account the expected number of listings by firms from given domicile on a given exchange is:

$$\text{STAT1A} = \sum_{ij} [(\text{DLR}_i - \text{DLR}_j) (((L_{ij} - E(L_{ij}))/ E(L_{ij}))]$$

where $E(L_{ij}) = [(\sum_k L_{ik})(\sum_k L_{kj})/(\sum_{km} L_{km} - \sum_k L_{jk})]$. An analogous statistic for testing Hypothesis 2, STAT2A, restricts $(\text{DLR}_i - \text{DLR}_j)$ to be 1 when $\text{DLR}_i > \text{DLR}_j$. STAT1A based on the data in panel A of Table 7–7 is 33.539. From 1,000 random shufflings of DLR, this original value has a statistical significance level of $p = .090$, supportive of Hypothesis 1. STAT2A based on the data in panel A of Table 7–7 is 40.978. From 1,000 random shufflings of DLR, this original value has a statistical significance level of $p = .023$, supportive of Hypothesis 2.

41. *Wall Street Journal*, December 21, 1990, p. C5.

42. *Wall Street Journal*, March 13, 1991, p. C13.

43. A similar concern has been expressed by FASB Chairman Dennis Beresford: "It is widely reported that many foreign companies are reluctant to offer their securities in U.S. public markets or list them on U.S. exchanges because they are unwilling to comply with the voluminous and detailed U.S. accounting and disclosure requirements or submit to the SEC's jurisdiction. This is said to put the U.S. exchanges and securities industry at a competitive disadvantage." (Beresford, 1990).

44. K. Salwen, "Breeden Rejects Big Board Plan to Relax Listing Standards for Foreign Concerns," *Wall Street Journal*, May 3, 1991, p. C20.

45. Fuhrman, P., *op cit.*

46. Block, S., "SEC Proposal Aids Investors in Foreign Issues," *Wall Street Journal*, June 5, 1991, p. C12; Labaton, S., "U.S. May Ease Rules Affecting Foreign Stocks," *New York Times*, June 5, 1991, p. A1.

REFERENCES

Adler, M., and B. Dumas. (1983). "International Portfolio Choice and Corporate Finance: A Synthesis." *Journal of Finance*. June, pp. 925–84.

American Accounting Association. (1977). "Report of Committee on International Accounting Operations and Education 1975–76." *Accounting Review*. Supplement, pp. 343–61.

Balakrishnan, R., T. S. Harris, and P. K. Sen. (1990). "The Predictive Ability of Geographical Segment Disclosures." *Journal of Accounting Research*. Autumn, pp. 305–25.

Barrett, E. M. (1976). "Financial Reporting Practices: Disclosure and Comprehensiveness in an International Setting." *Journal of Accounting Research*. Spring, pp. 10–26.

Beresford, D. (1990). "Financial Reporting, Comparability and Competition." Speech presented at the University of Washington and the University of California in Berkeley, October 18–19.

Biddle, G. C., and S. M. Saudagaran. (1989). "The Effects of Financial Disclosure Levels on Firms' Choices Among Alternative Foreign Stock Exchanges." *Journal of International Financial Management and Accounting*. Spring, pp. 55–87.

Cairns, D., M. Lafferty, and P. Mantle. (1984). *Survey of Accounts and Accountants 1983–84*. London: Lafferty Publications.

Choi, F. D. S. (1973a). "Financial Disclosure in Relation to a Firm's Capital Costs." *Accounting and Business Research*. Autumn, pp. 282–92.

Choi, F. D. S. (1973b). "Financial Disclosure and Entry to the European Capital Market." *Journal of Accounting Research*. Autumn, pp. 159–75.

Choi, F. D. S., and V. B. Bavishi. (1982). "Diversity in Multinational Accounting." *Financial Executive*. August, pp. 45–49.

Choi, F. D. S., and R. M. Levich. (1990). *The Capital Market Effects of International Accounting Diversity*. Chicago, IL: Dow Jones-Irwin.

Choi, F. D. S., and G. G. Mueller. (1984). *International Accounting*. Englewood Cliffs, NJ: Prentice-Hall.

Choi, F. D. S., and A. I. Stonehill. (1982). "Foreign Access to U.S. Securities Markets: The Theory, Myth and Reality of Regulatory Barriers." *Investment Analyst*. July, pp. 17–26.

Daley, L. A., and G. G. Mueller. (1982). "Accounting in the Arena of World Politics: Crosscurrents of International Standard Setting Activities." *Journal of Accountancy*. February, pp. 40–53.

Eiteman, D. K., and A. I. Stonehill. (1989). *Multinational Business Finance*. Reading, MA: Addison-Wesley.

Evans, T. G., and M. E. Taylor. (1982). "Bottom Line Compliance with the IASC: A Comparative Review." *International Journal of Accounting, Education and Research*. Fall, pp. 115–28.

Fantl, I. L. (1971). "The Case Against International Uniformity." *Management Accounting*. May, pp. 13–16.

Frank, W. G. (1979). "An Empirical Analysis of International Accounting Principles." *Journal of Accounting Research*. Autumn, pp. 593–605.

Goodrich, P. S. (1986). "Cross-national Financial Linkages: An Empirical Political Analysis." *British Accounting Review*. Autumn, pp. 42–60.

Gray, S. J. (1980). "The Impact of International Accounting Differences from a Security-Analysis Perspective: Some European evidence." *Journal of Accounting Research*. Spring, pp. 64–76.

Gray, S. J. (1988). "Towards a Theory of Cultural Influence on the Development of Accounting Systems Internationally." *Abacus*. March, pp. 1–15.

Gray, S. J., L.B. McSweeney, and J. C. Shaw. (1984). *Information Disclosure and the Multinational Corporation*. New York: Wiley.

Howe, J. S., and K. Kelm. (1987). "The Stock Price Impacts of Overseas Listings." *Financial Management*. Autumn, pp. 51–56.

Kraayenhof, J. (1960). "International Challenges for Accounting." *Journal of Accountancy*. January, pp. 34–38.

Lafferty, M., and D. Cairns. (1980). *Financial Times Survey of Annual Reports 1980*. London: Financial Times Business Information.

Mason, A. K. (1978). *The Development of International Financial Reporting Standards*. International Center for Research in Accounting, University of Lancaster.

McComb, D. (1979). "The International Harmonization of Accounting: A Cultural Dimension." *International Journal of Accounting, Education And Research*. Spring, pp. 1–16.

McMonnies, P. N. (1977). "EEC, UEC, ASC, IASC, IASG, AISG, ICCAP-IFAC, Old Uncle Tom Cobbleigh and All." *Accounting and Business Research*. Summer, pp. 162–67.

Meek, G. K., and S. Gray. (1989). "Globalization of Stock Markets and Foreign Listing Requirements: Voluntary Disclosures by Continental European Companies Listed on the London Stock Exchange." *Journal of International Business Studies*. Summer, pp. 315–36.

Meek, G. K., and S. M. Saudagaran. (1990). "A Survey of Research on Financial Reporting in a Transnational Context." *Journal of Accounting Literature*. pp. 145–82.

Moulin, D. J., and M. B. Solomon. (1989). "Practical Means of Supporting International Standards." *CPA Journal*. December, pp. 38–48.

Mueller, G. G. (1967). *International Accounting*. New York: Macmillan.

Nair, R. D., and W. G. Frank. (1980). "The Impact of Disclosure and Measurement Practices on International Accounting Classifications." *Accounting Review*. July, pp. 426–50.

Nobes, C. W. (1983). "A Judgmental International Classification of Financial

Reporting Practices." *Journal of Business Finance and Accounting.* Spring, pp. 1–19.

Nobes, C. W., and R. H. Parker. (1985). *Comparative International Accounting.* Oxford: Philip Allan.

Noreen, E. (1989). *Computer Intensive Methods for Testing Hypotheses.* New York: John Wiley & Sons.

Saudagaran, S. M. (1988). "An Empirical Study of Selected Factors Influencing the Decision to List on Foreign Stock Exchanges." *Journal of International Business Studies.* Spring, pp. 101–27.

Saudagaran, S. M. (1991). "The SEC and the Globalization of Financial Markets." *Research in Accounting Regulation.* pp. 31–53.

Securities and Exchange Commission. (1982). SEC Docket, 24, no. 15, March 16, pp. 1262–1349.

Securities and Exchange Commission. (1987). *Internationalization of the Securities Markets.* Report of the Staff of the U.S. Securities and Exchange Commission to the Senate Committee on Banking, Housing and Urban Affairs and the House Committee on Energy and Commerce, Washington DC.

Siegel, S. (1956). *Nonparametric Statistics for the Behavioral Sciences.* New York: McGraw-Hill.

Stamp, E. (1972). "Uniformity in International Accounting Standards." *Journal of Accountancy.* April, pp. 64–67.

Stapleton, R., and M. Subrahmanyam. (1977). "Market Imperfections, Capital Market Equilibrium and Corporation Finance." *Journal of Finance,* May, pp. 307–19.

Stilling, P., R. Norton, and L. Hopkins. (1984). *Financial Times World Accounting Survey.* London: Financial Times Business Information.

Stonehill, A. I., and K. Dullum. (1982). *Internationalizing the Cost of Capital.* New York: John Wiley and Sons.

Taylor, S. L. (1987). "International Accounting Standards: An Alternative Rationale." *Abacus.* September, pp. 157–71.

Thomas, B. S. (1983). "Increased Access to United States Capital Markets: A Brief Look at the SEC's New Integrated Disclosure Rules for Foreign Issuers." *Journal of Comparative Business and Capital Market Law.* June, pp. 129–35.

Tonkin, D. J. (1989). *World Survey of Published Accounts.* London: Lafferty Publications.

Turner, J. N. (1983). "International Harmonization: A Professional Goal." *Journal of Accountancy.* January, pp. 58–67.

Wyatt, A. (1989). "International Accounting Standards: A New Perspective." *Accounting Horizons.* September, pp. 105–08.

COMMENT

Sara Hanks

There is at present a heated debate on the question of whether the United States Securities and Exchange Commission (SEC) should accept financial statements prepared in accordance with non-U.S. generally accepted accounting principles (GAAP). Public offerings of securities or their listing on a U.S. stock exchange requires registration with the SEC, and the registration process involves the reconciliation to U.S. GAAP of financial statements prepared in accordance with foreign GAAP.

Many institutions (both U.S. and foreign) argue that by requiring reconciliation, the SEC is putting the U.S. capital markets at a competitive disadvantage, and encouraging capital-seekers to access non-U.S. markets, which deprives U.S. investors of investment opportunities. The SEC's response is that reconciliation is necessary for investor protection, so that investors may make reasonable comparisons of alternative investment opportunities.

There appears to be a general belief among regulators and academics that comparability of financial statements is a desirable end. Some commentators, however, hold that mandating harmonized or reconciled financial statements in the absence of harmonization of the underlying financial systems (for example, to take account of the special issues that arise when an authority requires the same financial statements for both reporting and taxation purposes) can be meaningless if not downright misleading. These papers do not address the policy question of whether reconciliation per se is good or necessary. They do, however, provide some very interesting information to those debating the question of requiring reconciliation.

I looked at both these papers not as an academic, but as a former regulator concerned with policy questions and a current advocate of the relaxation of some of the SEC's requirements. What I was looking for was whether these papers proved or cast any light on the contention being made that (1) U.S. stock exchanges are losing market share because of U.S. disclosure requirements, including reconciliation of financial statements, and (2) that those disclosure requirements (especially reconciliation) are not necessary in order for the SEC to perform its function of investor protection. The papers did indeed provide useful input on these questions, but in both cases I wish they had gone further.

DISCUSSION OF CHAPTER 7

Professors Saudargaran and Biddle pose two hypotheses, the first suggesting that decisions to list on foreign stock exchanges are influenced by financial disclosure levels, and the second suggesting that this effect should operate only for companies whose domestic disclosure levels are lower than those of a given foreign exchange. Examination of a cross-section of companies listed on more than one stock exchange supports the first hypothesis, while the second hypothesis is only supported by companies whose status changed (e.g., who became newly-listed) during the period studied.

The second hypothesis is the more important of the two from the point of view of policy makers. It is generally assumed that higher disclosure levels tend to deter companies from listing, but this common assumption needs to be backed up by factual findings.

The fact that the hypothesis proved accurate only when changes in listing status were examined is not troublesome; in fact it supports the hypothesis more strongly. This is because it controls for historical anomalies that might otherwise skew the results. It is not uncommon for regulatory authorities, when they improve or increase their disclosure requirements, to make those requirements only applicable on an ongoing basis: regulated entities meeting the old requirements may be permitted to continue to comply with those requirements for a specified or indefinite period and only entities newly joining the regulatory scheme are subjected to the new requirements. United States regulatory authorities often practice this form of "grandfathering" of regulated entities. Additionally, some companies may have made listing decisions a number of years ago, when not only may disclosure levels have changed in the meantime, but perhaps not all exchanges were available to those companies at the time the decision was made (for political reasons, for example, or because not all the exchanges existed then).

Thus, because Professors Saudargaran and Biddle rank exchanges' disclosure levels as if they were static (which gives rise to another problem, discussed below), looking at recent changes in listing status provides controls for historical changes in disclosure levels, and provides a more useful result.

Assigning exchanges static disclosure levels (in effect, assuming that for the whole period studied, the United Kingdom, for example, had more stringent requirements than the Netherlands) gives rise to another problem, although it is difficult to suggest how it might be controlled for. The 1980's were a period of rapid changes in the regulation of securities markets, especially among European Community countries. Many of these changes are identified and discussed in the paper. It may well be that some markets have "changed rank" during that period, and it might be a useful exercise, if any of the 142 respondents who ranked relative disclosure levels can recall comparative regulation a decade ago, to ask whether their assessment of comparative stringency in 1981 would have been any different. Incidentally, since it is now 1992, I would also ask specifically whether the persons ranking disclosure levels actually did so as of 1987, the end of the period studied, and not as of a later date.

Even if we focus on new listings, however, I think we lose a potentially very useful source of information (and base for policy-making) because of the composition of the study's sample. The study looks at cross-listings by companies from the major capital markets on exchanges within those major capital markets. The paper clearly states that the study focused on the listing decisions of large, internationally traded firms. This is regrettable on two counts. First, because including companies from lesser capital markets may well result in different findings. Second, because those different findings might provide helpful input on the debate over reconciliation.

Most commentators would agree that the eight major markets identified are the world's most stringent in terms of financial disclosure levels. Applying the findings that supported the paper's second hypothesis to the case of companies from less regulated markets, we would expect those companies to chose the major markets ranked lowest on the stringency-of-disclosure scale. This is not, however, the case. The third-ranked United Kingdom has a very large number of (non-major market) foreign listings. Additionally, (and this is based purely on anecdotal evidence), companies from less-regulated Latin American markets appear to be choosing to list on the most-stringent U.S. exchanges in preference to any of the European exchanges.

Possible reasons for this phenomenon could be prestige, geographic proximity, or the degree to which the less-regulated market's GAAP is more or less close to U.S. GAAP (U.S. GAAP because many of the other major markets permit reconciliation to IASC standards). Other possible causes might include the relationship of the company's domestic legal system to that of the market where it intends to list: for example, do companies from common law countries tend to prefer to list in other common law markets where they are more likely to understand liability for failures in disclosure compliance?

Clearly, there are a number of variables here, not all of which can be examined or controlled for, but in order for this research to become a useful policy-making tool (which it should), it should be expanded. The results of this study clearly show that the level of financial disclosure in the United States affects competitiveness of U.S. markets and the options open to U.S. investors.

DISCUSSION OF CHAPTER 6

Professors Bhusham and Lessard ask the very interesting and as yet inadequately explored question, "What do investors need in the way of financial disclosure?" As discussed above, the SEC is of the opinion that reconciliation is necessary in the interest of investor protection. This study finds that professional investors, while they regard reconciliation, like all forms of addition information as useful, they do not regard it as essential. Notably, few professional investors attempt to do their own reconciliation. The reason for this includes the fact that local financial statements and local valuation are still most important, for reasons that include accounting diversity, but are not limited to it. This latter point is relevant to the debate as to whether reconciliation of diverse systems is meaningless, and managers surveyed by this paper did (marginally) view reconciliation as being less important than more uniform disclosure or harmonization.

This paper is important to policy makers for two reasons. First, it attempts to distinguish what investors need as opposed to what they would like, and secondly, it focuses on the cost of reconciliation. Since reconciliation is not costless, a weighing of its benefits as against its costs is necessary. The authors reach the conclusion that the SEC's emphasis on reconciliation is not well-founded. Before we can agree with this statement, however, more work is necessary.

SOME QUESTIONS

If we establish, as do Professors Saudargaran and Biddle, that the U.S. markets are uncompetitive because of their levels of disclosure, then we need to ask what to do to rectify that situation. In order to challenge the SEC's insistence on reconciliation most effectively, we have to ask what investors regard as absolutely essential. Under what circumstances would investors feel unable to make an informed investment decision? What line items in financial statements do they regard as essential?

These questions may be partially answered by discovering what managers are doing with the information they do get. If they aren't reconciling financial statements themselves, how are they using foreign accounts? Are they mastering local accounting principles, and if so, which are important? Do they restate financial statements in any way at all?

An interesting area to explore further is whether, as prices become set by markets other than the issuer's home market, local financial statements become of less importance.

Another area for investigation is based on the fact that the SEC frequently focuses on the individual investor, and believes that it is for his sake that reconciliation is important. Although it is difficult to prove a negative, it would help the debate very much if we could firmly establish (as seems to be the case) that individual investors do not use financial statements (whether domestic or foreign, reconciled or unreconciled) and that, therefore, the SEC is focusing on the wrong constituency, while it should be concentrating on the professional managers that are the subject of this paper.

Both these papers involve research that will be very useful for U.S. and other policy-makers and I hope to see both areas of investigation explored further.

COMMENT

Richard M. Levich

The papers in this section are concerned with how accounting differences and securities market regulations affect capital market participants. My comments will be grouped under three headings. First, I will summarize the major findings of each paper and comment briefly on the methodology and significance of the results. Second, I will outline how accounting and regulatory factors establish economic forces that affect capital market participants. These forces entail both costs and benefits for participants, and participants have adopted various important coping mechanisms that temper these economic forces. In the third section, I consider a broader question—that is, whether economic forces are sufficient to achieve the goals of international capital market efficiency and integration, or whether policy changes are a necessary ingredient.

SUMMARY OF THE PAPERS

In Chapter 6, Ravi Bhusham and Donald Lessard focus on investment managers. In a survey of investment managers, the authors find that managers would prefer reduced international accounting diversity. However, Bhusham and Lessard conclude that reduced diversity is not critical for investment managers to reach their objectives.

The Bhusham and Lessard chapter draws on a survey of both U.S. and U.K. based investment managers. The sample is not particularly large—44

U.S. responses (out of 94 institutions invited) and 14 U.K. responses (out of 29 institutions invited)—but it may reflect a large proportion of the top investment managers in both countries. The authors' reliance on a survey approach possibly reflects the difficulty of extracting hard data from investment managers on their share holdings and how these have responded to cross-country accounting differences and changes over time.

Bhusham and Lessard surmise that there may be a relationship between "investment style" and the impact of accounting diversity. Investment style (for example, whether the firm uses fundamental rather than top-down techniques for stock selection) can be ascertained with reasonable assurance from a survey questionnaire. Determining whether investment decisions would be affected by the availability of alternative accounting information is more problematic, as managers may not respond truthfully or accurately to such a hypothetical question. Bhusham and Lessard are not, however, seeking pin-point accuracy here; they wish to determine whether managers feel that the unification of various accounting principles would have a large or small impact, as measured on a five-point scale.

The accounting principles that Bhusham and Lessard focus on are (a) uniform and comparable disclosure across countries, (b) reconciliation of non-U.S. financial statements to U.S. GAAP, and (c) harmonization of local GAAP principles to a single standard. Their overall results suggest that a clear majority (60 percent) believe that each of these three approaches could have a considerable impact on their investment *practices*. And the results seem to be broadly consistent with the information about managers' investment styles, e.g., managers who rely more heavily on earnings and cash flow information believe that more uniformity of disclosure would effect their investment decisions.

One short-coming of the survey, that Bhusham and Lessard acknowledge, is that the managers are not asked how much they would be willing to pay for more uniform accounting information. By the same token, managers are not asked to estimate how much their *performance* might be improved if they (along with other investment managers) had access to more uniform accounting information. As Bhusham and Lessard state clearly, accounting information is costly to produce. The preference of investment managers for more uniform accounting information is not a sufficient condition for policy-making bodies to require it. While the data from their survey suggest that most investment managers view greater uniformity in accounting information as a good thing, Bhusham and Lessard conclude that "most managers appear to manage quite well with existing information sources." Unfortunately, the data supporting this important conclusion can only be imagined as the authors do not elaborate on this point. And the authors' real meaning is itself a little unclear. Do they mean that international investment *managers* are earning super-normal management fees or super-normal returns? Or do they mean that the international investment *industry* is expanding, as if not impeded by the barriers of accounting diversity? Even if international investment *managers* as agents are doing "quite well", how are the private international *investors* doing who are the ultimate owners of these funds?

In Chapter 7, Gary Biddle and Shahrokh Saudagaran focus on corporate issuers of debt and equity securities. The authors hypothesize that accounting rules and regulatory disclosure requirements impose costs on firms. Biddle and Saudagaran present statistical evidence that these factors have a significant effect on where a firm will decide to list their equity shares.

The authors' null hypothesis—that costs deter corporate issuers from listing on exchanges—would be a strongly maintained hypothesis by most economists. Biddle and Saudagaran propose a framework that allows for an asymmetric effect on firm's listing decisions, i.e., disclosure requirements are a cost only when the foreign country requires more that your home country of incorporation. This is especially important as U.S. firms face foreign regulators that practice reciprocity regarding the selection of GAAP and typically maintain lower levels of disclosure requirements. Non-U.S. firms, by comparison, face U.S. regulators that require U.S. GAAP as a policy of national treatment with high maintained levels of disclosure.

The empirical section of the Biddle and Saudagaran paper presents a compelling case for the maintained hypothesis. The sample size is large and the econometric tests are handled with imagination and care. Overall, it is simply hard to quarrel with results that seem so rational.

ECONOMIC FORCES EFFECTING MARKET PARTICIPANTS

Costs and Benefits for Market Participants

Both sets of authors recognize that there are both costs and benefits in the provision of accounting information to the market. Thus, decisions about accounting information involve trade-offs. And the trade-offs effect market participants in a variety of ways.[1]

First, consider corporations, the participants examined by Biddle and Saudagaran. Corporations, as issuers of financial instruments, want to raise financial capital at low cost. When raising debt, either in their home bond market, in a foreign bond market or in the international or Eurobond market, corporations seek the most favorable overall terms—comprising interest rate, size of issue, maturity and so forth.[2] When raising new equity, corporations attempt to sell their shares at the maximum price.[3] And once these shares have been issued, corporations strive to maximize their value.

The provision of more complete information could be beneficial to the firm on the issuance of new securities, as additional information reduces the perceived risk of the issuer and raises the price that an investor is willing to pay. The preparation of information, however, is costly to the firm. The out-of-pocket cost is only the most obvious component. The firm (especially the non-U.S. firm) fears the negative effect that additional disclosures might have on its competitive position, its dealings with labor unions, regulators, and other constituencies. Thus the firm's efforts to raise new funds cheaply, may trade-off against the firm's efforts to maximize the value of its existing shares.

Second, consider investment managers, the participants examined by Bhusham and Lessard. Investment managers want to maximize their own profits which might depend on their ability to show strong investment performance, commonly associated with returns per unit of risk. Investment managers might prefer more information to improve their performance. But information is costly to collect, costly to analyze, and may not reduce the uncertainty of investment returns.

It is indeed possible to argue that investment managers face a conflict on the matter of accounting information. More accounting information, to the extent that it is useful, might lead to greater financial market efficiency and not greater profits for investment managers. In fact, managers that have special expertise for deciphering the current set of diverse accounting practices, may see the returns on their specialized human capital decline as more public information is available. The trade-off then for investment managers is whether a reduction in international accounting and regulatory diversity would increase the demand for international investment management services by enough to compensate for the loss of super-normal returns on human capital.

Another set of market participants, market regulators, face diverse incentives depending upon their objectives. A regulatory group might want to maximize their regulatory domain, perhaps measured by market capitalization or trading volume. The present example of this objective is the struggle in Europe between France, Germany, and the United Kingdom to be *the* financial center of the European Community. These centers will compete on a number of dimensions, but one will be the net regulatory burden (NRB) they impose on participants in their markets.[4]

Markets with a high NRB will capture a small market share, since both corporate issuers and investors will avoid them. A market with a low NRB, such as the Eurobond market, may prosper as a market for large, well-known issuers and large, professionally managed investment funds. For other individual investors and corporate issuers, there will be a trade-off between the NRB (reflected by the amount and nature of information disclosures required) and the market share. A low NRB may attract more corporate issuers to a market place. But if investors have difficulty distinguishing good and bad investments (because of low disclosure and/or uninformative GAAP), then investors will avoid the market place and trade elsewhere. This is the competitive regulatory dialectic in action.

Another objective of regulatory bodies, often associated with the U.S. Securities Exchange Commission (SEC), is investor protection. Even though one might agree that more information provides better protection for investors, differences of a more basic sort exist.[5] The U.S. SEC strongly believes that U.S. investors are served best when the accounting statements of foreign firms are reconciled to, if not expressed in, U.S. GAAP. Interviews conducted by Choi and Levich (1990) in Japan suggest that Japanese policymakers believe that Japanese investors would be at a *disadvantage* if they were deprived of seeing the accounting statements of foreign firms in their original GAAP presentations. The Japanese logic seems to be that if foreign share prices are determined primarily by foreign investors, in the foreign market, using foreign accounting statements, then Japanese investors are served best by using the exact same materials. If the firm's native accounting practices carry real cash flow implications (as in Choi and Lee, see Chapter 5), then the Japanese approach seems to have merit.

A final set of market participants, the stock exchanges themselves, as profit making organizations, also face costly trade-offs. A stock exchange may seek to maximize its profits by maximizing the market capitalization of shares listed, and the volume of trading activity in those shares. The stock exchange is a competitive organization, but it competes subject to constraints placed on it by regulators. These constraints have indeed been effective in the United States.[6] A U.S. stock exchange can increase its marketing efforts (for example, by putting an advance office in London) as an attempt to reduce the costs for foreign firms considering a U.S. listing. Alternatively, the exchanges could pursue costly lobbying activity to affect public policy changes.

Coping Mechanisms by Market Participants

As market participants face trade-offs in their individual attempts to maximize subject to accounting and regulatory diversity, it is hardly surprising that numerous coping mechanisms have been developed over the years. A few of these are discussed for each category of market participant. The general question that must be addressed is: How well do these coping mechanisms help each participant to achieve their overall objective?

Investors have adopted numerous techniques for international portfolio allocation, many of which do not rely on the comparability of accounting statement across countries, or the reconciliation of accounting statements. Large investors might cope by using a top-down approach that relies on country allocations (derived from GNP or market capitalization measures) or an indexation approach.[7] A bottom-up approach that relies on country specialists with a mastery of local accounting principles is another way to cope. The country specialist could base investment allocations on an analysis of current accounting numbers, or on a comparison with earlier periods. The analyst might instead base his decisions on "accounting-free" numbers, such as free cash flows.

This general approach seems to depend on the superiority of local valuation principles. This assumption could be supported by circumstantial (but untested) evidence. The apparent home country bias in investor portfolios (Uppal, Chapter 2), may imply that home country investors play the dominant role in price setting. Accounting treatments may have real consequences (Choi and Lee, Chapter 5), and so analysts destroy information when they re-state foreign company statements into another GAAP. In essence then, the local GAAP, as it determines local taxes and after-tax cash flows, plays the role of a "non-traded asset" that the locally incorporated firm takes advantage of, but which a foreign incorporated firm can not.

Issuers have also adopted many techniques for coping with the restricted access to foreign capital markets associated with accounting diversity. As Biddle and Saudagaran note, however, this is less of problem for U.S. firms than it is for non-U.S. firms. Firms that are reluctant to provide greater disclosures or accounting statements reconciled to or prepared in another GAAP may put greater reliance on bank lending or private placements. The main bank relationship of Japanese and German companies is one example. When capital is mobile internationally, the firm may attempt to attract foreign investors directly to the firm's home capital market. While one often thinks of markets being integrated by the firm travelling to a foreign country's exchange, the integration process could also work in reverse, by having foreign investors trade in shares directly on the firm's home market. This approach is more likely to attract large institutional investors with the capacity to handle matters of clearing and settlement, custody, transfer, collection of dividends, and their conversion into foreign exchange—all outside of the United States. Firms may prefer large institutional investors over a retail investor base, thinking that the former are less likely to dump their shares after the first large shock.

And issuers can also cope by using offshore markets for Eurocurrency loans, Eurobond issues, and Euroequity placements.[8] In many cases, this coping mechanism has actually been the optimal avenue for corporate financing, as the firm obtains a lower cost of funds than in the United States *and* avoids the added information and regulatory costs of a U.S. issue.

The maturation of the offshore markets has been an important factor leading U.S. regulators to cope by adopting less stringent regulations that reduce the NRB on corporate issuers and investors. For example, Rule 415 on "shelf registration" (adopted in 1983) helped to reduce the paperwork costs and time delays associated with U.S. bond issues. And more recently, Rule 144A (adopted in 1990) permits large institutional investors to form a secondary market for trading what were formerly illiquid private placement offerings. Both of the new regulations could be viewed as part of the regulatory dialectic, in this case an attempt by the United States to stop the further migration of issuing activity offshore.

While stock exchanges would like to cope and compete in the same way, often their actions are circumscribed by government regulation. This is the case in this United States, where the New York Stock Exchange would like wider latitude to trade foreign shares (especially the shares of the world's major 1,000 companies) even though accounting statements reconciled with U.S. GAAP and full disclosures are not provided.[9]

Outside of the United States, stock exchanges cope by maintaining the freedom to list shares even though a full reconciliation to local GAAP is not provided. As noted earlier, foreign stock exchanges practice reciprocity, and so they may agree to list shares based on the prevailing accounting information, or with a variable amount of additional information.[10]

CONCLUDING REMARKS

The main question that continues to concern policymakers is whether policy changes to harmonize accounting principles and/or disclosure requirements are necessary or desirable at this time. In this section, the paper by Biddle and Saudagaran shows convincing evidence that regulatory practices entail costs that influence the international listing patterns of corporate equity. So policies are important as they influence the NRB and the market shares of listing and trading activity worldwide. Also in this section, the survey by Bhusham and Lessard suggests that investment managers would like greater international uniformity of accounting practices and disclosures. But the authors remind us that this is not a necessary condition for investment managers to carry out their charge—that is, coping mechanisms are available.

The objective of future research should be to determine quantitatively whether accounting differences act as a non-tariff-style barrier between national capital markets. Do accounting principles and disclosure differences cause national capital markets (which one can assume to be reasonably efficient on an individual basis) to be poorly integrated, so that the market price of risk and a firm's cost of capital vary significantly across capital market locations? More quantitative tests can be imagined. Such as—Does the market risk premia differ more across markets where accounting diversity is greater? Are the measures of market integration weaker where accounting diversity is greater?

Until these results are available, it would seem that policy measures to harmonize accounting practices ought to proceed with caution. As Choi and Lee (Chapter 5) have demonstrated, accounting differences might generate a real cash advantage or disadvantage for a firm. It would be a mistake to harmonize accounting principles on these points, making it more difficult for analysts to observe the real economic forces affecting the firm.

NOTES

1. For a more complete discussion of the impact of accounting diversity on capital market participants, see Choi and Levich (1990).
2. For the sake of simplicity, we ignore the various 'sweeteners' such as warrants or options that could be attached to any bond. We also ignore the value of keeping several sources of funding open among banks or investors in various parts of the world that could lower the risk of raising funds successfully.
3. Again, we simplify by assuming plain vanilla equity issues rather than those with different voting rights, convertibility features, and so forth.
4. For a discussion of the net regulatory burden concept applied in this context, see Levich and Walter (1990).
5. These views were expressed in interviews documented in Choi and Levich (1990).
6. See the remarks by Cochrane in the roundtable discussion, p. 233, this volume.
7. Small investors can hire an international investment specialist using open-end or closed-end mutual funds.
8. For a historical review of the Eurocurrency and Eurobond markets, see Levich (1985 and 1990). See Marr, Trimble, and Varma (1992) for an introduction to the Euroequity market.
9. See Cochrane, p. 233, this volume, for a full discussion of this proposal.
10. See Meek and Gray (1989) for a discussion of the discretionary practices on the London Stock Exchange and the voluntary disclosures of non-U.K. firms.

REFERENCES

Choi, Frederick D. S., and Richard M. Levich. (1990). *The Capital Market Effects of International Accounting Diversity*. Homewood, IL: Dow Jones-Irwin.

Levich, Richard M. (1985). "A View from the International Capital Markets," in I. Walter (ed.), *Deregulating Wall Street*. New York: John Wiley.

Levich, Richard M. (1990). "The Euromarkets After 1992," in J. Dermine (ed.), *European Banking in the 1990s*. Oxford: Basil Blackwell.

Levich, Richard M., and Ingo Walter. (1990). "Tax-Driven Regulatory Drag: European Financial Centers in the 1990s," in Horst Siebert (ed.), *Reforming Capital Income Taxation*. Tübingen Germany: J.C.B. Mohr Publishing.

Marr, Wayne, John Trimble, and Raj Varma. (1992). "Innovation in Global Financing: The Case of Euroequity Offerings." *Journal of Applied Corporate Finance*. Spring, pp. 50–54.

Meek, G. K., and S. J. Gray. (1989). "Globalization of Stock markets and Foreign Listing Requirements: Voluntary Disclosures by Continental European Companies Listed on the London Stock Exchange." *Journal of International Business Studies*. 20, no. 2, Summer, pp. 315–36.

PART FOUR

POLICY ALTERNATIVES AND STRATEGIC OPTIONS FOR A WORLD WITH ACCOUNTING DIFFERENCES

ROUNDTABLE DISCUSSION

THE U.S.-CANADA MULTIJURISDICTIONAL DISCLOSURE SYSTEM

Robert P. Fisher, Jr.

The Multijurisdictional Disclosure System (MJDS) is an agreement between the United States and Canada designed to reduce the cost and burden of disclosure requirements for new securities issues and to enhance the opportunities for cross-border securities activities between the United States and Canada. The 90-page agreement (written in both English and French) came into effect in June 1991 after more than two years of intense debate among all of the concerned parties—investors, issuers, securities dealers, lawyers, and the regulatory bodies—of the two countries. Even though the Toronto and New York stock exchanges had broadly similar disclosure requirements, the differences were sufficient to impose costs upon issuers that desired to tap both markets. The objective of the MJDS is to reduce these costs and permit the new-issue markets in Canada and the United States to function more like a single market.

In the short time available for comments, I will first briefly describe the main features of the MJDS. I will then review market practices for securities issues in the United States and Canada. And finally, I will outline some examples of financings under the MJDS and give you my views on how the agreement has performed in its first 15 months and what problems remain.

The essential principle of the MJDS is that of reciprocity. For "large" companies, defined as companies having a market capitalization in excess of 360 million Canadian dollars (C$), or approximately 300 million U.S. dollars (US$), the MJDS provides that home country disclosure requirements should be considered adequate for disclosure in the other country. So, for example, the Canadian disclosure provided by Bell Canada would be sufficient for U.S. investors, and the U.S. disclosure provided by NYNEX would be sufficient for Canadian investors. At the present time [October 1992], these reciprocal privileges are available only to investment grade issuers. Non-investment grade issuers must still reconcile their accounting statements, as prepared under U.S. and Canadian generally accepted accounting principles (GAAP). But this requirement may be relaxed in 1993.

Since taking effect in June 1991, there have been no filings by U.S. firms for a Canadian offering. There have been 29 filings of MJDS securities by Canadian firms with the U.S. Securities and Exchange Commission (SEC) as set forth in Table 1. So far, these 29 filings have resulted in 15 financings. Eight of these (worth $1.3 billion) were for investment grade bonds. Another two issues (totaling $400 million) were for non-investment grade bonds. And five equity issues (valued at $800) were completed.

Market issuing practices in Canada and the United States may vary depending upon whether the issue is for debt or equity. With debt, the main concern is whether the debt is to be denominated in U.S. dollars or Canadian dollars. Once the currency decision has been made, debt issuing practices are similar between U.S. and Canadian underwriters. With equity, however, practices differ considerably across countries. An equity issuer in the United States will first file with the SEC and then proceed on a series of road shows to meet with major investment groups— really financial marketing designed to promote the value of the firm. The firm builds an underwriting syndicate and makes a pricing decision on the equity before the prospectus is issued.

In Canada, however, underwriters compete on a *bought deal* basis. In a bought deal, underwriters contact the issuer and offer to buy a block of shares at a discounted price. The underwriters, having acquired the shares, assume the risk of distributing them.

The issuers, having effectively disposed of the shares, are certain of the amount of equity capital raised. Both Canadian counterparties seem to like this arrangement. The bought deal eliminates pricing uncertainty for the issuer and lets the issuer collect competitive bids. The Canadian underwriter gets a competitive tool to use against an American underwriter, who typically has not been permitted to distribute securities in the United States on a

TABLE 1
Multijurisdictional Disclosure System Offerings

Issuer by Form	Date
F-7	
Bovar, Inc.	08/25/92
Sceptre Resources, Ltd.	06/30/92
Cabre Exploration Ltd.	04/27/92
Chauvco Resources Ltd.	02/27/92
Triton Canada Resources Ltd.	02/11/92
Northgate Exploration Ltd.	01/10/91
Lasmo Canada Inc.	09/11/91
Noranda Forest Inc.	07/17/91
F-8	
International Corona Corp.	06/11/92
Morgan Hydrocarbons Inc.	03/24/92
F-9	
Noranda Forest Inc.	09/18/92
Noranda Inc.	07/09/92
Canadian Pacific Forest Products Ltd.	06/09/92
Canadian Pacific Ltd.	05/22/92
Bell Canada	05/14/92
TECK Corp.	04/30/92
MacMillian Bloedel Ltd.	12/09/91
F-10	
Nova Corporation of Alberta	09/15/92
	04/21/92
Rogers Communications Inc.	08/09/92
	04/09/92
Laidlaw Inc.	08/08/92
	02/04/92
SHL Systemhouse, Inc.	06/19/92
Magna International Inc.	06/09/92
	12/23/91
Domtar Inc.	03/04/92
LAC Minerals Ltd.	12/03/91
Pan Canadian Petroleum Ltd.	11/22/91

bought-deal basis. Thus Canadian underwriters can retain an edge in a market that is smaller and less liquid than the U.S. market.

A few illustrations of securities offerings will illustrate how the MJDS has performed. The first use of the MJDS was by the TECK Corporation, a large (C$1 billion capitalization) mining company based in Vancouver, British Columbia. The company was developing a copper mine in Chile that required US$300 million in financing. The company had US$150 of its own funds and decided to finance the remaining US$150 through debt in the U.S. market. The TECK Corporation was not listed on any U.S. exchanges, and so availing themselves of the MJDS made it easier for them to tap the U.S. market. This bond issue was completed as a public offering under the MJDS rather than a private placement under Rule 144a as investors in the public market accept a lower coupon and fewer covenants from issuers in return for the liquidity of a publicly-traded security.

Another example is Magna International, a Canadian auto components maker with shares listed on the New York Stock Exchange. Magna sought to raise US$100 in equity using the MJDS, with US$50 being raised on each side of the border. The company filed a prospectus in each of Canada and the United States. But because of strong demand in Canada and a lack of demand in the United States, Magna completed the offering as a bought deal with Canadian underwriters, and placed the entire amount in Canada alone.

Even though the MJDS has been in place for only a short period, it is still possible to draw a few conclusions regarding its operation and its future. First, while there have 29 MJDS filings in 15 months, all of these have been from Canadian issuers. The Canadian securities dealers are not too happy about this, since there is a belief that Canadian firms are often taken advantage of by U.S. financiers.

On the debt side, market participants believe that securities issued under the MJDS has been successful in terms of their pricing and market reception. One factor possibly deterring firms from using the MJDS is that the requirement to reconcile U.S. and Canadian GAAP has been left in place for non-investment grade issuers. However, this provision will lapse on June 30, 1993 unless specifically extended by the U.S. and Canadian authorities, and it remains to be seen whether this change will spur cross-border issues.

On the equity side, the MJDS has not had a major impact. But here, the reason seems to be that underwriting practices differ so much between the Canada and the United States, rather than vast differences in accounting or disclosure practices. Again, however, it is possible that some issuers are waiting until June 30, 1993 (or the following fiscal year starting December 31, 1993), when GAAP reconciliation requirements may be relaxed further under the MJDS. Some concerns related to equity are clearly non-GAAP related. Disclosure of executive compensation is one such example. In the United States, the five highest paid company officials have to reveal their individual compensation, whereas in Canada, only the collective compensation for the five individuals must be disclosed. Historically, if the Canadian company has listed its shares in the United States, disclosure of individual compensation was required. And this is not popular with Canadian corporations where such information is believed to be irrelevant to the investment decision. This is an evolving area where some Canadian corporations are comfortable with U.S. style disclosures and others are comfortable with Canadian style disclosures.

The short experience with the MJDS reveals a system that is working for debt issues but having no major impact on the equity market. Companies have availed themselves of the MJDS mechanism which suggests that there have been lower funding expenses from these offerings, however no estimates of the magnitude of these savings have been made. While the MJDS has been a useful step in harmonizing some securities market practices in Canada and United States, it is also clear that a number of differences remain in GAAP (particularly as applied to investment grade versus non-investment grade firms), corporate disclosures, and underwriting practices. These differences continue to act as a force on the markets.

ROUNDTABLE DISCUSSION

QUANTITATIVE RECONCILIATION

Bevis Longstreth

I am going to discuss the SEC's quantitative reconciliation requirement contained in items 17 and 18 of Form 20–F. This requirement applies to any foreign issuer seeking to sell securities in the U.S. public markets or to list on the New York or other stock exchange or NASDAQ. Simply put, the requirement for quantitative reconciliation means that a foreign issuer, whose financial statements are prepared according to non-U.S. accounting principles, must reconcile those financial statements in all important particulars to U.S. generally accepted accountings principles (GAAP) and the provisions of Regulation S–X. This single requirement has served as a powerful disincentive to non-U.S. issuers, particularly those in Germany, for listing their shares on the New York Stock Exchange. For example, to date no German issuer (as of October 1992) has ever chosen to list in this country or to offer its securities in our public markets. Given the number of globally recognized world-class issuers from Germany, their absence from the U.S. markets is striking. The explanation, however, is simple: the requirement that German issuers conform their financial statements to U.S. GAAP by quantitative reconciliation. This step, the German issuers believe, forces them to produce two sets of financial figures for net income and material balance sheet items. To do so, they believe, is confusing to investors, to German tax authorities and politicians and to the issuers' various other constituencies. In addition, they believe, the quantitative reconciliation requirement undermines the credibility of their published financial statements in their home country.

Recently, I participated in the development of a proposal involving a limited waiver by the SEC of the quantitative reconciliation requirement to enable 'qualifying world-class" issuers from various countries around the world to list on the Big Board using their home country financials. This effort addressed the problem of German issuers, but the proposal we developed was equally applicable to all world-class issuers, and the the arguments in favor of the proposal would be equally applicable to issuers from other countries. We defined a "qualifying non-U.S. world-class issuer" as one that met each of three tests designed to establish (1) its large size, measured by market capitalization, (2) the existence of an international following among investors, and (3) the absence of a large following among U.S. investors or a large U.S. business presence.

The market capitalization test would require that the aggregate world-wide market value of the issuer's common stock held by nonaffiliates be the equivalent of $1 billion U.S. dollars or more. The international investor following test would require that common stock of the issuer be listed on either the London Exchange or the Tokyo Exchange in addition to the exchange of its home country. Here the purpose was to ensure a wide market following beyond the home market, wide dissemination of current market information, and the pricing of securities based upon all publickly available information.

The absence of U.S. presence test was intended to alleviate any concern of unfairness to U.S. companies for the SEC to grant the requested waiver of the quantitative reconciliation requirement. To meet this test, an issuer would have to satisfy either a trading market standard, designed to show the absence of a large U.S. investor following, or a business presence standard, designed to show the absence of a significant U.S. presence.

In developing the proposal, we asked Donald R. Lessard, Professor of International Management at the Alfred P. Sloan School of Management, Massachusetts Institute of Technology, to conduct a study of the implications of market efficiency for U.S. disclosure by non-U.S. world-class issuers.[1] We believed that market efficiency in the trading of stock of world-class issuers was the key to developing a credible argument favoring waiver of the quantitative reconciliation requirement.

Beyond market efficiency, the case for waiver, which the SEC has power under Rule 3–13 of Regulation S–X to grant, was based on a number of other factors that, we believe, made it clear that the public interest would be significantly served if the SEC were to grant the waiver.

The argument, in a nutshell, is that U.S. investors do not need quantitative reconciliation to be adequately informed about world-class issuers and would be far better protected if they could access securities of those issuers here rather than in foreign markets. The SEC rejected this argument, turning down the requested waiver. If this argument is correct, history will record that the SEC, at a time of critical importance to the global position of the U.S. capital markets, acted against the interests of those it is charged to serve—U.S. investors—and in the process hurt the U.S. capital markets. What follows is a summary of the argument's main themes.

First, we point out that the waiver requested is a narrow one—just the quantitative reconciliation requirement. A foreign issuer still would have to make qualitative disclosure, emphasizing in words the major differences in accounting treatment, and would still have to comply with all other requirements of Form 20–F.

Second, we argue that German accounting principles and its system of accounting are coherent, rigorous, applied with consistency, and create transparency. They produce different numerical results from U.S. GAAP. Those results differ mainly due to a greater conservatism. But, and this is one key point, German results are as valid and reliable as U.S. results. And the other key point is that the German accounting profession, in performing its auditing and certification functions, is fully as demanding, diligent, and suspicious as are its counterparts in the United States. The same general argument could be advanced with respect to the accounting principles and auditing standards used by practically all the "world-class foreign issuers," although not all would be as conservative as the German model.

Third, Dr. Lessard's study on the efficiency of markets with respect to securities of world-class non-U.S. issuers reached a number of important conclusions.

As to the efficiency of markets, he concluded that
1. publicly available information about world-class non-U.S. issuers is impounded in the market price for their securities to a degree comparable to that for world-class U.S. issuers; and
2. such information is adequate, without reconciliation to U.S. GAAP to assure efficient pricing to a degree comparable to that for world-class U.S. issuers.

It is well known that the SEC embraced the efficiency of U.S. markets in its historic step, taken in 1981, of integrating the Securities Act of 1933 with the Securities Exchange Act of 1934, allowing a prospectus prepared for use in a public offering under the 1933 Act to incorporate by reference documents filed with the SEC under the 1934 Act. Dr. Lessard's study provides a solid basis for extending this principle to international markets, at least in the case of world-class securities.

With respect to the value of quantitative reconciliation to investors, Professor Lessard found that

1. diversity in GAAP is only one factor among many of equal or greater importance that differ across borders and must be taken into account in a comparative analysis of issuers from different countries;
2. such other factors include tax policy, fiscal policy, regulatory objectives, managerial systems, performance incentives, and other cultural aspects of the environment in which issuers operate within their home countries;
3. the particular GAAP used in a country can only be understood in the context of all these other factors;
4. therefore, quantitative reconciliation will often convey an illusion of comparability that, in fact, does not exist.

This last point is very powerful—indeed, too powerful for the SEC to deal with comfortably—because it suggests the quantitative reconciliation requirement has a greater capacity to mislead than to clarify the investor's mind.

Finally, we argue that, if the waiver is granted, U.S. investors will be better protected because they will be able to access securities of non-U.S. world-class issuers in our country. There are several important implications to their listing in the United States:

1. Investors will have more information, readily available, including cashflow statements, bad debt reserves, schedules showing valuation and qualifying accounts and reserves, segment reporting, and MD&A.
2. Granting the waiver will reduce transaction costs and custody charges (custody charges abroad are about four times greater than in the United States).
3. U.S. broker-dealers will be stimulated to develop and disseminate far greater information on these foreign issuers.
4. Investors will have the protection of the SEC and our securities laws, including Rule 10b–5 and the application of sanctions for fraud and other wrongdoing. None of this is now available.

The United States is the leading capital market center in the world, but competition is growing. Among U.S. investors there is now developing a

huge pent-up demand for foreign securities, particularly of world-class issuers. There will be a one-time shift into foreign securities—one time, due to
the growing recognition of the lessons of modern portfolio theory and diversification. The shift will be from the current 3 to 5 percent to at least some
15 to 20 percent in the pension fund market alone, which is more than a $2
trillion market. If the shift has to occur by investors and managers going
abroad to acquire shares in foreign markets, they are not likely to come back
to the United States. Custody, brokerage, and advisory relationships will
have been established and are likely to be continued. The experience of the
interest equalization tax serves as a useful analog. This tax, adopted in the
1960s, drove U.S. corporations offshore in search of financing, creating the
Eurodollar market. The business never came back. Another, more limited,
example is the move by Citibank of its credit card operations from New
York to South Dakota, as a result of New York usury law restrictions. Even
though those laws were changed very soon after Citibank left, the bank
never moved those operations back to New York.

Once the case is made that U.S. investors are helped rather than hurt by
the waiver, the SEC should be applauded for granting the waiver, even on
Capitol Hill.

The absence of U.S. investor following or business presence test, in the
proposal's definition of world-class foreign issuer, protects against the
charge that U.S. companies would be put at unfair disadvantage. Of course,
in the case of German issuers, so, too, does the conservatism of German
accounting.

The SEC treats "quantitative reconciliation" as a constitutional bulwark
of investor protection—any deviation from which would expose U.S. investors to dire harm. Professor Lessard's paper shows this just is not true.
Moreover, over its entire history, the SEC has demonstrated a willingness to
accommodate to foreign ways of doing things. In 1935 the SEC decided that
Rule 16 and the proxy rules would not apply to foreign companies. More
recently, Rule 144A, Regulation S, the concept release on tender and exchange offers, and the treatment of investment companies are examples of a
willingness to modfy our rules in the interest of opening up U.S. markets to
foreign issuers.

It is also revealing to consider one method the SEC permits for U.S.
investors to commit capital to foreign issuers. This method is the open- or
closed-end investment company organized and offered to the U.S. public for
the purpose of investing in issuers of a particular foreign country. Take the
Germany Fund, for example. An investor in the Germany Fund is given no

information on the companies whose securities are in the fund. He is given no financials for these companies. Since these companies are not listed here, the managers of the Germany Fund do not receive financials quantitatively reconciled to U.S. GAAP. Thus, with SEC blessing, the U.S. investor accessing German issuers in this way is investing blindly.

On the other hand, if the German companies were encouraged to list in the U.S. market, a great deal more information would be available to fund managers and other investors compared to the information that they have now.

By insisting on "all or nothing," the SEC is discouraging listings—in effect giving U.S. investors "nothing" and forcing them offshore. If the SEC's purpose is protection of U.S. investors, this result is perverse. The United States is out of step with the rest of the world. Home-country accounting principles for issuers is accepted in all of the other great markets around the world. If every country insisted on quantitative reconciliation, the confusion would grow as the global reach of an issuer grew. It would become unmanageable. Common sense suggests that there be one set of financials for each issuer, prepared under home-country accounting principles and used in other countries, with a "qualitative" statement of material differences between the home-country principles, practices and methods and those of the country where the issuer is raising capital or listing its shares for trading.

NOTE

1. Donald R. Lessard, "The Implications of Market Efficiency for U.S. Disclosure by Non-U.S. World-Class Issuers," unpublished manuscript (November 9, 1990).

ROUNDTABLE DISCUSSION

HELPING TO KEEP U.S. CAPITAL MARKETS COMPETITIVE: LISTING WORLD-CLASS NON-U.S. FIRMS ON U.S. EXCHANGES

James L. Cochrane

U.S investor interest in foreign equity securities has grown dramatically in recent years and continued expansion of international trading is expected during the 1990s. Despite this growth, specific Securities and Exchange Commission (SEC) regulations limit the trading of foreign securities in the United States.

While U.S. capital markets are currently the most liquid, technologically advanced markets in the world, we put at risk these advantages and our position as a global capital market if we do not aggressively seek to change certain regulations.

Which regulations limit the trading of non-U.S. firms on U.S. exchanges?

The most onerous is the requirement that foreign companies can not sell or list their securities on U.S. exchanges or NASDAQ unless they register these securities with the SEC and agree to quantitatively reconcile their financial statements to U.S. generally accepted accounting principles (U.S. GAAP).

What is the practical impact of these restrictions?

Very few foreign companies seek to sell or list their securities in the United States. For example, although there are over 2,000 non-U.S. companies which meet New York Stock Exchange listing standards, only about 155 of these are traded on a U.S. exchange or NASDAQ. In contrast, every major European exchange trades over 200 foreign issues; London, the most internationally receptive market, trades over 900. While Europe is actively grappling with the difficulties of reconciling diverse regulatory policies across countries, the United States seems to be ignoring these issues, hoping the rest of the world will simply stop being different. Our unwillingness to tackle these issues of international diversity is forcing business to London, Frankfurt, Tokyo and elsewhere. And every time a U.S. investor trades in a foreign market center and sets up a brokerage or custodial relationship, he or she encourages the success of these other markets and strikes a blow to the long-term competitive prospects of U.S. markets.

Is there any way to trade foreign securities in the U.S. if they are not registered with the SEC?

Some foreign securities are allowed to trade in the United States using home-country disclosure documents that are not reconciled to U.S. GAAP—but only if they trade in the pink sheet market (an illiquid segment of the over-the-counter market where there are few quotes and no last-sale reporting and which involves higher costs and wider spreads for investors). Because of the lack of transparency and liquidity in this market, it does not provide a real alternative to foreign markets.

What can be done to change this situation?

The objective of U.S. public policy in this area should be to permit "world-class" non-U.S. issuers to access the U.S. capital markets without requiring the quantitative reconciliation of home-country financial statements to U.S. GAAP. This would apply to the registration of securities under both the Securities Exchange Act of 1934 ("Exchange Act") and the Securities Act of 1933 (the "Securities Act").

What is a world-class company?

By most reasonable criteria, about 200 of the largest and best-known non-U.S. companies can be considered world-class. One approach to identifying a world-class company would be if:
- it has revenues of $5 billion (for the most recent fiscal year) and a market capitalization of $2 billion; and
- it has average weekly trading volume outside the United States of at least $1 million or 200,000 shares.

The SEC should adopt special disclosure standards for such world-class non-U.S. corporate issuers.

What should these special disclosure standards look like?

Current regulations require issuers to submit certain information, including financial information, to the SEC. However, these regulations also recognize that not all information submitted by all issuers need be the same. For example, the Exchange Act allows the SEC to accept information of "comparable character" to the standard disclosure information under certain circumstances.

World-class foreign issuers should be required to register securities in accordance with current disclosure requirements—with one exception. The sole exception would be that the quantitative reconciliation requirements would not be applicable. Instead, for world-class issuers, independently-audited home-country financial statements would be accepted as long as these include a written explanation of the material differences between home-country accounting practices and U.S. GAAP.

Would special requirements for these world-class foreign issuers be imposed?

Yes, in addition to the SEC amending its rules and forms to permit the registration of foreign world-class securities, the exchanges might amend their listing standards in a complementary fashion. For example, the issuer might sign a listing agreement requiring, among other things, that it include in its annual report to U.S. shareholders a description of the differences between its home-country accounting requirements and U.S. GAAP.

Exchanges might also consider adopting a special "suitability" requirement for investors who engage in transactions in securities of foreign world-class issuers. With a suitability requirement, before recommending transactions in these securities, member firms would have to have a reasonable basis for believing that the customer has such knowledge and experience in financial matters that he or she could be expected to understand the characteristics of the security and be financially able to bear the risks of the recommended position.

At the time of the initial trade in foreign world-class securities, it might be also desirable to require member firms to send customers a notice indicating that the issuer prepares its financial statements in accordance with its home-country accounting standards, and not U.S. GAAP. Similarly, it might be desirable to encourage the newspapers to include these stock listings in a separate section or provide a footnote indicating that foreign world-class securities are subject to different disclosure requirements.

Will special treatment for non-U.S. world-class companies disadvantage U.S. companies?

No. Preserving the international competitiveness of U.S. capital markets is clearly in the long-term interests of U.S. corporations. Maintaining the attractiveness of U.S. markets for issuers and investors are two inseparable goals. If we stand by and watch foreign financial centers emerge as the dominant international markets, U.S. issuers will increasingly be forced abroad to access capital—just as U.S. investors are forced abroad to access foreign stocks today.

Home-country disclosure documents for world-class private issuers can and should be considered of "comparable character" to U.S. disclosure documents. They may not be the same—or even as good from our point of view. But as long as they are coherent and independently audited and meet other minimum requirements, we should accept them—until more stringent international standards have been adopted.

World-class issues are already widely held by international investors. If disclosure documents for these issuers are not of "comparable character" to U.S. issues, then investors demand an appropriate risk premium before investing. This will be true if the issues are traded in the U.S.—or if we continue to force trading offshore. In short, the efficiency of international capital markets will impose a penalty on companies which provide lower quality disclosure documents.

Will making it easier for U.S. investors to buy foreign stocks make the value of U.S. stocks fall?

U.S. investors will, we believe, continue increasing their holdings of foreign stocks—regardless of whether these stocks are listed on U.S. exchanges. The only question is if this increased international activity will occur in U.S. markets. It is unlikely that increased international diversification alone will cause values in U.S. markets to fall. Foreign investors will likely be diversifying their holding into U.S. stocks over the same period.

What are the benefits of such a regulatory change?

First, it would be consistent with recent SEC proposals to lessen the regulatory burden of disclosure for emerging U.S. companies and to allow foreign mutual funds to solicit U.S. investors if their home-country regulation is comparable to U.S. regulation.

Second, it would bring U.S. regulatory practices more into line with those of other major capital markets. U.S. companies can issue stocks and list them on exchanges in Japan and in Europe without conforming to local rules of accounting, even though U.S. financial statements are not prepared on the basis of principles considered from a Japanese or European viewpoint. (It should be noted, however, that the European Community is considering withholding this regulatory treatment of U.S. companies unless the SEC extends similar privileges to European Community companies.)

Most importantly, removing the obstacles to increased international trading in the United States would help the U.S. capital market maintain its position as a major international financial center.

What about investor protection?

Exempting world-class foreign companies from U.S. GAAP reconciliation will not hurt U.S. investors. First, there is a growing consensus among experts that requiring foreign companies to file additional U.S. GAAP reconciliations (in most cases after their home-country documents are made public) is of little value to investors. Academic studies generally confirm that these filings have no material impact on the price of the stock, which is typically set by informed investors in the home market in any case.

Diversity in GAAP is only one factor among many that must be taken into account by international investors. Companies operate in different legal and regulatory environments, under different social norms and contracts. They have different accounting definitions and standards in large part because these standards reflect different business realities. For these reasons, international accountants generally warn that mechanically translating—or quantitatively reconciling—foreign accounting data to U.S. GAAP will often convey an illusion of comparability that does not exist. To understand a foreign company's financial position, one must ultimately come to terms with the home-country's accounting standards.

Second, current restrictions harm U.S. investors. Individual investors can now buy and sell world-class foreign issues through their local brokers, but the trades will likely occur in the illiquid pink sheet market—where the spreads are punishing. Institutional investors already buy and sell foreign stocks overseas, but they incur additional costs because of cumbersome foreign custody and clearance and settlement arrangements.

In sum, requiring U.S. GAAP reconciliation for world-class foreign companies is not only harming U.S. competitiveness, it is serving no valid regulatory purpose. It is raising trading costs (and lowering returns) for U.S. investors, while at the same time forcing them to deal in markets with less effective overall regulation.

ROUNDTABLE DISCUSSION

INTERNATIONAL REGULATORY INITIATIVES

Paul Guy

Let me first say a few words about the International Organization of Securities Commissions commonly known as "IOSCO."

IOSCO was created in 1974 as an initiative to stimulate cooperation between North and South American securities regulators. It became an international organization in 1984. As of this moment, almost 100 members from all continents are gathered in IOSCO to pursue the following objectives:

1. to cooperate together to ensure better regulation of the markets, on the domestic as well as on the international level, in order to maintain fair and efficient markets;
2. to exchange information on their respective experiences in order to promote the development of domestic markets;
3. to unite their efforts to establish standards and an effective surveillance of international securities transactions;
4. to provide mutual assistance to ensure the integrity of the markets by a rigorous application of the standards and by effective enforcement against offenses.

THE RIO DECLARATION

One of the first initiatives of IOSCO was the adoption in November 1986 of a resolution concerning mutual assistance. Because it was adopted at a meeting of the Executive Committee in Rio, this resolution is commonly known as the "Rio Declaration." This was truly the first concrete step in international cooperation between securities and futures regulators. This resolution recognizes the need to promote investor protection by effective markets and intermediaries surveillance and by active enforcement of securities and futures regulations. Regulators who sign the resolution undertake, on a reciprocal basis, to provide assistance in gathering information related to market surveillance and protection from fraudulent securities and futures transactions. Most of the regular members of IOSCO have now signed this resolution.

ANOTHER IMPORTANT STEP

The second major initiative was the setting up of two important committees:
1. The Technical Committee; and
2. The Development Committee.

THE TECHNICAL COMMITTEE

The Technical Committee was set up in 1987 with the aim of reviewing major problems related to international securities and futures transactions and to propose in the shortest possible time practical solutions to these problems. It is made up of top level representatives of all the agencies that regulate the most developed markets of the world. It is active in the following areas:
1. Multinational disclosure and accounting;
2. Regulation of secondary markets;
3. Regulation of market intermediaries;
4. Enforcement and exchange of information.

THE DEVELOPMENT COMMITTEE

The Development Committee was set up in 1989 to deal with problems facing the emerging markets and to try to provide workable solutions to these problems. It is active in the following areas:

1. Incentives for market development;
2. Efficient clearing and settlement systems;
3. The impact of internationalization on the regulation of emerging markets;
4. Minimum standards of disclosure.

SUBCOMMITTEE ON ACCOUNTING AND AUDITING

The Working Group on Accounting and Auditing was set up in 1987, to work with a view to identifying accounting and auditing standards that securities regulators might be willing to accept in the case of multinational offerings and multiple listings. This working group became a subcommittee of the Working Group on Multinational Disclosure and Accounting as a result of the Strategic Assessment carried out by the Technical Committee in 1990.

As part of its activities, the working group has sought to determine whether a sufficiently comprehensive set of generally accepted international accounting standards existed, so that financial statements prepared in accordance with these standards would be acceptable by the securities and futures regulators in certain circumstances. To achieve this objective, the Technical Committee decided to work with the International Accounting Standards Committee in developing acceptable accounting standards.

In addition, the group also sought to develop, in collaboration with the International Auditing Practices Committee (IAPC) of the International Federation of Accountants (IFAC), an acceptable set of international auditing standards. The subcommittee concluded that the auditing standards of IAPC were the most suited to the purpose of determining a set of generally accepted international auditing standards.

AUDITING STANDARDS

The subcommittee undertook a detailed review of the professional standards that an auditor should comply with when auditing financial statements. The subcommittee received considerable assistance from the IAPC Committee set up to participate in the review. Potentially significant deficiencies were analyzed and rated as being either highly relevant or moderately relevant for action. A summary report was prepared and presented to the IAPC, which in turn developed action plans to respond to the identified issues. Sixteen of the nineteen issues identified have been dealt with. The remaining three items, which deal with the comparative presentation of audited and unaudited financial information, audit considerations relating to service organizations and the auditor's responsibility for the prevention, detection and reporting of material misstatements resulting from illegal acts, are the subject of exposure drafts issued or to be issued.

As far as the question of reporting is concerned, the subcommittee has concluded that it is not necessary at this time to agree on uniform international reporting standards. This leaves two additional questions to be dealt with in the future: independence and qualifications. On independence, the subcommittee wishes to wait for a number of studies that are being conducted by various securities regulatory authorities. The results of these studies will have to be reviewed before the subcommittee considers ethical standards developed by IFAC. On the issue of the qualifications of auditors, the subcommittee will work with IFAC in the future to attempt to develop international qualifications which could be accepted by all participating jurisdictions.

We believe that IFAC has responded to the potentially significant deficiencies identified by the subcommittee, including the three issues subject of exposure drafts. The subcommittee will therefore recommend the endorsement of the International Standards on Auditing next week at the IOSCO Annual Conference in London. The purpose of the endorsement would be to encourage the securities regulatory authorities which are members of IOSCO to adopt policies providing for the acceptance, in the case of cross-border offerings and continuous reporting for foreign issuers, of audits conducted in accordance with International Standards on Auditing. The subcommittee will continue to monitor and review exposure drafts and new or amended auditing standards. It would also continue to work with IFAC on the questions of reporting, independence and qualifications.

This is a major achievement and it should facilitate multinational offerings and multiple listings. However, a more significant achievement will be reached when the Technical Committee agrees to a similar resolution concerning international accounting standards.

ACCOUNTING STANDARDS

The issue of accounting standards is a more complex and difficult one. When it started its association with IASC, the subcommittee identified three broad areas requiring action by IASC before most developed market regulators should consider acceptance of international accounting standards in the preparation of financial statements in the case of international offers of equity securities and multiple listings. These are:

1. The reduction of free choices of accounting treatment under existing standards and the establishment of a benchmark treatment where the standards continue to allow a choice of accounting treatment for like transactions and events;

2. The revision of existing standards to improve disclosure requirements and implementation guidance (more detailed guidance with respect to general standards which lead to reasonable comparability in similar facts and circumstances);

3. The continuation of the process of identifying accounting areas not covered by existing standards, prioritizing these issues, and developing new standards to achieve a sufficiently complete set of standards.

The publication by IASC of E32 on the Comparability of Financial Statements in January 1989 was the first step in the development of acceptable international accounting standards. It was followed by the adoption by IASC of the Statement of Intent on Comparability of Financial Statements in July 1990. This dealt with the first issue identified by IOSCO. To be able to work efficiently with the question of detail and disclosure, the IASC set up an Improvements Steering Committee to which the subcommittee on accounting and auditing is actively participating. This substantial involvement enables the subcommittee to provide timely views of the appropriateness of decisions being reached and the course of the projects.

This work is progressing very satisfactorily and we can expect IASC to have revised and approved most of the accounting standards included in the E32 project in 1993. Although we would have liked to move more rapidly, it is also important to recognize the need for an adequate due process to take place. Otherwise, the credibility of the process may be put in doubt.

Some major issues remain to be considered by the Technical Committee:

1. Whether or not reconciliation to IASC benchmark standards will be required, and consideration of exceptions, if any.

2. The relative authority of the explanation and standards sections of the IASC literature. In many jurisdictions, the standards are considered mandatory guidance and the explanation is considered non-mandatory guidance.

3. The identification of projects that may be prerequisite to an initial

determination that the standards are sufficiently complete for consideration.

Is it necessary for all this work to be completed by IASC before the Technical Committee can consider the acceptance of international accounting standards? In my view it is not. We could very well proceed by stages. For example, the Technical Committee could indicate that it accepts the standards that were part of E32 when that work is completed. Other new or revised standards could be accepted as soon as they have been reviewed by the subcommittee and are considered satisfactory in the view of the Technical Committee. In the case of an offering of equity securities where financial statements are prepared in accordance with international accounting standards, questions that are not dealt with in the international standards would have to be reconciled to the standards in effect in the jurisdiction where the offering is made, if requested by the relevant authority. For example, if a cash flow statement is a requirement of the foreign jurisdiction and no international standard exist on cash flow, then the cash flow statement would have to be prepared in accordance with the standards of the foreign jurisdiction or reconciled to it.

In proceeding this way and by indicating to the IASC the future work that we feel is most important to be completed, we could move a long way in facilitating multinational equity offerings. To do this, members of the Technical Committee must be willing to compromise. They must forget their own personal interest, without, in any way, sacrificing the protection of investors, and work towards making it easier for international corporations to issue equity securities in foreign markets. One argument that we hear very often is that the local issuers will want to be treated the same way if easier requirements are put in place for some international foreign corporations. I do not think this is a valid concern. As long as the principal market for the securities of the foreign corporation remains the home market, it is entirely appropriate that different requirements be agreed to. Domestic corporations would benefit from the same rules in the foreign market.

I do not think that there is any other valid choice. Reconciliation to many national accounting standards by international corporations is just too high a price to pay to have access to a foreign market. If no agreement is reached on a set of acceptable international accounting standards, the number of international equity offerings and the number of foreign listings will remain marginal.

In fact, we have seen many cases, in particular in large privatization offers, where foreign regulators have been willing to make exceptions to accommodate these offerings. The situation we are speaking of is not very different. The acceptance of international accounting standards would be limited to multinational offers of equity securities and listings by international size corporations. Since we are only proposing to determine a set of acceptable international accounting standards to facilitate these situations, it should be much easier to agree on the international standards.

INDEX